£3.95

SOIL MECHANICS

SOIL MECHANICS

R.F. CRAIG

Lecturer in Civil Engineering
University of Dundee

VNR VAN NOSTRAND REINHOLD COMPANY
New York - Cincinnati - Toronto - London - Melbourne

© R.F. Craig, 1974

ISBN 0 442 30011 5 cloth
ISBN 0 442 30013 1 paperback

Library of Congress Catalogue Card No. 73–11582

Published by Van Nostrand Reinhold Company Ltd.,
25–28 Buckingham Gate, London SW1E 6LQ.

Printed in Great Britain by
William Clowes & Sons Ltd.,
London, Colchester and Beccles

Contents

Preface

This book is intended primarily to serve the needs of the undergraduate Civil Engineering student and aims at the clear explanation, in adequate depth, of the fundamental principles of Soil Mechanics. The understanding of these principles is considered to be an essential foundation upon which future practical experience in soils engineering can be built. The choice of material involves an element of personal opinion but the contents of this book should cover the requirements of most undergraduate courses to honours level. It is assumed that the student has no prior knowledge of the subject but has a good understanding of basic Mechanics. The book includes a comprehensive range of worked examples and problems set for solution by the student to consolidate understanding of the fundamental principles and illustrate their application in simple practical situations. The International system of units is used throughout the book. A list of references is included at the end of each chapter as an aid to the more advanced study of any particular topic. It is intended also that the book will serve as a useful source of reference for the practising engineer.

The author wishes to record his thanks to the various publishers, organisations and individuals who gave permission for the use of figures and tables of data, and to acknowledge his dependence on those authors whose works provided sources of material. The author also wishes to express his gratitude to Dr. Ian Christie of the University of Edinburgh for reading the draft manuscript and offering a number of suggestions for improvement. Thanks are also due to Mr. L. N. M. Pariti for checking all the calculations and to Miss Evelyn Clark and Mrs. Sandra Nicoll for their careful work in typing the manuscript.

Robert F. Craig

Dundee
March 1973

Acknowledgements

Figures 7.25, 9.10 and 9.12 are published by permission of the American Society of Civil Engineers.

Figure 9.5 and Table 2.2 are published by permission of the Boston Society of Civil Engineers.

Tables 2.1, 4.2 and 8.1 are extracts from CP 2004:1972, 'Foundations', reproduced by permission of the British Standards Institution, 2 Park Street, London, W1A 2 BS.

Figure 8.7 is published by permission of the Director of the Building Research Establishment.

Table 1.1, parts of section 1.4 and Figure 8.12 are based on material in the Proceedings of the Fourth International Conference on Soil Mechanics and Foundation Engineering and are published by permission of Butterworth and Company, London.

Figure 6.7 is reproduced by permission of Professor R. E. Fadum, North Carolina State University.

Table 7.1 and Figures 8.6 and 9.14 are published by permission of the Council of the Institution of Civil Engineers.

Table 5.2 is extracted from CP2: 'Earth Retaining Structures' and is published by permission of the Institution of Structural Engineers.

Figure 6.8 is reproduced by permission of Professor N. M. Newmark, University of Illinois.

Figure 6.11 is reproduced by permission of Dr. W. Steinbrenner, Linz, Austria.

Figures 2.22, 3.6, 5.19, 8.10 and 8.11 are published by permission of John Wiley and Sons Inc., New York.

CHAPTER 1

Basic Characteristics of Soils

1.1 The Nature of Soils

To the Civil Engineer soil is any uncemented or weakly cemented accumulation of mineral particles formed by the weathering of rocks, the void space between the particles containing water and/or air. Weak cementation can be due to carbonates or oxides precipitated between the particles or due to organic matter. If the products of weathering remain at their original location they constitute a residual soil. If the products are transported and deposited in a different location they constitute a transported soil, the agents of transportation being gravity, wind, water and glaciers. During transportation the size and shape of particles can undergo change and the particles can be sorted into size ranges.

The destructive process in the formation of soil from rock may be either physical or chemical. The physical process may be erosion by the action of wind, water or glaciers, or disintegration caused by alternate freezing and thawing in cracks in the rock. The resultant soil particles retain the same composition as that of the parent rock. Particles of this type are approximately equidimensional and are described as being of 'bulky' form: the particles may be angular, subangular or rounded. The particles occur in a wide range of sizes, from boulders down to the fine rock flour formed by the grinding action of glaciers. The structural arrangement of bulky particles (Fig. 1.1) is described as *single grain* each particle being in direct contact with adjoining particles, without there being any bond or cohesion between them. The structure may be loose, medium dense or dense, depending on the way in which the particles are packed together.

The chemical process results in changes in the mineral form of the parent rock due to the action of water (especially if it contains traces of acid or alkali), oxygen and carbon dioxide. Chemical weathering results in the formation of groups of crystalline particles of colloidal size (< 0.002 mm) known as the clay minerals. The clay mineral kaolinite, for example, is formed by the breakdown of felspar by the action of water and carbon dioxide. Most clay mineral particles are of 'plate-like' form having a high specific surface (i.e. a high surface area to mass ratio) with the result that their properties are influenced significantly by surface forces. Long 'needle-shaped' particles can also occur but are comparatively rare.

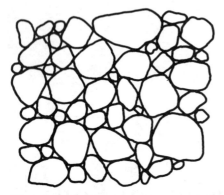

Figure 1.1   Single grain structure.

The basic structural units of most clay minerals consist of a silica tetrahedron and an alumina octahedron (Fig. 1.2a). Silicon and aluminium may be partially replaced by other elements in these units, this being known as isomorphous substitution. The basic units combine to form sheet structures which are represented symbolically in Fig. 1.2b. The various clay minerals are formed by the stacking of combinations of the basic sheet structures with different forms of bonding between the combined sheets. The structures of the principal clay minerals are represented in Fig. 1.3.

Kaolinite consists of a structure based on a single sheet of silica tetrahedrons combined with a single sheet of alumina octahedrons. There is very limited isomorphous substitution. The combined silica–alumina sheets are held together fairly tightly by hydrogen bonding: a kaolinite particle may consist of over one hundred stacks. *Illite* has a basic structure consisting of a sheet of alumina octahedrons between and combined with two sheets of silica tetrahedrons. In the octahedral sheet there is partial substitution of aluminium by magnesium and iron, and in the tetrahedral sheet there is partial substitution of silicon by aluminium. The combined sheets are linked together

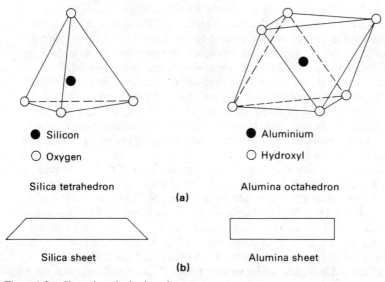

● Silicon

○ Oxygen

Silica tetrahedron

● Aluminium

○ Hydroxyl

Alumina octahedron

(a)

Silica sheet

Alumina sheet

(b)

Figure 1.2   Clay minerals: basic units.

by fairly weak bonding due to (non-exchangeable) potassium ions held between them. *Montmorillonite* has the same basic structure as illite. In the octahedral sheet there is partial substitution of aluminium by magnesium. The space between the combined sheets is occupied by water molecules and (exchangeable) cations other than potassium. There is a very weak bond between the combined sheets due to these ions. Considerable swelling of montmorillonite can occur due to additional water being adsorbed between the combined sheets.

The surfaces of clay mineral particles carry residual negative charges, mainly as a result of the isomorphous substitution of aluminium or silicon atoms by atoms of lower valency, but also due to disassociation of hydroxyl ions. Unsatisfied charges due to 'broken bonds' at the edges of the particles also occur. The negative charges result in cations present in the water in the void space being attracted to the particles. The cations are not held strongly and, if the nature of the water changes, can be replaced by other cations, a phenomenon referred to as *cation exchange*.

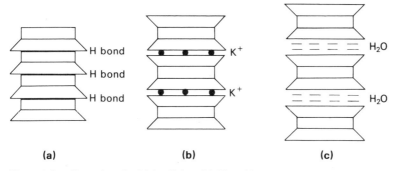

Figure 1.3   Clay minerals: (a) kaolinite, (b) illite, (c) montmorillonite.

The cations are attracted to a clay mineral particle because of the negative surface charges but at the same time tend to move away from each other because of their thermal energy. The net effect is that the cations form a dispersed layer adjacent to the particle, the cation concentration decreasing with increasing distance from the surface until the concentration becomes equal to that in the 'normal' water in the void space. The term *double layer* describes the negatively-charged particle surface and the dispersed layer of cations. For a given particle the thickness of the cation layer depends mainly on the valency and concentration of the cations: an increase in valency (due to cation exchange) or an increase in concentration will result in a decrease in layer thickness. Temperature also affects cation layer thickness, an increase in temperature resulting in a decrease in layer thickness.

Layers of water molecules are held round a clay mineral particle by hydrogen bonding and (because water molecules are dipolar) by attraction to the negatively-charged surfaces. In addition the exchangeable cations attract water (i.e. they become hydrated). The particle is thus surrounded by a layer of *adsorbed water*. The water nearest the particle is strongly held and appears to have a high viscosity: the viscosity decreases with increasing distance from the particle surface to that of 'free' water at the boundary of the adsorbed layer. Adsorbed water molecules can move relatively freely parallel to the particle surface but movement perpendicular to the surface is restricted.

Forces of repulsion and attraction act between adjacent clay mineral particles. Repulsion occurs between the like charges of the double layers, the force of repulsion

depending on the characteristics of the layers. An increase in cation valency or concentration will result in a decrease in repulsive force, and vice versa. Attraction between
particles is due to short-range Van der Waals forces; these forces are independent of
the double layer characteristics and decrease rapidly with increasing distance between
particles. In environments where the pH of the water is low the edges of kaolinite
particles can become positively-charged and this can result in edge-to-face attraction
between adjacent particles. The forces of attraction are responsible for the cohesive
nature of soils containing a significant proportion of clay mineral particles.

The net interparticle forces govern the structural form assumed by clay mineral
particles in a soil, the two extreme structures being represented diagrammatically in
Fig. 1.4. The *dispersed* structure results when there is net repulsion between particles

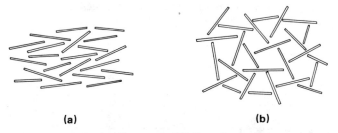

(a)   **(b)**

Figure 1.4   (a) Dispersed structure, (b) flocculent structure.

and the *flocculent* structure when there is net attraction. However these structures
can be modified due to the particles being moved closer together by the application of
external forces: the attractive forces between the particles are increased as a result of
the closer spacing. The presence of bulky particles can also influence the structural
arrangement. A flocculent structure is more compressible and is more sensitive to
disturbance than a dispersed structure. As repulsive forces are high when the ion
concentration of the water is low, a clay soil in a fresh water environment will have a
lower degree of flocculation than a soil of similar composition in a salt water environment. A change in the nature of the water can result in a change in the soil structure.

Particle sizes in soils can vary from over 100 mm to less than 0·001 mm. In
British Standards the size ranges detailed in Fig. 1.5 are specified. In Fig. 1.5 the

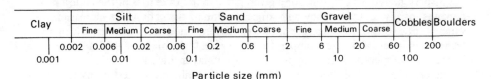

Particle size (mm)

Figure 1.5   Particle size ranges.

terms 'clay', 'silt', etc. are used only to describe the *sizes* of particles between specified
limits. However the same terms are also used to describe particular *types* of soil. For
example clay is a type of soil possessing cohesion and plasticity which normally
consists of particles in both the *clay size* and *silt size* ranges. If the proportion of silt
size particles is large the soil may be described as a silty clay. Most types of soil
consist of a graded mixture of particles from two or more size ranges. All clay size
particles are not necessarily clay mineral particles: the finest rock flour particles may
be of clay size. If clay mineral particles are present they usually exert a considerable

influence on the properties of a soil, an influence out of all proportion to their percentage by weight in the soil.

Soils consisting of particles mostly in the gravel size and sand size ranges are referred to as *coarse-grained*. Those consisting of particles mostly in the silt size and clay size ranges are referred to as *fine-grained* soils.

1.2 Particle Size Analysis

The particle size analysis of a soil sample involves determining the percentage by weight of particles within the different size ranges. The particle size distribution of a coarse-grained soil can be determined by the method of *sieving*. The soil sample is passed through a series of standard test sieves having successively smaller mesh sizes. The weight of soil retained in each sieve is determined and the cumulative percentage by weight passing each sieve is calculated. If fine-grained particles are present in the soil, the sample should be treated with a deflocculating agent and washed through the sieves.

The particle size distribution of a fine-grained soil or the fine-grained fraction of a coarse-grained soil can be determined by the method of *sedimentation*. The method is based on Stokes' law which governs the velocity at which spherical particles settle in a suspension: the larger the particles the greater is the settling velocity and vice versa. The law does not apply to particles smaller than 0·0002 mm, the settlement of which is influenced by Brownian movement. The size of a particle is given as the diameter of a sphere which would settle at the same velocity as the particle. The soil sample is pre-treated to remove any organic material, calcium compounds and soluble salts. The sample is then made up as a suspension in distilled water to which a deflocculating agent has been added to ensure that all particles settle individually. The suspension is placed in a sedimentation tube. From Stokes' law it is possible to calculate the time (t) for particles of a certain 'size' D (the equivalent settling diameter) to settle a specified depth in the suspension. If, after the calculated time t, a sample of the suspension is drawn off with a pipette at the specified depth below the surface, the sample will contain only particles smaller than the size D at a concentration unchanged from that at the start of sedimentation. If pipette samples are taken at the specified depth at times corresponding to other chosen particle sizes the particle size distribution can be determined from the weights of the residues. An alternative procedure to pipette sampling is the measurement of the specific gravity of the suspension by means of a special hydrometer, the specific gravity depending on the weight of soil particles in the suspension at the time of measurement. Full details of the determination of particle size distribution by both the sieving and sedimentation methods are given in BS 1377 [1.1].

The particle size distribution of a soil is presented as a curve on a semi-logarithmic plot, the ordinates being the percentage by weight of particles smaller than the size given by the abscissa. The flatter the distribution curve the larger the range of particle sizes in the soil; the steeper the curve the smaller the size range. A coarse-grained soil is described as *well-graded* if there is no excess of particles in any size range and if no intermediate sizes are lacking. In general a well-graded soil is represented by a smooth, concave distribution curve. A coarse-grained soil is described as *poorly-graded*, (a) if a high proportion of the particles have sizes within narrow limits (a *uniform* soil) or (b) if particles of both large and small sizes are present but with a relatively low proportion of particles of intermediate size (a *gap-graded* soil). Particle size is represented on a logarithmic scale so that two soils having the same degree of uniformity are represented by curves of the same shape regardless of their positions on the particle size distribution plot. Examples of particle size distribution curves appear in Fig. 1.7. The particle size corresponding to any specified value on the 'percentage smaller' scale can be read from the particle size distribution curve. The size such that 10% of the particles are smaller than that size is denoted by D_{10}. Other sizes such as D_{30} and D_{60} can be defined in a similar way. The size D_{10} is defined as the *effective size*. The general slope and shape of the distribution curve can be described by means of the *coefficient of uniformity* (C_U) and the *coefficient of curvature* (C_C), defined as follows:

$$C_U = \frac{D_{60}}{D_{10}} \tag{1.1}$$

$$C_C = \frac{D_{30}^2}{D_{60}D_{10}} \tag{1.2}$$

The higher the value of the coefficient of uniformity the larger the range of particle sizes in the soil. A well-graded soil has a coefficient of curvature between 1 and 3.

1.3 Plasticity of Fine Grained Soils

Plasticity is an important characteristic in the case of fine-grained soils, the term plasticity describing the ability of a soil to undergo unrecoverable deformation at constant volume without cracking or crumbling. Plasticity is due to the presence of clay mineral particles in the soil. The physical state of a fine-grained soil at a particular water content (defined as the ratio of the mass of water in the soil to the mass of solid particles) is known as its consistency. Depending on its water content a soil may exist in the liquid, plastic, semi-solid or solid state. The water contents at which the transitions between states occur vary from soil to soil. The consistency depends on the interaction between the clay mineral particles. Any decrease in water content results in a decrease in cation layer thickness and an increase in the net attractive forces between particles. For a soil to exist in the plastic state the magnitudes of the net interparticle forces must be such that the particles are free to slide relative to each other, with cohesion between them being maintained. A decrease in water content also results in a reduction in the volume of a soil in the liquid, plastic or semi-solid state.

Most fine-grained soils exist naturally in the plastic state. The upper and lower limits of the range of water content over which a soil exhibits plastic behaviour are defined as the *liquid limit* (*LL* or w_L) and the *plastic limit* (*PL* or w_P) respectively. The water content range itself is defined as the *plasticity index* (*PI* or I_P), i.e.:

$$I_P = w_L - w_P$$

However the transitions between the different states are gradual and the liquid and plastic limits must be defined arbitrarily. The natural water content (*w*) of a soil relative to the liquid and plastic limits can be represented by means of the *liquidity index* (*LI* or I_L), where:

$$I_L = \frac{w - w_P}{I_P}$$

The degree of plasticity of the clay size fraction of a soil is expressed by the ratio of the plasticity index to the percentage of clay size particles in the soil: this ratio is called the *activity*.

The transition between the semi-solid and solid states occurs at the *shrinkage limit*, defined as the water content at which the volume of the soil reaches its lowest value as it dries out.

The liquid and plastic limits are determined by means of arbitrary test procedures, fully detailed in BS 1377. The soil sample is dried sufficiently to enable it to be crumbled and broken up, using a mortar and a rubber pestle, without crushing individual particles: only material passing a No. 36 BS sieve (0·42 mm) is used in the tests.

The apparatus for the liquid limit test consists of a brass cup, mounted on an edge pivot: the cup rests initially on a hard rubber base. A mechanism enables the cup to be lifted to a height of 10 mm and dropped onto the base. The test soil is mixed with distilled water to form a thick paste and stored for 24 hours. Some of the paste is then placed in the cup, levelled off horizontally and divided by cutting a groove (on the diameter through the pivot of the cup) using a standard grooving tool. The two halves of the soil gradually flow together as the cup is repeatedly dropped onto the base at a rate of two drops per second. The number of drops, or blows, required to close the bottom of the groove over a distance of 13 mm is recorded. Repeat determinations should be made until two successive determinations give the same number of blows: the water content of the soil in the cup is then determined. The test is repeated at least four times, the water content of the paste being increased for each test: the number of blows should be within the limits of 50 and 10. Water content is plotted against the logarithm of the number of blows and the best straight line fitting the plotted points is drawn. An example appears in Fig. 1.8. The liquid limit is defined as the water content at which 25 blows are required to close the groove over a distance of 13 mm. BS 1377 also gives details of the determination of liquid limit based on a single test, provided the number of blows is between 35 and 15.

For the determination of the plastic limit the test soil is mixed with distilled water until it becomes sufficiently plastic to be moulded. A ball of the soil is rolled into a thread 3 mm in diameter between the hand and a glass plate. The soil is moulded together again and the process repeated until the thread crumbles when its diameter is 3 mm. The water content of the crumbled soil is then determined, this water content being defined as the plastic limit. The average of two separate determinations should be taken.

The determination of the liquid and plastic limits may be difficult in the case of soils having low percentages of clay mineral particles. The degree of plasticity of such soils can be indicated by means of the linear shrinkage test, detailed in BS 1377. A sample of the soil is mixed with distilled water to form a smooth paste at a water content approximating to the (estimated) liquid limit. The sample is placed in a brass mould having a semi-circular cross section of 13 mm radius and 140 mm long. The sample is dried out completely and the linear shrinkage (*LS*) is calculated as:

$$LS = 1 - \frac{\text{length after drying}}{\text{initial length}}$$

If the linear shrinkage is expressed as a percentage, an approximate value of the plasticity index is:

$$PI = 2 \cdot 13 \, LS$$

1.4   Soil Classification

The object of soil classification is to divide soils into groups such that all the soils in a particular group have similar characteristics, by which they may be identified, and exhibit similar behaviour in given engineering situations. A classification system also provides a common language for the exchange of information and experience regarding soils. Soil classification, however, should be regarded as the first step only in the evaluation of a soil as the classification tests (particle size analysis and liquid and plastic limit tests) use samples of the soil in a disturbed form: the properties of the soil in its in-situ condition may not be accurately represented. Numerical values of parameters representing permeability, shear strength and compressibility may also be required, depending on the problem under consideration: the determination of such parameters is considered in subsequent chapters.

Most soil classification systems divide soils into a number of groups each denoted by a group symbol. A soil is identified and allocated to the appropriate group on the basis of particle size distribution and plasticity, these characteristics being determined either by standard tests in the laboratory or by simple, and less accurate, visual and manual procedures in the field.

In addition to the appropriate group symbol, a general description of the soil and its in-situ condition should be given. This description should include the colour of the soil, details of the predominant particle shape and if possible the mineral composition of the particles. The soil in situ may be homogeneous or stratified. Sands and gravels may be loose, medium dense, dense or weakly-cemented. Clays may be described as very soft (exudes between the fingers when squeezed in the fist), soft (easily moulded in the fingers), firm (moulded in the fingers only by strong pressure), stiff (cannot be moulded in the fingers) or hard. It is also important to describe the arrangement of the minor geological details (referred to as the soil fabric) present in the soil as a whole as these details can influence the engineering behaviour of the soil to a considerable extent. Features such as layering, fissuring and inclusions should be described. Two examples of soil descriptions are given below.

'Reddish-brown, dense homogeneous, well-graded, clean sand consisting of sub-angular particles.'
'Dark-grey, firm, silty clay of low plasticity with small fissures and silt inclusions.'

Certain soils contain a significant proportion of finely-divided organic matter. Peat, a fibrous aggregate of decayed vegetable matter (i.e. not derived from rock) is normally included in soil classification systems.

In the Unified Soil Classification System [1.8] used in the United States the group symbols consist of a primary and a secondary descriptive letter. The letters and their meaning are given below.

Primary Letter	*Secondary Letter*
G: gravel	*W*: well-graded
S: sand	*P*: poorly-graded
M: silt	*M*: non-plastic fines
C: clay	*C*: plastic fines
O: organic	*L*: low plasticity
Pt: peat	*H*: high plasticity

The essential features of the Unified system are given in Table 1.1. Reference must also be made to the plasticity chart shown in Fig. 1.6.

The recommended procedure for field classification is detailed below. Initially the size of the largest particle in the sample should be estimated and any boulders and cobbles removed, their percentage by weight in the sample being estimated.

(1) Spread the sample on a flat surface and, based on observation, classify the soil as coarse-grained if more than 50% of the particles are visible to the naked eye: otherwise classify the soil as fine-grained.

(2) If coarse-grained, classify as gravel if more than 50% of the coarse fraction is of gravel size (larger than about 2·5 mm): otherwise classify as sand. If fine-grained see (6) below.

(3) If gravel or sand, classify as 'clean' (i.e. with little or no fines) or 'with appreciable fines'.

(4) Classify clean gravel or sand as either well-graded or poorly-graded.

(5) Classify gravel or sand with appreciable fines according to the nature of the fines as in (6) below.

(6) For a fine-grained soil or the fine-grained fraction of a coarse-grained soil classify on the basis of behaviour in the dilatancy, dry strength and toughness tests described below.

(7) Highly organic soils are identified by their colour, odour, spongy feel and fibrous texture and are classified as peat.

(8) Soils exhibiting the characteristics of two groups should be given a boundary classification denoted by dual symbols connected by a hyphen.

Dilatancy Test

Particles larger than about 0·5 mm (No. 36 BS sieve size) are removed and a small pat of moist soil is prepared. Enough water should be added to make the soil soft but not sticky. The pat is placed in the open palm of one hand and shaken horizontally by striking vigorously against the other hand several times. A positive reaction occurs when a film of water appears on the surface of the pat which changes to a 'livery' consistency and appears glossy. If the pat is now squeezed between the fingers the water and glossiness disappear from the surface, the pat becomes stiff and eventually cracks or crumbles. The rapidity with which water appears during shaking and disappears during squeezing should be noted. Very fine clean sands give the quickest and most positive reaction. Inorganic silts and rock flour give a moderately quick reaction. Plastic clays give no reaction.

Dry Strength Test

Particles larger than about 0·5 mm (No. 36 BS sieve size) are removed and a small specimen of soil is moulded to the consistency of putty, water being added if necessary. The soil is allowed to dry completely, by oven, sun or air drying, then its strength is assessed by breaking and crumbling between the fingers. The dry strength depends on the nature and the proportion of colloidal size particles in the soil. High dry strength indicates a clay with a high degree of plasticity: the dry strength decreases with decreasing plasticity. Inorganic silts show only slight dry strength and have a smooth feel when powdered. Silty sands also show only slight dry strength but have a gritty feel when powdered.

Table 1.1   Unified soil classification system

Description			Group symbols	Laboratory criteria			Notes
				Fines (%)	Grading	Plasticity	
Coarse grained (More than 50% larger than No. 200 BS sieve size)	Gravels (More than 50% of coarse fraction of gravel size)	Well-graded gravels, sandy gravels, with little or no fines	GW	0–5	$C_U > 4$ $1 < C_C < 3$		Dual symbols if 5–12% fines. Dual symbols if above 'A' line and $4 < PI < 7$
		Poorly-graded gravels, sandy gravels, with little or no fines	GP	0–5	Not satisfying GW requirements		
		Silty gravels, silty sandy gravels	GM	> 12		Below 'A' line or $PI < 4$	
		Clayey gravels, clayey sandy gravels	GC	> 12		Above 'A' line and $PI > 7$	
	Sands (More than 50% of coarse fraction of sand size)	Well-graded sands, gravelly sands, with little or no fines	SW	0–5	$C_U > 6$ $1 < C_C < 3$		
		Poorly-graded sands, gravelly sands, with little or no fines	SP	0–5	Not satisfying SW requirements		
		Silty sands	SM	> 12		Below 'A' line or $PI < 4$	
		Clayey sands	SC	> 12		Above 'A' line and $PI > 7$	
Fine grained (More than 50% smaller than No. 200 BS sieve size)	Silts and clays (Liquid limit less than 50)	Inorganic silts, silty or clayey fine sands, with slight plasticity	ML	Use Plasticity Chart			
		Inorganic clays, silty clays, sandy clays of low plasticity	CL	Use Plasticity Chart			
		Organic silts and organic silty clays of low plasticity	OL	Use Plasticity Chart			
	Silts and clays (Liquid limit greater than 50)	Inorganic silts of high plasticity	NH	Use Plasticity Chart			
		Inorganic clays of high plasticity	CH	Use Plasticity Chart			
		Organic clays of high plasticity	OH	Use Plasticity Chart			
Highly organic soils		Peat and other highly organic soils	Pt				

(After Wagner [1.8])

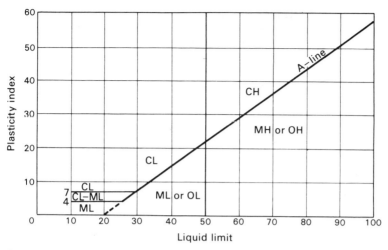

Figure 1.6   Plasticity chart.

Toughness Test

Particles larger than about 0·5 mm (No. 36 BS sieve size) are removed and a small specimen of soil is moulded to the consistency of putty. If the specimen is too dry water should be added and if too sticky the specimen should be allowed to dry to the required consistency. The specimen is rolled out between the open hands, or rolled out on a smooth surface, into a thread approximately 3 mm in diameter. The thread is repeatedly remoulded and re-rolled until it crumbles. The crumbled pieces are lumped together and subjected to kneading until the lump crumbles. The tougher the thread and the stiffer the kneaded lump just before they crumble the greater the activity of the colloidal size particles, indicating a clay of high plasticity. Weakness of the thread and quick loss of coherence of the kneaded lump indicate either an inorganic clay of low plasticity or an organic clay.

The characteristic behaviour of the fine-grained soil groups in the above tests are summarised in Table 1.2.

The British standard code of practice on site investigations CP2001 [1.2] classifies soils only in a very general way. Identification is based on the size and nature of the particles and on the density and structural features of the soil. Six principal soil types are recognised—boulders and cobbles, gravels, sands, silts, clays and peats.

Table 1.2   Field identification of fine-grained soils

Group	Dilatancy	Dry strength	Toughness
ML	Quick to slow	None to slight	None
CL	None to very slow	Medium to high	Medium
OL	Slow	Slight to medium	Slight
MH	Slow to none	Slight to medium	Slight to medium
CH	None	High to very high	High
OH	None to very slow	Medium to high	Slight to medium

(After Wagner [1.8])

Simple tests are detailed to enable the six types to be identified in the field. In CP 2001 a classification system relevant to road and airfield construction is also given, being a modification of a system developed by Casagrande [1.3].

In a suggested revision of the British system [1.4] the essential features of the Unified system are adopted but additional descriptive letters are introduced giving a more detailed classification: certain symbols are given slightly different meanings. The group symbols may consist of up to four descriptive letters.

Example 1.1

The results of the particle size analyses of four soils A, B, C and D are tabulated below. The results of limit tests on soil D are also given. The fine-grained fraction of soil C is non-plastic. Classify each soil according to the Unified system.

Soil		A	B	C	D
Particle size (mm)	BS sieve	Percentage smaller			
63·5	$2\frac{1}{2}$ in	100		93	
19·0	$\frac{3}{4}$ in	63		76	
6·3	$\frac{1}{4}$ in	40	100	66	
2·4	No. 7	26	99	60	
0·60	No. 25	12	89	54	
0·21	No. 72	5	9	47	100
0·075	No. 200	2	3	37	98
0·020				23	69
0·006				14	46
0·002				7	31

Soil D

Liquid Limit:					
Number of blows	40	31	23	19	12
Water content (%)	40·3	41·2	42·4	43·0	44·9
Plastic Limit:					
Water content (%)	23·9	23·0	24·4		

The particle size distribution curves are plotted in Fig. 1.7. For soils A, B and C the sizes D_{10}, D_{30} and D_{60} are read from the curves and the values of C_U and C_C are calculated.

Soil	D_{10}	D_{30}	D_{60}	C_U	C_C
A	0·47	3·5	16	34	1·6
B	0·23	0·30	0·41	1·8	0·95
C	0·003	0·042	2·4	800	0·25

For soil D the liquid limit is obtained from Fig. 1.8 in which water content is plotted against the logarithm of the number of blows. The percentage water content, to the nearest integer, corresponding to 25 blows is the liquid limit and is 42. The

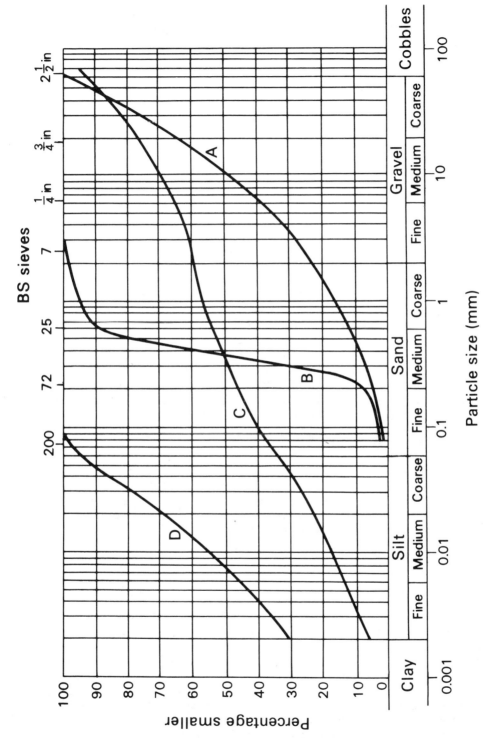

Figure 1.7   Particle size distribution curves (Example 1.1).

plastic limit is the average of the three percentage water contents, again to the nearest integer, i.e. 24. The plasticity index is the difference between the liquid and plastic limits, namely 18.

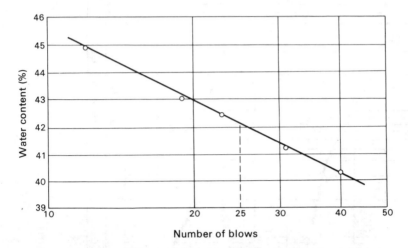

Figure 1.8   Determination of liquid limit (Example 1.1).

Soil A is classified as *GW*, a well-graded sandy gravel. More than 50% of the coarse-grained fraction is of gravel size and the fine-grained fraction is less than 5%. The coefficient C_U is greater than 4 and the coefficient C_C is between 1 and 3.

Soil B is classified as *SP*, a poorly-graded sand, 95% of the particles being of sand size; the fine-grained fraction is less than 5%. The coefficient C_U is less than 6 and the coefficient C_C is not between 1 and 3.

Soil C is classified as *GM* and is a glacial till, a soil consisting of particles in all size ranges. The coarse-grained fraction is 65% and the fine-grained fraction 35%. More than 50% of the coarse-grained fraction is of gravel size. The fine-grained fraction is non-plastic. Although C_U is very high, C_C is not between 1 and 3.

Soil D is classified as *CL*, a silty clay of low plasticity. The soil is 98% fine-grained, 67% being of silt size and 31% of clay size. The liquid limit is 42 and the plasticity index is 18, plotting just above the '*A*' line in the *CL* zone on the plasticity chart (Fig. 1.6).

1.5   Site Investigation

An adequate site investigation is an essential preliminary to any civil engineering project. The object is to determine the sequence of the strata, the extent and nature of each soil (and rock) and the soil water conditions. In addition, representative samples of the different soils are obtained for identification and for the determination of relevant parameters. The investigation must be carried out to a depth covering all strata likely to be significantly affected by the project. The various strata can be exposed by means of trial pits, borings or headings. The lateral extent of the investigation and the number of trial pits, borings or headings depends on the degree of variation of the strata in the horizontal direction. Two types of samples may be obtained once a particular stratum has been exposed—disturbed and undisturbed. Disturbed samples are obtained using techniques (direct excavation; auger or shell sampling) which modify or destroy the natural soil structure. Undisturbed samples are obtained using techniques (block or core sampling) which aim at preserving the natural structure and water content of the soil: however it is impossible to obtain an absolutely undisturbed sample. Full details of site investigation procedures are given in CP 2001 [1.2].

1.6   Phase Relationships

Soils can be of either two-phase or three-phase composition. In a completely dry soil there are two phases, namely the solid soil particles and pore air. A fully saturated soil is also two-phase, being composed of solid soil particles and pore water. A partially saturated soil is three-phase, being composed of solid soil particles, pore water and pore air. The components of a soil can be represented by a phase diagram as shown in Fig. 1.9a. The following relationships are defined with reference to Fig. 1.9a.

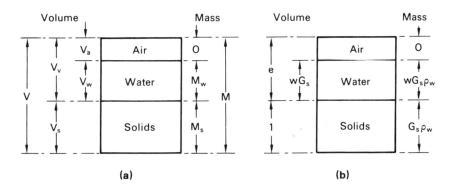

(a)   (b)

Figure 1.9   Phase diagrams.

The *water content* (*w*), or *moisture content* (*m*), is the ratio of the mass of water to the mass of solids in the soil, i.e.:

$$w = \frac{M_w}{M_s} \tag{1.3}$$

The water content is determined by weighing a sample of the soil then drying the sample in an oven at a temperature of 105–110°C and re-weighing. Drying should continue until the differences between successive weighings at four-hourly intervals are not greater than 0·1% of the original mass of the sample. A drying period of 24 hours is normally adequate for most soils. (See BS 1377.)

The *degree of saturation* (*S_r*) is the ratio of the volume of water to the total volume of void space, i.e.:

$$S_r = \frac{V_w}{V_v} \tag{1.4}$$

The degree of saturation can range between the limits of zero for a completely dry soil and 1 (or 100%) for a fully saturated soil.

The *void ratio* (e) is the ratio of the volume of voids to the volume of solids, i.e.:

$$e = \frac{V_v}{V_s} \tag{1.5}$$

The *porosity* (n) is the ratio of the volume of voids to the total volume of the soil, i.e.:

$$n = \frac{V_v}{V} \tag{1.6}$$

The void ratio and the porosity are inter-related as follows:

$$e = \frac{n}{1 - n} \tag{1.7}$$

$$n = \frac{e}{1 + e} \tag{1.8}$$

The *air content* (A) is the ratio of the volume of air to the total volume of the soil, i.e.:

$$A = \frac{V_a}{V} \tag{1.9}$$

The *bulk density* (ρ) of a soil is the ratio of the total mass to the total volume, i.e.:

$$\rho = \frac{M}{V} \tag{1.10}$$

Convenient units for density are kg/m^3 or Mg/m^3. The density of water (1000 kg/m^3 or 1.00 Mg/m^3) is denoted by ρ_w.

The specific gravity of the *solid soil particles* (G_s) is given by:

$$G_s = \frac{M_s}{V_s \rho_w} \tag{1.11}$$

Procedures for determining the value of G_s are detailed in BS 1377.

From the definition of void ratio, if the volume of solids is 1 unit then the volume of voids is e units. The mass of solids is then $G_s \rho_w$ and, from the definition of water content, the mass of water is $w G_s \rho_w$. The volume of water is thus $w G_s$. These volumes and masses are represented in Fig. 1.9b. The following relationships can now be obtained.

The degree of saturation can be expressed as:

$$S_r = \frac{w G_s}{e} \tag{1.12}$$

In the case of a fully saturated soil, $S_r = 1$, hence:

$$e = w G_s \tag{1.13}$$

The air content can be expressed as:

$$A = \frac{e - wG_s}{1 + e} \tag{1.14}$$

or, from equations 1.12 and 1.8:

$$A = n(1 - S_r) \tag{1.15}$$

The bulk density of a soil can be expressed as:

$$\rho = \frac{G_s(1 + w)}{1 + e} \rho_w \tag{1.16}$$

or, from equation 1.12:

$$\rho = \frac{G_s + S_r e}{1 + e} \rho_w \tag{1.17}$$

For a fully saturated soil ($S_r = 1$):

$$\rho_{sat} = \frac{G_s + e}{1 + e} \rho_w \tag{1.18}$$

For a completely dry soil ($S_r = 0$):

$$\rho_d = \frac{G_s}{1 + e} \rho_w \tag{1.19}$$

The *unit weight* (γ) of a soil is the ratio of the total weight (a force) to the total volume, i.e.:

$$\gamma = \frac{W}{V} = \frac{Mg}{V}$$

Equations similar to 1.16 to 1.19 apply in the case of unit weights, for example:

$$\gamma = \frac{G_s(1 + w)}{1 + e} \gamma_w \tag{1.16a}$$

$$\gamma = \frac{G_s + S_r e}{1 + e} \gamma_w \tag{1.17a}$$

where γ_w is the unit weight of water. Convenient units are kN/m^3, the unit weight of water being 9·8 kN/m^3.

When a soil in-situ is fully saturated the solid soil particles (volume 1 unit, weight $G_s \gamma_w$) are subjected to upthrust (γ_w). Hence the *buoyant unit weight* (γ') is given by:

$$\gamma' = \frac{G_s \gamma_w - \gamma_w}{1 + e} = \frac{G_s - 1}{1 + e} \gamma_w \tag{1.20}$$

i.e.:

$$\gamma' = \gamma_{sat} - \gamma_w \tag{1.21}$$

In the case of sands and gravels the *relative density* (RD or I_D) is used to express the relationship between the actual void ratio (e) and the limiting values e_{max} and e_{min}. The relative density is defined as:

$$RD = \frac{e_{max} - e}{e_{max} - e_{min}} \tag{1.22}$$

Thus the relative density of a soil in its densest possible state ($e = e_{min}$) is 1 (or 100%) and the relative density in its loosest possible state ($e = e_{max}$) is 0.

Example 1.2

In its natural condition a soil sample has a mass of 2290 g and a volume of $1 \cdot 15 \times 10^{-3}$ m^3. After being completely dried in an oven the mass of the sample is 2035 g. The value of G_s for the soil is 2·68. Determine the bulk density, unit weight, water content, void ratio, porosity, degree of saturation and air content.

$$\text{Bulk density, } \rho = \frac{M}{V} = \frac{2 \cdot 290}{1 \cdot 15 \times 10^{-3}} = 1990 \text{ kg/m}^3 \ 1.99 \text{ Mg/m}^3$$

$$\text{Unit weight, } \gamma = \frac{Mg}{V} = 1990 \times 9 \cdot 8 = 19{,}500 \text{ N/m}^3$$
$$= 19 \cdot 5 \text{ kN/m}^3$$

$$\text{Water content, } w = \frac{M_w}{M_s} = \frac{2290 - 2035}{2035} = 0 \cdot 125 \text{ or } 12 \cdot 5\%$$

From equation 1.16, void ratio, $e = G_s (1 + w)\dfrac{\rho_w}{\rho} - 1$

$$= \left(2 \cdot 68 \times 1 \cdot 125 \times \frac{1000}{1990}\right) - 1$$
$$= 1 \cdot 52 - 1$$
$$= 0 \cdot 52$$

$$\text{Porosity, } n = \frac{e}{1 + e} = \frac{0 \cdot 52}{1 \cdot 52} = 0 \cdot 34 \text{ or } 34\%$$

$$\text{Degree of saturation, } S_r = \frac{wG_s}{e} = \frac{0 \cdot 125 \times 2 \cdot 68}{0 \cdot 52} = 0 \cdot 645 \text{ or } 64 \cdot 5\%$$

$$\text{Air content, } A = n(1 - S_r) = 0 \cdot 34 \times 0 \cdot 355$$
$$= 0 \cdot 121 \text{ or } 12 \cdot 1\%$$

1.7 Soil Compaction

Compaction is the process of increasing the density of a soil by packing the particles closer together with a reduction in the volume of *air*: the volume of water remains unchanged. In the construction of fills and embankments loose soil is placed in layers (normally 200–300 mm thick), each layer being compacted to a specified standard by means of rollers (smooth-wheeled, sheepsfoot or pneumatic-tyred), vibrators (roller or plate) or rammers. The degree of compaction of a soil is measured in terms of dry density, i.e. the mass of solids only per unit volume of soil. If the bulk density of the soil is ρ and the water content w, then from equations 1.16 and 1.19 it is apparent that the dry density is given by:

$$\rho_d = \frac{\rho}{1 + w} \qquad\qquad (1.23)$$

The dry density after compaction depends on the type of soil, the water content and the effort supplied by the compaction equipment.

The compaction characteristics of a soil can be assessed by means of standard laboratory tests. The soil is compacted in a cylindrical mould using a standard compactive effort. In BS 1377 three compaction procedures are detailed. In the *standard* test the volume of the mould is $9 \cdot 44 \times 10^{-4}$ m^3 and the soil (with all particles larger than 20 mm removed) is compacted by a rammer consisting of a $2 \cdot 5$ kg mass falling freely through 305 mm: the soil is compacted in three equal layers, each layer receiving 25 blows with the rammer. In the *heavy* test the mould is the same as is used in the standard test but the rammer consists of a $4 \cdot 5$ kg mass falling 458 mm: the soil (with all particles larger than 20 mm removed) is compacted in five layers, each layer receiving 25 blows with the rammer. In the *vibrating hammer* test, which is suitable for sands and gravels, the volume of the mould is $2 \cdot 31 \times 10^{-3}$ m^3: the soil (with all particles larger than 40 mm removed) is compacted in three layers under a circular steel tamper fitted in the vibrating hammer, each layer being compacted for a period of 60 s.

After compaction using one of the three standard methods, the bulk density and water content of the soil are determined and the dry density calculated. For a given soil the process is repeated at least five times, the water content of the sample being increased each time. Dry density is plotted against water content and a curve of the form shown in Fig. 1.10 is obtained. This curve shows that for a particular method of compaction (i.e. a particular compactive effort) there is a particular value of water content, known as the *optimum water content* (w_{opt}) at which a maximum value of dry density is obtained. At low values of water content most soils tend to be stiff and

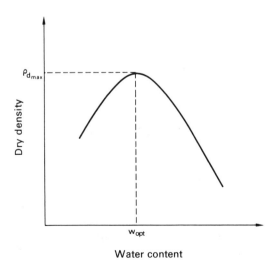

Figure 1.10   Dry density–water content relationship.

are difficult to compact. As the water content is increased the soil becomes more workable, facilitating compaction and resulting in higher dry densities. At high water contents, however, the dry density decreases with increasing water content, an increasing proportion of the soil volume being occupied by water.

If all the air in a soil could be expelled by compaction the soil would be in a state of full saturation and the dry density would be the maximum possible value for the given water content. However this degree of compaction is unattainable in practice. The maximum possible value of dry density is referred to as the 'zero air voids' dry density or the saturation dry density and can be calculated from the expression:

$$\rho_d = \frac{G_s}{1 + wG_s} \rho_w \qquad (1.24)$$

In general the dry density after compaction at water content w to an air content A can be calculated from the following expression, derived from equations 1.14 and 1.19:

$$\rho_d = \frac{G_s(1 - A)}{1 + wG_s} \rho_w \qquad (1.25)$$

The calculated relationship between zero air voids dry density and water content (for $G_s = 2\cdot65$) is shown in Fig. 1.11; the curve is referred to as the zero air voids line or the saturation line. The experimental dry density/water content curve for a particular compactive effort must lie completely to the left of the zero air voids line. The curves relating dry density at air contents of 5% and 10% with water content are also shown in Fig. 1.11, the values of dry density being calculated from equation 1.25. These curves enable the air content at any point on the experimental dry density/water content curve to be determined by inspection.

For a particular soil, different dry density/water content curves are obtained for different compactive efforts. Curves representing the results of BS 'standard' and 'heavy' compaction tests are shown in Fig. 1.11. The curve for the 'heavy' test is situated above and to the left of the curve for the 'standard' test. Thus a higher compactive effort results in a higher value of maximum dry density and a lower value of optimum water content: however the values of air content at maximum dry density are approximately equal.

The dry density/water content curves for a range of soil types using the same compactive effort (the BS 'standard' test procedure) are shown in Fig. 1.12. In general coarse-grained soils can be compacted to higher dry densities than fine-grained soils.

Laboratory compaction tests are not directly applicable to field compaction since the compactive efforts in the laboratory tests are different from those produced by the field equipment. Further, the laboratory tests are carried out only on material smaller than either 20 mm or 40 mm size. Laboratory test results provide only a rough guide to the water content at which the maximum dry density will be obtained in the field. The main value of laboratory tests is in the classification and selection of soils for use in fills and embankments.

The dry density achieved after field compaction expressed as a percentage of the maximum dry density in a particular laboratory test is defined as the *relative compaction*. The required standard of field compaction may be specified in terms of relative compaction: for example a specification may state that the dry density should not be less than 95% of the maximum dry density in the BS 'standard' compaction test. In addition, water content limits must be specified, compaction being allowed

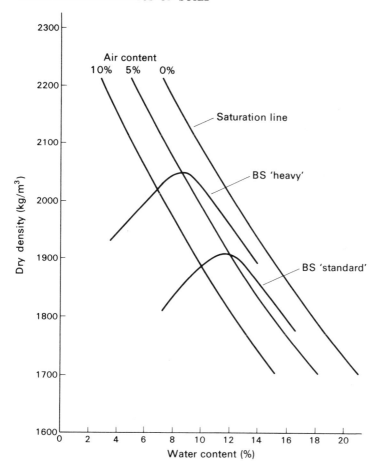

Figure 1.11   Dry density–water content curves for different compactive efforts.

to proceed only if the natural water content of the soil is within these limits. However specification based on the results of laboratory tests is not recommended because of the reasons given in the previous paragraph. An alternative method of specification is to give the maximum air content to which the soil must be compacted in the field. Water content limits must again be specified and, based on experience in Great Britain, it has been suggested that the limits should be based on the average natural water content measured below the top 1 m of unexcavated soil provided the soil at this depth is above the water table. For major projects field compaction trials should be carried out to determine the best compaction procedure. The performance of different types of field compaction equipment on different soils has been investigated by the Transport and Road Research Laboratory and much useful data has been published [1.6].

If the natural water content of the soil is less than the lower limit specified, water may be added. An alternative would be to allow the use of heavier compaction equipment, a greater compactive effort being associated with a lower optimum water content. If the natural water content is above the upper limit specified, compaction

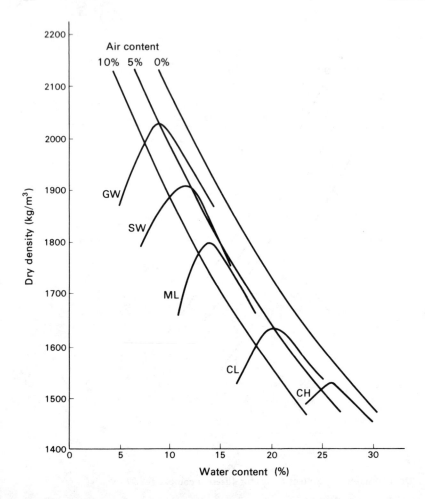

Figure 1.12   Dry density–water content curves for a range of soil types.

should be delayed to allow the soil to dry sufficiently as in this case there is no other way of obtaining adequate dry densities.

The standard of field compaction is controlled by means of frequent measurements of the bulk density and water content of the newly-compacted soil. A number of methods of measuring bulk density in the field are detailed in BS 1377.

Problems

1.1   The results of particle size analyses and, where appropriate, limit tests on samples of four soils are given below. Classify each soil according to the Unified system.

Soil		E	F	G	H
Particle size (mm)	BS sieve	Percentage smaller			
63·5	2½ in				
19·0	¾ in	100			
6·3	¼ in	94			
2·4	No. 7	75	100		
0·60	No. 25	32	89	100	
0·21	No. 72	14	70	96	
0·075	No. 200	3	42	78	100
0·020			21	46	88
0·006			11	25	71
0·002			4	13	58
Liquid limit			Non-plastic	32	78
Plastic limit				24	31

1.2   A soil has a bulk density of 1910 kg/m³ and a water content of 9·5%. The value of G_s is 2·70. Calculate the void ratio and degree of saturation of the soil. What would be the values of density and water content if the soil were fully saturated at the same void ratio?

1.3   Calculate the dry unit weight, the saturated unit weight and the buoyant unit weight of a soil having a void ratio of 0·70 and a value of G_s of 2·72. Calculate also the unit weight and water content at a degree of saturation of 75%.

1.4   A soil specimen is 38 mm in diameter and 76 mm long and in its natural condition weighs 168·0 g. When dried completely in an oven the specimen weighs 130·5 g. The value of G_s is 2·73. What is the degree of saturation of the specimen?

1.5   Soil has been compacted in an embankment at a bulk density of 2150 kg/m³ and a water content of 12%. The value of G_s is 2·65. Calculate the dry density, void ratio, degree of saturation and air content.

1.6   The following results were obtained from a standard compaction test on a soil. The value of G_s is 2·67. Plot the dry density/water content curve and give the optimum water content and maximum dry density. Plot also the curves of zero, 5% and 10% air content and give the value of air content at maximum dry density.

Mass (g)	1895	1970	1990	1985	1940
Water content (%)	12·8	14·5	15·6	16·8	19·2

The volume of the mould is $9·44 \times 10^{-4}$ m³.

References

1.1   British Standard 1377 (1967): *Methods of Testing Soils for Civil Engineering Purposes*, British Standards Institution, London.

1.2   British Standard Code of Practice, CP 2001 (1957): *Site Investigations*, British Standards Institution, London.

1.3   Casagrande, A. (1948): 'Classification and Identification of Soils', *Transactions ASCE*, Vol. 113, p. 901.

1.4   Dumbleton, M. J. (1968): *The Classification and Description of Soils for Engineering Purposes: a Suggested Revision of the British System*, Report LR 182, Transport and Road Research Laboratory, Crowthorne, Berkshire.

1.5   Grim, R. E. (1953): *Clay Mineralogy*, McGraw-Hill, New York.

1.6   Lewis, W. A. (1954): *Further Studies in the Compaction of Soil and the Performance of Compaction Plant*, Road Research Technical Paper No. 33, HMSO, London.

1.7   Rowe, P. W. (1972): 'The Relevance of Soil Fabric to Site Investigation Practice', *Geotechnique*, Vol. 22, No. 2.

1.8   Wagner, A. A. (1957): 'The Use of the Unified Soil Classification System by the Bureau of Reclamation', *Proceedings 4th International Conference SMFE, London*, Vol. 1, Butterworths.

CHAPTER 2

Seepage

2.1 Soil Water

All soils are *permeable* materials, water being free to flow through the interconnected pores between the solid particles. The pressure of the pore water is measured relative to atmospheric pressure and the level at which the pressure is atmospheric (i.e. zero) is defined as the *water table* (W.T.) or the *phreatic surface*. Below the water table the soil is assumed to be fully-saturated although it is likely that, due to the presence of small volumes of entrapped air, the degree of saturation will be marginally below 100%. The level of the water table changes according to climatic conditions but the level can change also as a consequence of constructional operations. A *perched* water table can occur locally, contained by soil of low permeability, above the normal water table level. *Artesian* conditions can exist if an inclined soil layer of high permeability is confined locally by an overlying layer of low permeability: the pressure in the artesian layer is governed not by the local water table level but by a higher water table level at a distant location where the layer is unconfined.

Below the water table the pore water may be static, the hydrostatic pressure depending on the depth below the water table, or may be seeping through the soil under hydraulic gradient: this chapter is concerned with the second case. Bernoulli's theorem applies to the pore water but seepage velocities in soils are normally so small that velocity head can be neglected. Thus:

$$h = \frac{u}{\gamma_w} + z \tag{2.1}$$

where:

h = total head,
u = pore water pressure,
γ_w = unit weight of water ($9 \cdot 8$ kN/m^3),
z = elevation head above a chosen datum.

Above the water table, water can be held at negative pressure by capillary tension: the smaller the size of the pores the higher the water can rise above the water table. The capillary rise tends to be irregular due to the random pore sizes occurring in a soil. The soil can be almost completely saturated in the lower part of the capillary zone but in general the degree of saturation decreases with height. When water percolates through the soil from the surface towards the water table some of this water can be held by surface tension around the points of contact between particles. The negative pressure of water held above the water table results in attractive forces between the particles: this attraction is referred to as soil suction and is a function of pore size and water content.

2.2   Permeability

In one dimension, water flows through a fully-saturated soil in accordance with Darcy's empirical law:

$$q = Aki \tag{2.2}$$

or,

$$v = \frac{q}{A} = ki$$

where:

q = volume of water flowing per unit time,
A = cross-sectional area of soil corresponding to the flow q,
k = coefficient of permeability,
i = hydraulic gradient,
v = discharge velocity.

The units of the coefficient of permeability are those of velocity (m/s).

The coefficient of permeability depends primarily on the average size of the pores, which in turn is related to the distribution of particle sizes, particle shape and soil structure. In general, the smaller the particles the smaller is the average size of the pores and the lower is the coefficient of permeability. The presence of a small percentage of fines in a coarse-grained soil results in a value of k significantly lower than the value for the same soil without fines. For a given soil the coefficient of permeability is a function of void ratio. If a soil deposit is stratified the permeability for flow parallel to the direction of stratification is higher than that for flow perpendicular to the direction of stratification. The presence of fissures in a clay results in a much higher value of permeability compared with that of the unfissured material.

The coefficient of permeability also varies with temperature, upon which the viscosity of the water depends. If the value of k measured at 20°C is taken as 100% then the values at 10°C and 0°C are 77% and 56% respectively. The coefficient of permeability can also be represented by the equation:

$$k = \frac{\gamma_w}{\eta} K \tag{2.3}$$

where γ_w is the unit weight of water, η is the viscosity of water and K (units m^2) is an absolute coefficient depending only on the characteristics of the skeleton of solid particles.

The values of k for different types of soil are typically within the ranges shown in Table 2.1. The values of k extend over many orders of magnitude, for example the value for a gravel can be 10^{10} times that for an unfissured clay.

On the microscopic scale the water seeping through a soil follows a very tortuous path between the solid particles but macroscopically the flow path (in one dimension)

Table 2.1   Coefficient of permeability (m/s) (CP 2004: 1972)

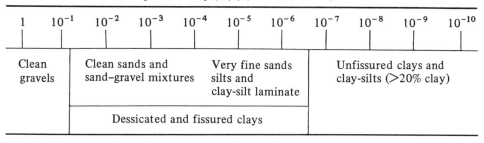

1	10^{-1}	10^{-2}	10^{-3}	10^{-4}	10^{-5}	10^{-6}	10^{-7}	10^{-8}	10^{-9}	10^{-10}

Clean gravels	Clean sands and sand–gravel mixtures	Very fine sands silts and clay-silt laminate	Unfissured clays and clay-silts (>20% clay)
	Dessicated and fissured clays		

can be considered as a straight line. The average velocity at which the water flows through the soil pores is obtained by dividing the volume of water flowing per unit time by the average area of voids (A_v) on a cross-section normal to the macroscopic direction of flow: this velocity is called the seepage velocity (v'). Thus:

$$v' = \frac{q}{A_v}$$

The porosity of a soil is defined in terms of volume:

$$n = \frac{V_v}{V}$$

However, on average, the porosity can also be expressed as:

$$n = \frac{A_v}{A}$$

Hence:

$$v' = \frac{q}{nA} = \frac{v}{n}$$

or,

$$v' = \frac{ki}{n} \tag{2.4}$$

Determination of Coefficient of Permeability

1.   Laboratory Methods

The coefficient of permeability for coarse-grained soils can be determined by means of the *constant head* permeability test (Fig. 2.1a). The soil specimen, at the appropriate density, is contained in a perspex cylinder of cross-sectional area A: the specimen rests on a coarse filter or a wire mesh. A steady vertical flow of water, under a constant total head, is maintained through the soil and the volume of water flowing per unit time (q) is measured. Tappings from the side of the cylinder enable the hydraulic gradient (h/l) to be measured. Then from Darcy's law:

$$k = \frac{ql}{Ah}$$

A series of tests should be run, each at a different rate of flow. Prior to running the test a vacuum is applied to the specimen to ensure that the degree of saturation under flow will be close to 100%. If a high degree of saturation is to be maintained the water used in the test should be de-aired.

For fine-grained soils the *falling-head* test (Fig. 2.1b) should be used. In the case of fine-grained soils, undistributed specimens are normally tested and the containing cylinder in the test may be the sampling tube itself. The length of the specimen is l

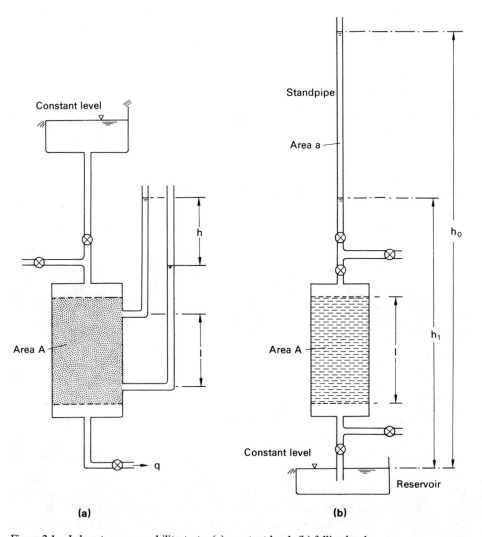

Figure 2.1   Laboratory permeability tests: (a) constant head, (b) falling head.

and the cross-sectional area A. A coarse filter is placed at each end of the specimen and a standpipe of internal area a is connected to the top of the cylinder. The water drains into a reservoir of constant level. The standpipe is filled with water and a measurement is made of the time (t_1) for the water level (relative to the water level in the reservoir) to fall from h_0 to h_1. At any intermediate time t the water level in the standpipe is given by h and its rate of change by $-dh/dt$. At time t the difference in total head between the top and bottom of the specimen is h. Then applying Darcy's law:

$$-a\frac{dh}{dt} = Ak\frac{h}{l}$$

$$\therefore \qquad -a\int_{h_0}^{h_1}\frac{dh}{h} = \frac{Ak}{l}\int_{0}^{t_1}dt$$

$$\therefore \qquad k = \frac{al}{At_1}\ln\frac{h_0}{h_1}$$

$$= 2\cdot 3\,\frac{al}{At_1}\log\frac{h_0}{h_1}$$

Again, precautions must be taken to ensure that the degree of saturation remains close to 100%. A series of tests should be run using different values of h_0 and h_1 and/or standpipes of different diameters.

The coefficient of permeability of fine grained soils can also be determined indirectly from the results of consolidation tests (see Chapter 7).

2. In-situ Methods

The reliability of laboratory permeability determinations depends on the extent to which the test specimens are representative of the in-situ soil mass as a whole. For important projects the in-situ determination of permeability may be justified.

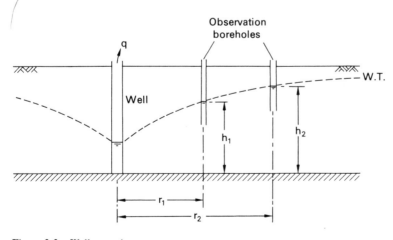

Figure 2.2   Well pumping test.

One in-situ method is the *well pumping test* which is suitable for use in homogeneous coarse-grained soil strata. The method involves continuous pumping from a well which penetrates to the bottom of the stratum and observing the water levels in a number of adjacent boreholes. Pumping is continued until steady seepage conditions become established. Seepage takes place radially towards the well and the boreholes are located, therefore, on a number of radial lines from the centre of the well: at least two boreholes are required on each line. A section through the well and two boreholes is shown in Fig. 2.2. Drawdown of the water table takes place as the result of pumping and when the steady state is established the water levels in the boreholes correspond to the new water table position. The boreholes are located at distances r_1 and r_2 from the well and the respective water table levels are at heights of h_1 and h_2 above the bottom of the stratum.

The analysis is based on the assumption that the hydraulic gradient at any distance r from the well is constant with depth and is equal to the slope of the water table, i.e.:

$$i_r = \frac{dh}{dr}$$

where h is the height of the water table at radius r. This is known as the Dupuit assumption and is reasonably accurate except at points close to the well. At distance r from the well the area through which flow takes place is $2\pi rh$. Then applying Darcy's law:

$$q = 2\pi rhk \frac{dh}{dr}$$

$$\therefore \qquad q \int_{r_1}^{r_2} \frac{dr}{r} = 2\pi k \int_{h_1}^{h_2} h \, dh$$

$$\therefore \qquad q \ln\left(\frac{r_2}{r_1}\right) = \pi k \left(h_2^2 - h_1^2\right)$$

$$\therefore \qquad k = \frac{2 \cdot 3q \log\left(r_2/r_1\right)}{\pi(h_2^2 - h_1^2)}$$

This equation is applied to each pair of boreholes and an average value of k is obtained.

Other in-situ methods include constant head and variable head *borehole tests*. In one procedure, water is allowed to flow, under constant head, into (or out of) the stratum under test through the bottom of a borehole, the sides of which are lined with a pipe casing. The arrangement is illustrated in Fig. 2.3a: the lower end of the borehole should not be less than $5d$ from either the top or bottom of the stratum, where d is the internal diameter of the casing. The water level in the borehole is maintained constant, the difference between this level and water table level being h. The rate of flow (q) required to maintain the constant water level is measured. The coefficient of permeability can then be calculated from the following equation, developed from electrical analogy experiments:

$$k = \frac{q}{2 \cdot 75 \, dh}$$

Care must be taken to ensure that clogging of the soil face at the bottom of the bore-hole does not occur due to the deposition of sediment from the water. If desired, water may be pumped into the borehole under pressure.

In a variable head test the rate of flow from the stratum into the borehole is measured by observing the time (t) for the water level in the borehole, relative to water table level, to change from a value h_1 to a value h_2. Hvorslev [2.4] published formulae for the determination of permeability in a number of borehole situations: two examples are given below. A cased borehole, of internal diameter d, penetrating a short distance D (not exceeding $1 \cdot 5$ m) below the water table in a stratum assumed to be of infinite depth, is shown in Fig. 2.3b: the coefficient of permeability for this situation is given by:

$$k = \frac{\pi d}{11 t} \ln \left(\frac{h_1}{h_2} \right)$$

A borehole with a cased length and an uncased or perforated extension of length L (where $L > 4d$) in a stratum assumed to be of infinite depth, is shown in Fig. 2.3c: the coefficient of permeability for this situation is given by:

$$k = \frac{d^2}{8 L t} \ln \left(\frac{2L}{d} \right) \ln \left(\frac{h_1}{h_2} \right)$$

The permeability of a coarse-grained soil can also be obtained from in-situ measurements of *seepage velocity*, using equation 2.4. The method involves excavating uncased boreholes (or trial pits) at two points A and B (Fig. 2.3d), seepage taking place from A towards B. The hydraulic gradient is given by the difference in the steady state water levels in the boreholes divided by the distance AB. Dye or any other suitable tracer is inserted into borehole A and the time taken for the dye to appear in borehole B is measured. The seepage velocity is then the distance AB divided by this time. The porosity of the soil can be determined from density tests. Then:

$$k = \frac{v' n}{i}$$

2.3 Seepage Theory

The general case of seepage in two dimensions will now be considered. Initially it will be assumed that the soil is homogeneous and isotropic with respect to permeability, the coefficient of permeability being k. In the x–z plane, Darcy's law can be written in the generalised form:

$$v_x = k i_x = - k \frac{\partial h}{\partial x} \tag{2.5a}$$

$$v_z = k i_z = - k \frac{\partial h}{\partial z} \tag{2.5b}$$

(total head h decreasing in the directions of v_x and v_z).

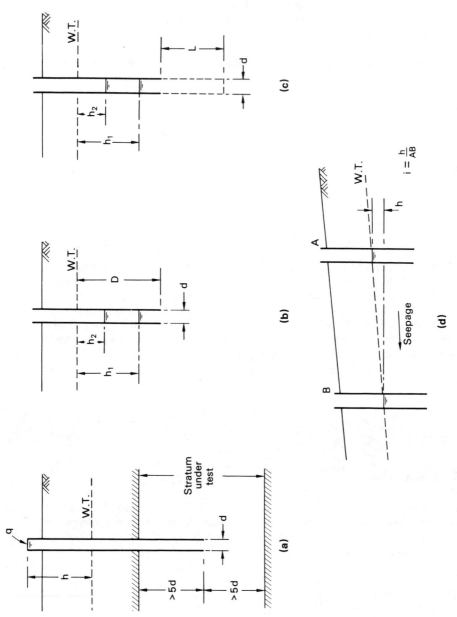

Figure 2.3   Borehole tests.

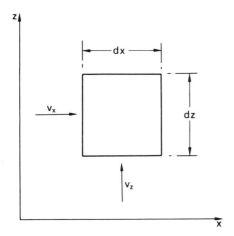

Figure 2.4   Seepage through a soil element.

An element of fully-saturated soil having dimensions dx, dy and dz in the x, y and z directions respectively, with flow taking place in the x, z plane only, is shown in Fig. 2.4. The components of discharge velocity of water entering the element are v_x and v_z and the rates of change of discharge velocity in the x and z directions are $\partial v_x/\partial x$ and $\partial v_z/\partial z$ respectively. The volume of water entering the element per unit time is:

$$v_x \, dy \, dz + v_z \, dx \, dy$$

and the volume of water leaving per unit time is:

$$\left(v_x + \frac{\partial v_x}{\partial x} dx\right) dy \, dz + \left(v_z + \frac{\partial v_z}{\partial z} dz\right) dx \, dy$$

If the element is undergoing no volume change and if water is assumed to be incompressible, the difference between the volume of water entering the element per unit time and the volume leaving must be zero.
Therefore:

$$\frac{\partial v_x}{\partial x} + \frac{\partial v_z}{\partial z} = 0 \tag{2.6}$$

Equation 2.6 is the *equation of continuity* in two dimensions. If, however, the volume of the element is undergoing change, the equation of continuity becomes:

$$\left(\frac{\partial v_x}{\partial x} + \frac{\partial v_z}{\partial z}\right) dx \, dy \, dz = \frac{dV}{dt} \tag{2.7}$$

where dV/dt is the volume change per unit time.
Consider, now, the function $\phi(x, z)$, called the *potential function*, such that:

$$\frac{\partial \phi}{\partial x} = v_x = -k \frac{\partial h}{\partial x} \tag{2.8a}$$

$$\frac{\partial \phi}{\partial z} = v_z = - k \frac{\partial h}{\partial z} \tag{2.8b}$$

From equations 2.6 and 2.8 it is apparent that:

$$\frac{\partial^2 \phi}{\partial x^2} + \frac{\partial^2 \phi}{\partial z^2} = 0 \tag{2.9}$$

i.e. the function $\phi(x,z)$ satisfies the Laplace equation.

Integrating equation 2.8:

$$\phi(x,z) = -kh(x,z) + C$$

where C is a constant. Thus, if the function $\phi(x,z)$ is given a constant value, equal to ϕ_1 (say), it will represent a curve along which the value of total head (h_1) is constant. If the function $\phi(x,z)$ is given a series of constant values, ϕ_1, ϕ_2, ϕ_3, etc., a family of curves is specified along each of which the total head is a constant value (but a different value for each curve). Such curves are called *equipotentials*.

A second function $\psi(x,z)$, called the *flow function*, is now introduced, such that:

$$-\frac{\partial \psi}{\partial x} = v_z = - k \frac{\partial h}{\partial z} \tag{2.10a}$$

$$\frac{\partial \psi}{\partial z} = v_x = - k \frac{\partial h}{\partial x} \tag{2.10b}$$

It can be shown that this function also satisfies the Laplace equation.

The total differential of the function $\psi(x,z)$ is:

$$d\psi = \frac{\partial \psi}{\partial x} dx + \frac{\partial \psi}{\partial z} dz$$

$$= - v_z dx + v_x dz$$

If the function $\psi(x,z)$ is given a constant value ψ_1 then $d\psi = 0$ and:

$$\frac{dz}{dx} = \frac{v_z}{v_x} \tag{2.11}$$

Thus the tangent at any point on the curve represented by

$$\psi(x,z) = \psi_1$$

specifies the direction of the resultant discharge velocity at that point: the curve therefore represents the flow path. If the function $\psi(x,z)$ is given a series of constant values ψ_1, ψ_2, ψ_3, etc., a second family of curves is specified, each representing a flow path. These curves are called *flow lines*.

Referring to Fig. 2.5, the flow per unit time between two flow lines for which the values of the flow function are ψ_1 and ψ_2 is given by:

$$\Delta q = \int_{\psi_1}^{\psi_2} (-v_z\, dx + v_x\, dz)$$

$$= \int_{\psi_1}^{\psi_2} \left(\frac{\partial \psi}{\partial x} dx + \frac{\partial \psi}{\partial z} dz \right)$$

$$= \psi_2 - \psi_1$$

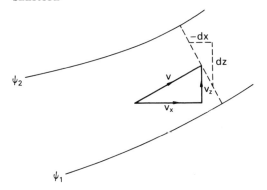

Figure 2.5   Seepage between two flow lines.

Thus the flow through the 'channel' between the two flow lines is constant.

The total differential of the function $\phi(x,z)$ is

$$d\phi = \frac{\partial\phi}{\partial x}\,dx + \frac{\partial\phi}{\partial z}\,dz$$

$$= v_x\,dx + v_z\,dz$$

If $\phi(x,z)$ is constant then $d\phi = 0$ and:

$$\frac{dz}{dx} = -\frac{v_x}{v_z} \tag{2.12}$$

Comparing equations 2.11 and 2.12 it is apparent that the flow lines and the equipotentials intersect each other at right angles.

Consider, now, two flow lines ψ_1 and $(\psi_1 + \Delta\psi)$ separated by the distance Δn. The flow lines are intersected orthogonally by two equipotentials ϕ_1 and $(\phi_1 + \Delta\phi)$ separated by the distance Δs, as shown in Fig. 2.6. The directions s and n are inclined at angle α to the x and z axes respectively. At point A the discharge velocity (in direction s) is v_s: the components of v_s in the x and z directions respectively are:

$$v_x = v_s \cos\alpha$$

$$v_z = v_s \sin\alpha$$

Now:

$$\frac{\partial\phi}{\partial s} = \frac{\partial\phi}{\partial x}\frac{\partial x}{\partial s} + \frac{\partial\phi}{\partial z}\frac{\partial z}{\partial s}$$

$$= v_s \cos^2\alpha + v_s \sin^2\alpha$$

$$= v_s$$

and:

$$\frac{\partial\psi}{\partial n} = \frac{\partial\psi}{\partial x}\frac{\partial x}{\partial n} + \frac{\partial\psi}{\partial z}\frac{\partial z}{\partial n}$$

$$= -v_s \sin\alpha\,(-\sin\alpha) + v_s \cos^2\alpha$$

$$= v_s$$

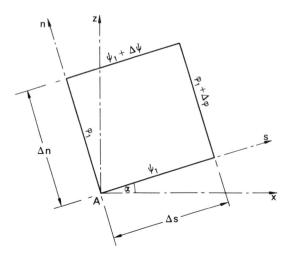

Figure 2.6.   Flow lines and equipotentials.

Thus:

$$\frac{\partial \psi}{\partial n} = \frac{\partial \phi}{\partial s}$$

or, approximately:

$$\frac{\Delta \psi}{\Delta n} = \frac{\Delta \phi}{\Delta s} \qquad\qquad (2.13)$$

2.4   Flow Nets

In principle, for the solution of a practical seepage problem the functions $\phi(x,z)$ and $\psi(x,z)$ must be found for the relevant boundary conditions. The solution is represented by a family of flow lines and a family of equipotentials, constituting what is referred to as a flow net. Possible methods of solution are complex variable techniques, the finite difference method, the finite element method, electrical analogy and the use of hydraulic models. However, the most widely used method of solution is by the trial-and-error sketching of the flow net, the general form of which can be deduced from a consideration of the boundary conditions.

The fundamental condition to be satisfied in a flow net is that every intersection between a flow line and an equipotential must be at right angles. In addition it is *convenient* to construct the flow net such that $\Delta \psi$ is the same value between any two adjacent flow lines and $\Delta \phi$ is the same value between any two adjacent equipotentials. It is also *convenient* to make $\Delta s = \Delta n$ in equation 2.13, i.e. the flow lines and equipotentials form 'curvilinear squares' throughout the flow net. Then for any curvilinear square:

$$\Delta \psi = \Delta \phi$$

Now, $\Delta\psi = \Delta q$ and $\Delta\phi = k\Delta h$, therefore:

$$\Delta q = k\Delta h \qquad (2.14)$$

The hydraulic gradient is given by:

$$i = \frac{\Delta h}{\Delta s} \qquad (2.15)$$

For the entire flow net:

> h = difference in total head between the first and last equipotentials,
> N_d = number of *equipotential drops*, each representing the same total head loss Δh,
> N_f = number of *flow channels*, each carrying the same flow Δq.

Then,

$$\Delta h = \frac{h}{N_d} \qquad (2.16)$$

and

$$q = N_f \Delta q$$

Hence, from equation 2.14:

$$q = kh\frac{N_f}{N_d} \qquad (2.17)$$

Equation 2.17 gives the total volume of water flowing per unit time (per unit dimension in the y direction) and is a function of the *ratio N_f/N_d*.

Example of a Flow Net

As an illustration the flow net for the problem detailed in Fig. 2.7a will be considered. The figure shows a line of sheet piling driven 6·00 m into a stratum of soil 8·60 m thick, underlain by an impermeable stratum. On one side of the piling the depth of water is 4·50 m; on the other side the depth of water (reduced by pumping) is 0·50 m.

The first step is to consider the boundary conditions of the flow region. At every point on the boundary AB the total head is constant, therefore AB is an equipotential; similarly CD is an equipotential. The datum to which total head is referred may be any level but in seepage problems it is convenient to select the downstream water level as datum. Then the total head on equipotential CD is zero (pressure head 0·50 m; elevation head − 0·50 m) and the total head on equipotential AB is 4·00 m (pressure head 4·50 m; elevation head −0·50 m). From point B, water must flow down the upstream face BE of the piling, round the tip E and up the downstream face EC. Water from point F must flow along the impermeable surface FG. Thus BEC and FG are flow lines. The shapes of other flow lines must be between the extremes of BEC and FG.

The first trial sketching of the flow net (Fig. 2.7b) can now be attempted using a procedure suggested by Taylor [2.6]. The estimated line of flow (HJ) from a point on AB near the piling is lightly sketched. This line must start at right angles to equi-

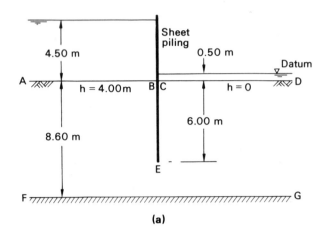

(a)

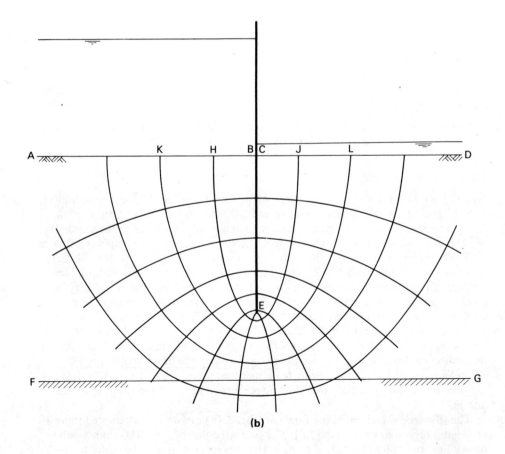

(b)

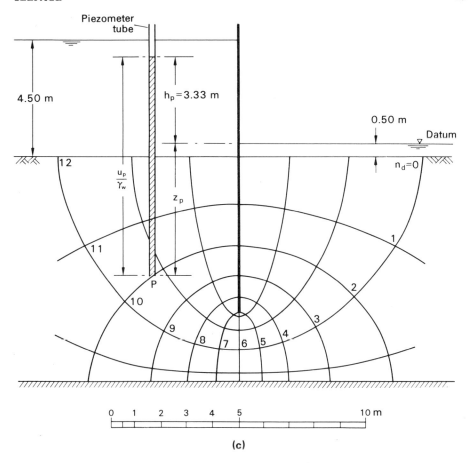

Piezometer tube

4.50 m

$h_p = 3.33$ m

0.50 m

Datum

$\dfrac{u_p}{\gamma_w}$

z_p

P

$n_d = 0$

1 2

11

10

9

8 7 6 5 4

3

2

1

0 1 2 3 4 5 10 m

(c)

Figure 2.7 Flow net construction: (a) section, (b) first trial, (c) final flow net.

potential AB and follow a smooth curve round the bottom of the piling. Trial equi-potential lines are then drawn between the flow lines BEC and HJ, intersecting both flow lines at right angles and forming curvilinear squares. If necessary the position of HJ should be altered slightly so that a whole number of squares is obtained between BH and CJ. The procedure is continued by sketching the estimated line of flow (KL) from a second point on AB and extending the equipotentials already drawn. The flow line KL and the equipotential extensions are adjusted so that all intersections are at right angles and all areas are square. The procedure is repeated until the boundary FG is reached. At the first attempt it is almost certain that the last flow line drawn will be inconsistent with the boundary FG as, for example, in Fig. 2.7b. By studying the nature of this inconsistency the position of the first flow line (HJ) can be adjusted in a way that will tend to correct the inconsistency. The entire flow net is then adjusted and the inconsistency should now be small. After a third trial the last flow line should be consistent with the boundary FG, as shown in Fig. 2.7c. In general, the areas between the last flow line and the lower boundary will not be square but the length/breadth ratio of each area should be constant within this flow channel. In constructing a flow net it is a mistake to draw too many flow lines: typically 4 to 5 flow channels are sufficient.

In the flow net in Fig. 2.7c the number of flow channels is 4·3 and the number of equipotential drops is 12: thus the ratio N_f/N_d is 0·36. The equipotentials are numbered from zero at the downstream boundary: this number is denoted by n_d. The loss in total head between any two adjacent equipotentials is:

$$\Delta h = \frac{h}{N_d} = \frac{4 \cdot 00}{12} = 0 \cdot 33 \text{ m}$$

The total head at every point on an equipotential numbered n_d is $n_d \Delta h$. The total volume of water flowing under the piling per unit time per unit length of piling is given by:

$$q = kh \frac{N_f}{N_d} = k \times 4 \cdot 00 \times 0 \cdot 36$$

$$= 1 \cdot 44 \, k \, \text{m}^3/\text{s}$$

A piezometer tube is shown at a point P on the equipotential denoted by $n_d = 10$. The total head at P is:

$$h_P = \frac{n_d}{N_d} h = \frac{10}{12} \times 4 \cdot 00 = 3 \cdot 33 \text{ m}$$

i.e. the water level in the tube is 3·33 m above the datum. The point P is distance z_P below the datum, i.e. the elevation head is $-z_P$. The pore water pressure at P can then be calculated from Bernoulli's theorem:

$$u_P = \gamma_w \{h_P - (-z_P)\}$$
$$= \gamma_w (h_P + z_P)$$

The hydraulic gradient across any square in the flow net involves measuring the average dimension of the square (equation 2.15). The highest hydraulic gradient (and hence the highest seepage velocity) occurs across the smallest square, and vice versa.

Example 2.1

The section through a sheet pile wall along a tidal estuary is given in Fig. 2.8. At low tide the depth of water in front of the wall is 4·00 m: the water table behind the wall lags 2·50 m behind tidal level. Plot the net distribution of water pressure on the piling.

The flow net is shown in the figure. The water level in front of the piling is selected as datum. The total head at water table level (the upstream equipotential) is 2·50 m (pressure head zero; elevation head +2·50 m). The total head on the soil surface in front of the piling (the downstream equipotential) is zero (pressure head 4·00 m; elevation head −4·00 m). There are 12 equipotential drops in the flow net.

The water pressures are calculated on both sides of the piling at selected levels numbered 1 to 7. For example at level 4 the total head on the back of the piling is:

$$h_b = \frac{8 \cdot 8}{12} \times 2 \cdot 50 = 1 \cdot 83 \text{ m}$$

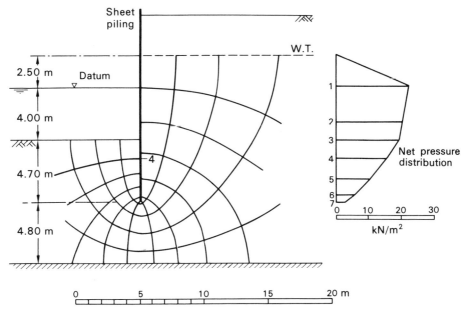

Figure 2.8   Example 2.1.

and the total head on the front is:

$$h_f = \frac{1}{12} \times 2 \cdot 50 = 0 \cdot 21 \text{ m}$$

The elevation head at level 4 is $-5 \cdot 5$ m.
Therefore the net pressure on the back of the piling is:

$$u_b - u_f = 9 \cdot 8 \ (1 \cdot 83 + 5 \cdot 5) - 9 \cdot 8 \ (0 \cdot 21 + 5 \cdot 5)$$
$$= 9 \cdot 8 \ (7 \cdot 33 - 5 \cdot 71)$$
$$= 15 \cdot 9 \text{ kN/m}^2$$

The calculations for the selected points are tabulated below and the net pressure diagram is plotted in Fig. 2.8.

Level	z (m)	h_b (m)	u_b/γ_w (m)	h_f (m)	u_f/γ_w (m)	$u_b - u_f$ (kN/m^2)
1	0	2·30	2·30	0	0	22·6
2	−2·70	2·10	4·80	0	2·70	20·6
3	−4·00	2·00	6·00	0	4·00	19·6
4	−5·50	1·83	7·33	0·21	5·71	15·9
5	−7·10	1·68	8·78	0·50	7·60	11·6
6	−8·30	1·51	9·81	0·84	9·14	6·6
7	−8·70	1·25	9·95	1·04	9·74	2·1

Example 2.2

The section through a dam in shown in Fig. 2.9. Determine the quantity of seepage under the dam and plot the distribution of uplift pressure on the base of the dam. The coefficient of permeability of the foundation soil is $2 \cdot 5 \times 10^{-5}$ m/s.

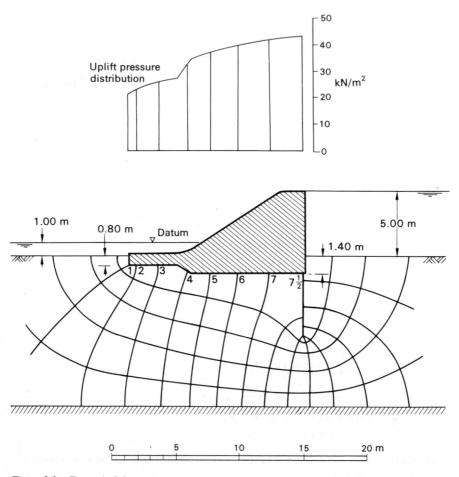

Figure 2.9   Example 2.2.

The flow net is shown in the figure. The downstream water level is selected as datum. Between the upstream and downstream equipotentials the total head loss is 4·00 m. In the flow net there are 4·7 flow channels and 15 equipotential drops. The seepage is given by:

$$q = kh\frac{N_f}{N_d}$$

$$= 2 \cdot 5 \times 10^{-5} \times 4 \cdot 00 \times \frac{4 \cdot 7}{15}$$

$$= 3 \cdot 1 \times 10^{-5} \text{ m}^3/\text{s (per m)}$$

The pore water pressure is calculated at the points of intersection of the equipotentials with the base of the dam. The total head at each point is obtained from the flow net and the elevation head from the section. The calculations are tabulated below and the pressure diagram is plotted in Fig. 2.9.

Point	h (m)	z (m)	$h - z$ (m)	$u = \gamma_w(h - z)$ (kN/m^2)
1	0·27	−1·80	2·07	20·3
2	0·53	−1·80	2·33	22·9
3	0·80	−1·80	2·60	25·5
4	1·07	−2·10	3·17	31·1
5	1·33	−2·40	3·73	36·6
6	1·60	−2·40	4·00	39·2
7	1·87	−2·40	4·27	41·9
$7\frac{1}{2}$	2·00	−2·40	4·40	43·1

Example 2.3

A river bed consists of a layer of sand 8·25 m thick overlying impermeable rock: the depth of water is 2·50 m. A long cofferdam 5·50 m wide is formed by driving two lines of sheet piling to a depth of 6·00 m below the level of the river bed and excavation to

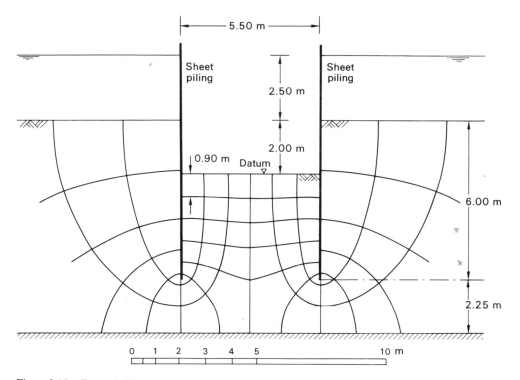

Figure 2.10   Example 2.3.

a depth of 2·00 m below bed level is carried out within the cofferdam. The water
level within the cofferdam is kept at excavation level by pumping.
If the flow of water into the cofferdam is 0·25
m^3/hour per unit length, what is the coefficient of permeability of the sand? What is
the hydraulic gradient immediately below the excavated surface?

The section and flow net appear in Fig. 2.10. In the flow net there are 6·0 flow
channels and 11 equipotential drops. The total head loss is 4·50 m. The coefficient
of permeability is given by:

$$k = q / \left(h \frac{N_f}{N_d} \right)$$

$$= \frac{0 \cdot 25}{4 \cdot 50 \times 6/11 \times 60^2} = 2 \cdot 8 \times 10^{-5} \text{ m/s}$$

The distance (Δs) between the last two equipotentials is measured as 0·9 m. The
required hydraulic gradient is given by:

$$i = \frac{\Delta h}{\Delta s}$$

$$= \frac{4 \cdot 50}{11 \times 0 \cdot 9} = 0 \cdot 45$$

2.5   Anisotropic Soil Conditions

It will now be assumed that the soil, although homogeneous, is anisotropic with
respect to permeability. Most natural soil deposits are anisotropic, with the coefficient
of permeability having a maximum value in the direction of stratification and a
minimum value in the direction normal to that of stratification: these directions are
denoted by x and z respectively, i.e.:

$$k_x = k_{max} \quad \text{and} \quad k_z = k_{min}$$

In this case the generalised form of Darcy's law is:

$$v_x = k_x i_x = - k_x \frac{\partial h}{\partial x} \tag{2.18a}$$

$$v_z = k_z i_z = - k_z \frac{\partial h}{\partial z} \tag{2.18b}$$

Also, in any direction s, inclined at angle α to the x direction, the coefficient of
permeability is defined by the equation:

$$v_s = - k_s \frac{\partial h}{\partial s}$$

Now:

$$\frac{\partial h}{\partial s} = \frac{\partial h}{\partial x}\frac{\partial x}{\partial s} + \frac{\partial h}{\partial z}\frac{\partial z}{\partial s}$$

i.e.

$$\frac{v_s}{k_s} = \frac{v_x}{k_x}\cos\alpha + \frac{v_z}{k_z}\sin\alpha$$

The components of discharge velocity are also related as follows:

$$v_x = v_s \cos\alpha$$
$$v_z = v_s \sin\alpha$$

Hence:

$$\frac{1}{k_s} = \frac{\cos^2\alpha}{k_x} + \frac{\sin^2\alpha}{k_z}$$

or,

$$\frac{s^2}{k_s} = \frac{x^2}{k_x} + \frac{z^2}{k_z} \tag{2.19}$$

The directional variation of permeability is thus described by equation 2.19 which represents the ellipse shown in Fig. 2.11.

Given the generalised form of Darcy's law (equations 2.18) the equation of continuity (2.6) can be written:

$$k_x\frac{\partial^2 h}{\partial x^2} + k_z\frac{\partial^2 h}{\partial z^2} = 0 \tag{2.20}$$

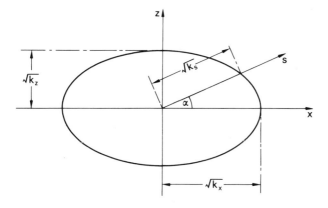

Figure 2.11   Permeability ellipse.

or,

$$\frac{\partial^2 h}{\left(\frac{k_z}{k_x}\right)\partial x^2} + \frac{\partial^2 h}{\partial z^2} = 0$$

Substituting:

$$x_t = x\sqrt{\frac{k_z}{k_x}} \tag{2.21}$$

the equation of continuity becomes:

$$\frac{\partial^2 h}{\partial x_t^2} + \frac{\partial^2 h}{\partial z^2} = 0 \tag{2.22}$$

which is the equation of continuity for an *isotropic* soil in an x_t, z plane.

Thus equation 2.21 defines a scale factor which can be applied in the x direction to transform a given anisotropic flow region into a fictitious isotropic flow region in which the Laplace equation is valid. Once the flow net (representing the solution of the Laplace equation) has been drawn for the transformed section the flow net for the natural section can be obtained by applying the inverse of the scaling factor. Essential data, however, can normally be obtained from the transformed section. The necessary transformation could also be made in the z-direction.

The value of coefficient of permeability applying to the transformed section, referred to as the equivalent isotropic coefficient, is:

$$k' = \sqrt{(k_x k_z)} \tag{2.23}$$

A formal proof of equation 2.23 has been given by Vreedenburgh [2.7]. The validity of equation 2.23 can be demonstrated by considering an elemental flow net field through which flow is in the x direction. The flow net field is drawn to the transformed and natural scales in Fig. 2.12, the transformation being in the x direction. The discharge velocity v_x can be expressed in terms of either k' (transformed section) or k_x (natural section), i.e.:

$$v_x = -k'\frac{\partial h}{\partial x_t} = -k_x\frac{\partial h}{\partial x}$$

where,

$$\frac{\partial h}{\partial x_t} = \frac{\frac{\partial h}{\partial x}}{\sqrt{\left(\frac{k_z}{k_x}\right)}}$$

Thus:

$$k' = k_x\sqrt{\frac{k_z}{k_x}} = \sqrt{(k_x k_z)}$$

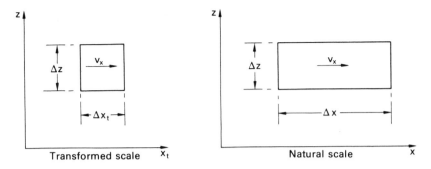

Figure 2.12   Elemental flow net field.

2.6   Non-homogeneous Soil Conditions

Two *isotropic* soil layers of thicknesses H_1 and H_2 are shown in Fig. 2.13, the respective coefficients of permeability being k_1 and k_2: the boundary between the layers is horizontal. (If the layers are anisotropic, k_1 and k_2 represent the equivalent isotropic coefficients for the layers.) The two layers can be considered as a single homogeneous anisotropic layer of thickness $(H_1 + H_2)$ in which the coefficients of permeability in the horizontal and vertical directions are $\bar{k}_x$ and $\bar{k}_z$ respectively.

For one-dimensional seepage in the horizontal direction, the equipotentials in each layer are vertical. If h_1 and h_2 represent total head at any point in the respective layers, then for a common point on the boundary $h_1 = h_2$. Therefore any vertical line through the two layers represents a common equipotential. Thus the hydraulic gradients in the two layers, and in the equivalent single layer, are equal: the equal hydraulic gradients are denoted by i_x.

The total horizontal flow per unit time is given by:

$$\bar{q}_x = (H_1 + H_2)\bar{k}_x i_x = (H_1 k_1 + H_2 k_2)i_x$$

$$\therefore \qquad \bar{k}_x = \frac{H_1 k_1 + H_2 k_2}{H_1 + H_2} \qquad\qquad (2.24)$$

For one-dimensional seepage in the vertical direction the discharge velocities in each layer, and in the equivalent single layer, must be equal if the requirement of continuity is to be satisfied. Thus:

$$v_z = \bar{k}_z \bar{i}_z = k_1 i_1 = k_2 i_2$$

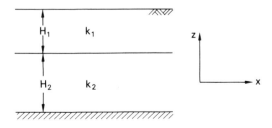

Figure 2.13   Non-homogeneous soil conditions.

where $\bar{i}_z$ is the average hydraulic gradient over the depth $(H_1 + H_2)$. Therefore:

$$i_1 = \frac{\bar{k}_z}{k_1}\bar{i}_z \quad \text{and} \quad i_2 = \frac{\bar{k}_z}{k_2}\bar{i}_z$$

Now the loss in total head over the depth $(H_1 + H_2)$ is equal to the sum of the losses in total head in the individual layers, i.e.:

$$\bar{i}_z(H_1 + H_2) = i_1 H_1 + i_2 H_2$$

$$= \bar{k}_z\bar{i}_z\left(\frac{H_1}{k_1} + \frac{H_2}{k_2}\right)$$

$$\therefore \qquad \bar{k}_z = (H_1 + H_2)\left/\left(\frac{H_1}{k_1} + \frac{H_2}{k_2}\right)\right. \qquad (2.25)$$

Similar expressions for $\bar{k}_x$ and $\bar{k}_z$ apply in the case of any number of soil layers. It can be shown that $\bar{k}_x$ must always be greater than $\bar{k}_z$, i.e. seepage can occur more readily in the direction parallel to stratification than in the direction perpendicular to stratification.

2.7   Transfer Condition

Consideration is now given to the condition which must be satisfied when seepage takes place diagonally across the boundary between two isotropic soils 1 and 2 having coefficients of permeability k_1 and k_2 respectively. The direction of seepage approaching a point B on the boundary ABC is at angle α_1 to the normal at B, as shown in Fig. 2.14: the discharge velocity approaching B is v_1. The components of v_1 along the boundary and normal to the boundary are v_{1s} and v_{1n} respectively. The direction of seepage leaving point B is at angle α_2 to the normal, as shown: the discharge velocity leaving B is v_2. The components of v_2 are v_{2s} and v_{2n}.

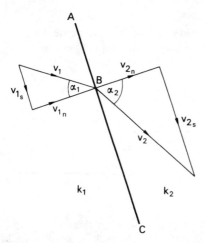

Figure 2.14   Transfer condition.

For soils 1 and 2 respectively:

$$\phi_1 = -k_1 h_1 \quad \text{and} \quad \phi_2 = -k_2 h_2$$

At the common point B, $h_1 = h_2$, therefore:

$$\frac{\phi_1}{k_1} = \frac{\phi_2}{k_2}$$

Differentiating with respect to s, the direction along the boundary:

$$\frac{1}{k_1} \frac{\partial \phi_1}{\partial s} = \frac{1}{k_2} \frac{\partial \phi_2}{\partial s}$$

i.e.:

$$\frac{v_{1s}}{k_1} = \frac{v_{2s}}{k_2}$$

For continuity of flow across the boundary the normal components of discharge velocity must be equal, i.e.:

$$v_{1n} = v_{2n}$$

Therefore:

$$\frac{1}{k_1} \frac{v_{1s}}{v_{1n}} = \frac{1}{k_2} \frac{v_{2s}}{v_{2n}}$$

Hence it follows that:

$$\frac{\tan \alpha_1}{\tan \alpha_2} = \frac{k_1}{k_2} \tag{2.26}$$

Equation 2.26 specifies the change in direction of the flow line passing through point B. This equation must be satisfied on the boundary by every flow line crossing the boundary.

Equation 2.13 can be written:

$$\Delta \psi = \frac{\Delta n}{\Delta s} \Delta \phi$$

i.e.:

$$\Delta q = \frac{\Delta n}{\Delta s} k \Delta h$$

If Δq and Δh are each to have the same values on both sides of the boundary then:

$$\left(\frac{\Delta n}{\Delta s} \right)_1 k_1 = \left(\frac{\Delta n}{\Delta s} \right)_2 k_2$$

and it is clear that curvilinear squares are possible only in one soil. If:

$$\left(\frac{\Delta n}{\Delta s} \right)_1 = 1$$

then:

$$\left(\frac{\Delta n}{\Delta s}\right)_2 = \frac{k_1}{k_2} \qquad (2.27)$$

If the permeability ratio is less than 1/10 it is unlikely that the part of the flow net in the soil of higher permeability need be considered.

2.8   Seepage Through Earth Dams

This problem is an example of unconfined seepage, one boundary of the flow region being a phreatic surface on which the pressure is atmospheric. In section the phreatic surface constitutes the top flow line and its position must be estimated before the flow net can be drawn.

Consider the case of a homogeneous isotropic earth dam on an impermeable foundation, as shown in Fig. 2.15. The impermeable boundary AB is a flow line and CD is the required top flow line. At every point on the upstream slope BC the total head is constant, therefore BC is an equipotential. If the downstream water level is taken as datum then the total head on equipotential BC is equal to h, the difference between the upstream and downstream water levels. The discharge surface AD, for the case shown in Fig. 2.15 only, is the equipotential for zero total head. At every point on the top flow line the pressure is zero (atmospheric), therefore total head is equal to elevation head and there must be equal vertical intervals Δz between the points of intersection between successive equipotentials and the top flow line.

A suitable filter must always be constructed at the discharge surface in an earth dam. The function of the filter is to keep the seepage entirely within the dam: water seeping out onto the downstream slope would result in the gradual erosion of the slope. A horizontal underfilter is shown in Fig. 2.15. Other possible forms of filter are illustrated in Figs. 2.19a and 2.19b: in these two cases the discharge surface AD is neither a flow line nor an equipotential since there are components of discharge velocity both normal and tangential to AD.

The boundary conditions of the flow region ABCD in Fig. 2.15 can be written as follows:

> Equipotential BC: $\phi = -kh$
> Equipotential AD: $\phi = 0$
> Flow line CD: $\psi = q$ (also, $\phi = -kz$)
> Flow line AB: $\psi = 0$

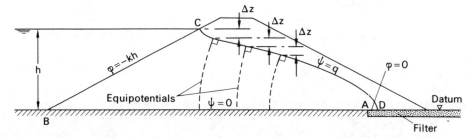

Figure 2.15   Homogeneous earth dam section.

The Conformal Transformation $r = w^2$

Complex variable theory can be used to obtain a solution to the earth dam problem. Let the complex number $w = \phi + i\psi$ be an analytic function of $r = x + iz$. Consider the function:

$$r = w^2$$

Thus:

$$(x + iz) = (\phi + i\psi)^2$$
$$= (\phi^2 + 2i\phi\psi - \psi^2)$$

Equating real and imaginary parts:

$$x = \phi^2 - \psi^2 \qquad\qquad\qquad (2.28)$$
$$z = 2\phi\psi \qquad\qquad\qquad (2.29)$$

Equations 2.28 and 2.29 govern the transformation of points between the r and w planes.

Consider the transformation of the straight lines $\psi = n$, where $n = 0, 1, 2, 3$ (Fig. 2.16a). From equation 2.29:

$$\phi = \frac{z}{2n}$$

and equation 2.28 becomes:

$$x = \frac{z^2}{4n^2} - n^2 \qquad\qquad\qquad (2.30)$$

Equation 2.30 represents a family of confocal parabolas. For positive values of z the parabolas for the specified values of n are plotted in Fig. 2.16b.

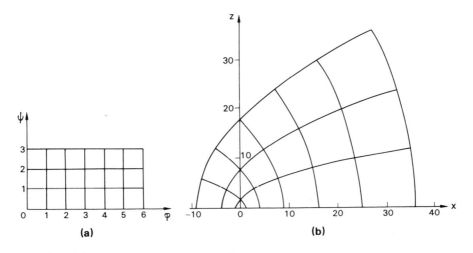

Figure 2.16   Conformal transformation $r = w^2$: (a) w plane, (b) r plane.

Consider also the transformation of the straight lines $\phi = m$, where $m = 0, 1, 2 \ldots 6$ (Fig. 2.16a). From equation 2.29:

$$\psi = \frac{z}{2m}$$

and equation 2.28 becomes:

$$x = m^2 - \frac{z^2}{4m^2} \tag{2.31}$$

Equation 2.31 represents a family of confocal parabolas conjugate with the parabolas represented by equation 2.30. For positive values of z the parabolas for the specified values of m are plotted in Fig. 2.16b. The two families of parabolas satisfy the requirements of a flow net.

Application to Earth Dam Section

The flow region in the w plane satisfying the boundary conditions for the earth dam section (Fig. 2.15) is shown in Fig. 2.17a. In this case the transformation function:

$$r = Cw^2$$

will be used, where C is a constant. Equations 2.28 and 2.29 then become:

$$x = C(\phi^2 - \psi^2)$$
$$z = 2C\phi\psi$$

The equation of the top flow line can be derived by substituting the conditions:

$$\psi = q$$
$$\phi = -kz$$

Thus:

$$z = -2Ckzq$$

$$\therefore \qquad C = -\frac{1}{2kq}$$

Hence:

$$x = -\frac{1}{2kq}(k^2z^2 - q^2)$$

$$x = \frac{1}{2}\left(\frac{q}{k} - \frac{k}{q}z^2\right) \tag{2.32}$$

The curve represented by equation 2.32 is referred to as Kozeny's basic parabola and is shown in Fig. 2.17b, the origin and focus both being at A.

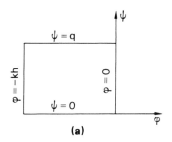

(a)

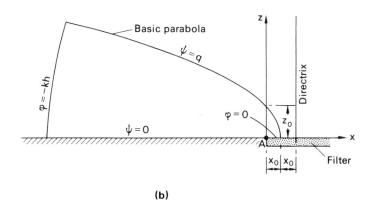

(b)

Figure 2.17   Transformation for earth dam section: (a) w plane, (b) r plane.

When $z = 0$ the value of x is given by:

$$x_0 = \frac{q}{2k}$$

$$\therefore \qquad q = 2kx_0 \tag{2.33}$$

where $2x_0$ is the directrix distance of the basic parabola. When $x = 0$ the value of z is given by:

$$z_0 = \frac{q}{k} = 2x_0$$

Substituting equation 2.33 in equation 2.32 yields:

$$x = x_0 - \frac{z^2}{4x_0} \tag{2.34}$$

The basic parabola can be drawn using equation 2.34 provided the coordinates of one point on the parabola are known initially.

An inconsistency arises due to the fact that the conformal transformation of the straight line $\phi = -kh$ (representing the upstream equipotential) is a parabola, whereas the upstream equipotential in the earth dam section is the upstream slope. Based on an extensive study of the earth dam problem, Casagrande [2.1] recommended that the initial point on the basic parabola should be taken at G (Fig. 2.18) where

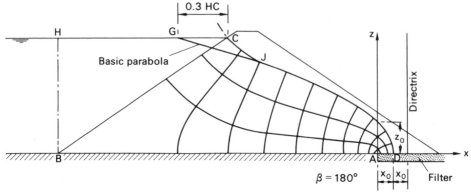

Figure 2.18   Flow net for earth dam section.

GC = 0·3 HC. The coordinates of point G, substituted in equation 2.34 enable the value of x_0 to be determined: the basic parabola can then be plotted. The top flow line must intersect the upstream slope at right angles: a correction CJ must therefore be made (using personal judgement) to the basic parabola. The flow net can then be completed as shown in Fig. 2.18.

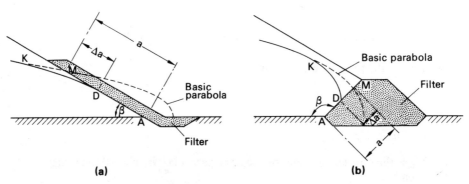

Figure 2.19   Downstream correction to basic parabola.

If the discharge surface AD is not horizontal, as in the cases shown in Fig. 2.19, a further correction KD to the basic parabola is required. The angle β is used to describe the direction of the discharge surface relative to AB. The correction can be made with the aid of values of the ratio MD/MA = $\Delta a/a$, given by Casagrande for the range of values of β (Table 2.2).

Table 2.2   Downstream correction to basic parabola

β	30°	60°	90°	120°	150°	180°
$\Delta a/a$	(0·36)	0·32	0·26	0·18	0·10	0

(After Casagrande [2.1])

Seepage Control in Earth Dams

The design of an earth dam section and, where possible, the choice of soils is aimed at reducing or eliminating the detrimental effects of seeping water. Where high hydraulic gradients exist there is a possibility that the seeping water may erode channels within the dam, especially if the soil is poorly compacted: the stability of the dam may then

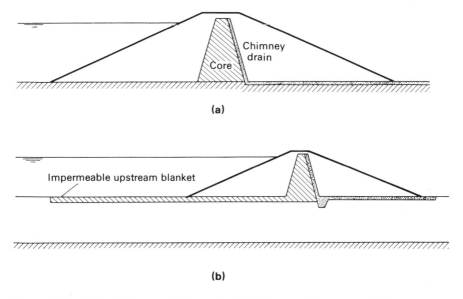

(a)

(b)

Figure 2.20   (a) Central core and chimney drain, (b) impermeable upstream blanket.

be impaired. The process of internal erosion is referred to as *piping*. A section with a central core of low permeability, aimed at reducing the volume of seepage, is shown in Fig. 2.20a. Practically all the total head is lost in the core and if the core is narrow, high hydraulic gradients will result. There is particular danger of erosion at the boundary between the core and the adjacent soil (of higher permeability) under a high exit gradient from the core. Protection against this danger can be given by means of a 'chimney' drain (Fig. 2.20a) at the downstream boundary of the core. The drain, designed as a filter to provide a barrier to soil particles from the core, also serves as an interceptor, keeping the downstream slope in an unsaturated state.

Most earth dam sections are non-homogeneous due to zoning, making the construction of the flow net more difficult. The basic parabola construction for the top flow line applies only to homogeneous sections but the condition that there must be equal vertical distances between the points of intersection of equipotentials with the top flow line applies equally to a non-homogeneous section. The transfer condition (equation 2.26) must be satisfied at all zone boundaries. In the case of a section with a central core of low permeability, the application of equation 2.26 means that the lower the permeability ratio the lower the position of the top flow line in the downstream zone (in the absence of a chimney drain).

If the foundation soil is more permeable than the dam, the control of underseepage is essential. Underseepage can be virtually eliminated by means of an 'impermeable' cut-off such as a grout curtain. Any measure designed to lengthen the seepage path, such as an impermeable upstream blanket (Fig. 2.20b), will result in a partial reduction in underseepage.

An excellent treatment of seepage control is given by Cedergren [2.2].

Filter Requirements

Filters or drains used to control seepage must satisfy two conflicting requirements:

(1) The size of the pores must be small enough to prevent particles being carried in from the adjacent soil;

(2) The permeability must be high enough to allow the rapid drainage of water entering the filter.

The following criteria have been found to be satisfactory for filters:

$$\frac{(D_{15})_f}{(D_{85})_s} < 4 \text{ to } 5 \tag{2.35}$$

$$\frac{(D_{15})_f}{(D_{15})_s} > 4 \text{ to } 5 \tag{2.36}$$

$$\frac{(D_{50})_f}{(D_{50})_s} < 25 \tag{2.37}$$

where f denotes 'filter' and s denotes 'adjacent soil'. Equation 2.35 is the requirement to prevent piping; equations 2.36 and 2.37 are requirements to ensure that the permeability of the filter is high enough for drainage purposes. The thickness of a filter can be determined from Darcy's law.

Filters comprising two or more layers with different gradings can also be used, the finest layer being on the upstream side of the filter: such an arrangement is called a graded filter.

Example 2.4

A homogeneous anisotropic earth dam section is detailed in Fig. 2.21a, the coefficients of permeability in the x and z directions being $4\cdot5 \times 10^{-8}$ m/s and $1\cdot6 \times 10^{-8}$ m/s respectively. Construct the flow net and determine the quantity of seepage through the dam. What is the pore water pressure at point P?

The scale factor for transformation in the x direction is:

$$\sqrt{\frac{k_z}{k_x}} = \sqrt{\frac{1\cdot6}{4\cdot5}} = 0\cdot60$$

The equivalent isotropic permeability is:

$$k' = \sqrt{(k_x k_z)}$$
$$= \sqrt{(4\cdot5 \times 1\cdot6)} \times 10^{-8} = 2\cdot7 \times 10^{-8} \text{ m/s}$$

The section is drawn to the transformed scale as in Fig. 2.21b. The focus of the basic parabola is at point A. The basic parabola passes through point G such that:

$$GC = 0\cdot3 \ HC = 0\cdot3 \times 27\cdot00 = 8\cdot10 \text{ m}$$

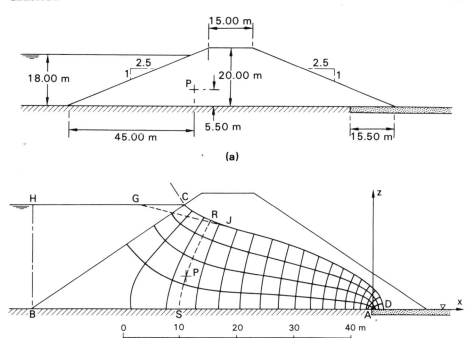

Figure 2.21   Example 2.4.

i.e. the coordinates of G are:

$$x = -40.80; \quad z = +18.00$$

Substituting these coordinates in equation 2.34:

$$-40.80 = x_0 - \frac{18.00^2}{4x_0}$$

Hence:

$$x_0 = 1.90 \text{ m}$$

Using equation 2.34 the coordinates of a number of points on the basic parabola are now calculated:

x	1·90	0	− 5·00	− 10·00	− 20·00	− 30·00
z	0	3·80	7·24	9·51	12·90	15·57

The basic parabola is plotted in Fig. 2.21b. The upstream correction is made and the flow net completed, ensuring that there are equal vertical intervals between the points of intersection of successive equipotentials with the top flow line. In the flow net there are 3·8 flow channels and 18 equipotential drops. Hence the quantity of seepage (per unit length) is:

$$q = k'h\frac{N_f}{N_d}$$

$$= 2\cdot7 \times 10^{-8} \times 18 \times \frac{3\cdot8}{18} = 1\cdot0 \times 10^{-7} \text{ m}^3/\text{s}$$

The quantity of seepage can also be determined from equation 2.33 (without the necessity of drawing the flow net):

$$q = 2k'x_0$$

$$= 2 \times 2\cdot7 \times 10^{-8} \times 1\cdot90 = 1\cdot0 \times 10^{-7} \text{ m}^3/\text{s}$$

Level AD is selected as datum. An equipotential RS is drawn through point P (transformed position). By inspection the total head at P is 15·60 m. At P the elevation head is 5·50 m, therefore the pressure head is 10·10 m and the pore water pressure is:

$$u_P = 9\cdot8 \times 10\cdot10 = 99 \text{ kN/m}^2$$

Alternatively the pressure head at P is given directly by the vertical distance of P below the point of intersection (R) of equipotential RS with the top flow line.

Example 2.5

Draw the flow net for the non-homogeneous earth dam section detailed in Fig. 2.22 and determine the quantity of seepage through the dam. Zones 1 and 2 are isotropic having coefficients of permeability $1\cdot0 \times 10^{-7}$ m/s and $4\cdot0 \times 10^{-7}$ m/s respectively.

The ratio $k_2/k_1 = 4$. The basic parabola is not applicable in this case. Three fundamental conditions must be satisfied in the flow net.

(1) There must be equal vertical intervals between points of intersection of equipotentials with the top flow line.

(2) If the part of the flow net in zone 1 consists of curvilinear squares then the part in zone 2 must consist of curvilinear rectangles having a length/breadth ratio of 4.

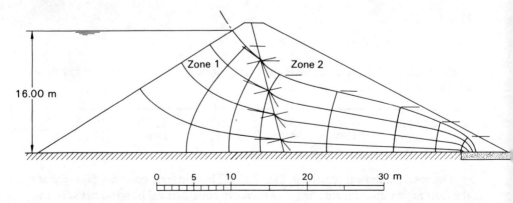

Figure 2.22   Example 2.5 (After Cedergren [2.2]).

(3) For each flow line the transfer condition (equation 2.26) must be satisfied at the inter-zone boundary.

The flow net is shown in Fig. 2.22. In the flow net there are 3·6 flow channels and 8 equipotential drops. The quantity of seepage per unit length is given by:

$$q = k_1 h \frac{N_f}{N_d}$$

$$= 1 \cdot 0 \times 10^{-7} \times 16 \times \frac{3 \cdot 6}{8} = 7 \cdot 2 \times 10^{-7} \text{ m}^3/\text{s}$$

(If curvilinear squares are used in zone 2 then curvilinear rectangles having a length/breadth ratio of 0·25 must be used in zone 2 and k_2 must be used in the seepage equation.)

2.9   Frost Heave

Frost heave is the rise of the ground surface due to frost action. The freezing of water is accompanied by a volume increase of approximately 9%: therefore in a saturated soil the void volume above the level of freezing will increase by the same amount, representing an overall increase in the volume of the soil of $2\frac{1}{2}\%$ to 5% depending on the void ratio. However, under certain circumstances, a much greater increase in volume can occur due to the formation of ice lenses within the soil.

In a soil having a high degree of saturation the pore water freezes immediately below the surface when the temperature falls below $0°C$. The soil temperature increases with depth but during a prolonged period of sub-zero temperatures the zone of freezing gradually extends downwards. The limit of frost penetration in Great Britain is normally assumed to be 0·5 m although under exceptional conditions this depth may approach 1·0 m. The temperature at which water freezes in the pores of a soil depends on the pore size, the smaller the pores the lower the freezing temperature: water therefore freezes initially in the larger pores, remaining unfrozen in the smaller pores. If conditions allow, water migrates towards the ice in the larger voids, attracted by the surface forces on the ice crystals, where it freezes and adds to the volume of ice. Continued migration gradually results in the formation of ice lenses and a rise in the ground surface. The process continues only if the bottom of the zone of freezing is within the zone of capillary rise, so that water can migrate upwards from below the water table. The magnitude of frost heave decreases as the degree of saturation of the soil decreases. When thawing eventually takes place the soil previously frozen will contain an excess of water with the result that it will become soft and its strength will be reduced.

In the case of coarse-grained soils with little or no fines, virtually all the pores are large enough for freezing to take place throughout the soil and the only volume increase is due to the 9% increase in the volume of water on freezing. In the case of soils of very low permeability, water migration is restricted by the slow rate of flow: consequently the development of ice lenses is restricted. However the presence of fissures can result in an increase in the rate of migration. The worst conditions for water migration occur in soils having a high percentage of silt-size particles: such soils usually have a network of small pores, yet, at the same time, the permeability is not too low. A well-graded soil is reckoned to be frost-susceptible if more than 3% of the particles are smaller than 0·02 mm. A poorly-graded soil is susceptible if more than 10% of the particles are smaller than 0·02 mm.

Problems

2.1   In a falling head permeability test the initial head of $1 \cdot 00$ m dropped to
$0 \cdot 35$ m in 3 hours, the diameter of the standpipe being 5 mm. The soil specimen was
200 mm long by 100 mm in diameter. Calculate the coefficient of permeability of
the soil.

2.2   A deposit of soil is 16 m deep and overlies an impermeable stratum: the
coefficient of permeability is 10^{-6} m/s. A sheet pile wall is driven to a depth of
$12 \cdot 00$ m in the deposit. The difference in water level between the two sides of the
piling is $4 \cdot 00$ m. Draw the flow net and determine the quantity of seepage under the
piling.

2.3   Draw the flow net for seepage under the structure detailed in Fig. 2.23 and
determine the quantity of seepage. The coefficient of permeability of the soil is
$5 \cdot 0 \times 10^{-5}$ m/s. What is the uplift force on the base of the structure?

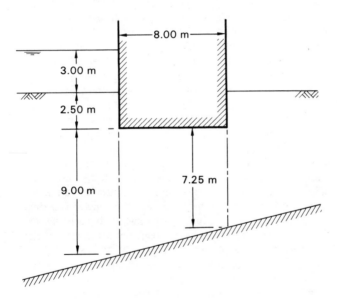

Figure 2.23   Problem 2.3.

2.4   The section through a long cofferdam is shown in Fig. 2.24, the coefficient
of permeability of the soil being $4 \cdot 0 \times 10^{-7}$ m/s. Draw the flow net and determine
the quantity of seepage entering the cofferdam.

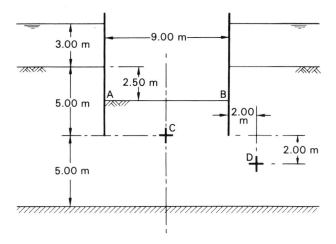

Figure 2.24 Problem 2.4.

2.5   The section through part of a cofferdam is shown in Fig. 2.25, the coefficient of permeability of the soil being $2 \cdot 0 \times 10^{-6}$ m/s. Draw the flow net and determine the quantity of seepage.

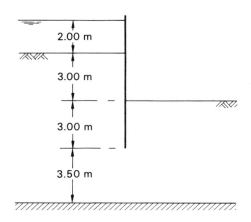

Figure 2.25 Problem 2.5.

2.6   The dam shown in section in Fig. 2.26 is located on anisotropic soil. The coefficients of permeability in the x and z directions are $5 \cdot 0 \times 10^{-7}$ m/s and $1 \cdot 8 \times 10^{-7}$ m/s respectively. Determine the quantity of seepage under the dam.

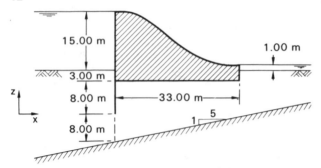

Figure 2.26   Problem 2.6.

2.7   An earth dam is shown in section in Fig. 2.27 the coefficients of perme-
ability in the horizontal and vertical directions being $7·5 \times 10^{-6}$ m/s and $2·7 \times 10^{-6}$ m/s
respectively. Construct the top flow line and determine the quantity of seepage
through the dam.

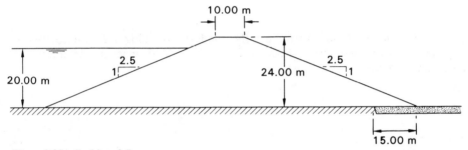

Figure 2.27   Problem 2.7.

2.8   Determine the quantity of seepage under the dam shown in section in
Fig. 2.28. Both layers of soil are isotropic the coefficients of permeability of the
upper and lower layers being $2·0 \times 10^{-6}$ m/s and $1·6 \times 10^{-5}$ m/s respectively.

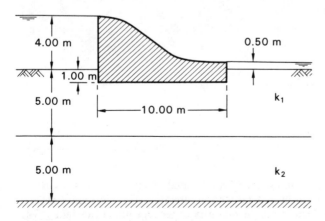

Figure 2.28   Problem 2.8.

References

2.1   Casagrande, A. (1940): 'Seepage Through Dams', in *Contributions to Soil Mechanics 1925–1940*, Boston Society of Civil Engineers.

2.2   Cedergren, H. R. (1967): *Seepage, Drainage and Flow Nets*, John Wiley and Sons, New York.

2.3   Harr, M. E. (1962): *Groundwater and Seepage*, McGraw-Hill, New York.

2.4   Hvorslev, M. J. (1951): *Time Lag and Soil Permeability in Ground-Water Observations*, Bulletin No. 36, Waterways Experimental Station, U.S. Corps of Engineers, Vicksburg, Mississippi.

2.5   Sherard, J. L., Woodward, R. J., Gizienski, S. F. and Clevenger, W. A. (1963): *Earth and Earth-Rock Dams*, John Wiley and Sons, New York.

2.6   Taylor, D. W. (1948): *Fundamentals of Soil Mechanics*, John Wiley and Sons, New York.

2.7   Vreedenburgh, C. G. F. (1936): 'On the Steady Flow of Water Percolating through Soils with Homogeneous-Anisotropic Permeability', *Proceedings 1st International Conference SMFE, Cambridge, Massachusetts*, Vol. 1.

CHAPTER 3

Effective Stress

3.1 Introduction

A soil can be visualised as a skeleton of solid particles enclosing continuous voids which contain water and/or air. For the range of stresses usually encountered in practice the individual solid particles and water can be considered incompressible: air, on the other hand, is highly compressible. The volume of the soil skeleton as a whole can change due to rearrangement of the solid particles into new positions, mainly by rolling and sliding, with a corresponding change in the forces acting between particles. The actual compressibility of the soil skeleton will depend on the structural arrangement of the solid particles. In a fully-saturated soil, since water is considered to be incompressible, a reduction in volume is possible only if some of the water can escape from the voids. In a dry or a partially-saturated soil a reduction in volume is always possible due to compression of the air in the voids, provided there is scope for particle rearrangement.

Shear stress can be resisted only by the skeleton of solid particles, by means of forces developed at the inter-particle contacts. Normal stress may be resisted by the soil skeleton through an increase in the inter-particle forces. If the soil is fully-saturated the water filling the voids can also withstand normal stress by an increase in pressure.

3.2 The Principle of Effective Stress

The importance of the forces transmitted through the soil skeleton from particle to particle was recognised in 1923 when Terzaghi presented the principle of effective stress, an intuitive relationship based on experimental data. The principle applies only to *fully-saturated* soils and relates the following three stresses:

(1) the *total normal stress* (σ) on a plane within the soil mass, being the force per unit area transmitted in a normal direction across the plane, imagining the soil to be a solid (single-phase) material;

(2) the *pore water pressure* (u), being the pressure of the water filling the void space between the solid particles;

(3) the *effective normal stress* (σ') on the plane, representing the stress transmitted through the soil skeleton only.

The relationship is:

$$\sigma = \sigma' + u \tag{3.1}$$

The principle can be represented by the following physical model. Consider a 'plane' XX in a fully-saturated soil, passing through points of inter-particle contact only, as shown in Fig. 3.1. The wavy plane XX is really indistinguishable from a true plane on the mass scale due to the relatively small size of individual soil particles. A normal force P applied over an area A may be resisted partly by inter-particle forces and partly by the pressure in the pore water. The inter-particle forces are very random in both magnitude and direction throughout the soil mass but at every point of contact on the wavy plane may be split into components normal and tangential to the direction of the true plane to which XX approximates: the normal and tangential components are N' and T respectively. Then the effective normal stress is interpreted

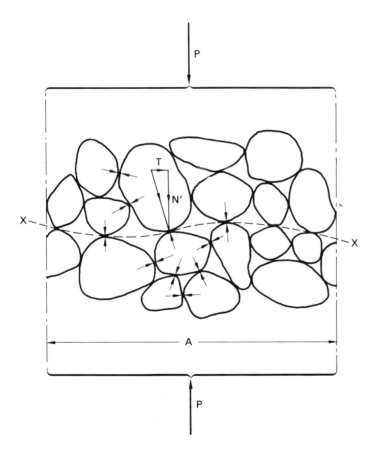

Figure 3.1   Interpretation of effective stress.

as the sum of all the components N' within the area A, divided by the area A, i.e.

$$\sigma' = \frac{\Sigma N'}{A} \tag{3.2}$$

The total normal stress is given by:

$$\sigma = \frac{P}{A} \tag{3.3}$$

If point contact is assumed between the particles, the pore water pressure will act on the plane over the entire area A. Then for equilibrium in the direction normal to XX:

$$P = \Sigma N' + uA$$

or,

$$\frac{P}{A} = \frac{\Sigma N'}{A} + u$$

i.e.

$$\sigma = \sigma' + u$$

The pore water pressure which acts equally in every direction will act on the entire surface of any particle but is assumed not to change the volume of the particle: also, the pore water pressure does not cause particles to be pressed together. The error involved in assuming point contact between particles is negligible in soils, the total contact area normally being between 1 and 3% of the cross-sectional area A. It should be understood that σ' does not represent the true contact stress between two particles, which would be the random but very much higher stress N'/a, where a is the actual contact area between the particles. Clay mineral particles, when they are present in a soil, may not be in direct contact due to their surrounding adsorbed layers but it is assumed that inter-particle force can be transmitted through the highly-viscous adsorbed water.

Effective Vertical Stress due to Self-weight of Soil

Consider a soil mass having a horizontal surface and with the water table at surface level. The total vertical stress (i.e. the total normal stress on a horizontal plane) at depth z is equal to the weight of all material (solids + water) per unit area above that depth, i.e.:

$$\sigma_v = \gamma_{\text{sat}} \, z$$

The pore water pressure at any depth will be hydrostatic since the void space between the solid particles is continuous, therefore at depth z:

$$u = \gamma_w z$$

Hence from equation 3.1 the effective vertical stress at depth z will be:

$$\sigma_v' = \sigma_v - u$$
$$= (\gamma_{\text{sat}} - \gamma_w)z = \gamma' z$$

where γ' is the buoyant unit weight of the soil.

3.3 Response of Effective Stress to a Change in Total Stress

As an illustration of how effective stress responds to a change in total stress, consider the case of a fully-saturated soil subject to an *increase* in total vertical stress and in which the lateral strain is zero, volume change being due entirely to deformation of the soil in the vertical direction. This condition may be assumed in practice when there is a change in total vertical stress over an area which is large compared with the thickness of the soil layer in question.

It is assumed initially that the pore water pressure is constant at a value governed by a constant position of the water table. This initial value is called the *static pore water pressure*. When the total vertical stress is increased the solid particles immediately try to take up new positions closer together. However, if water is incompressible and the soil is laterally confined no such particle rearrangement, and therefore no increase in the inter-particle forces, is possible unless some of the pore water can escape. Since the pore water is resisting the particle rearrangement the pore water pressure is increased above the static value immediately the increase in total vertical stress takes place. The increase in pore water pressure will be equal to the increase in total vertical stress, i.e. the increase in total vertical stress is carried entirely by the pore water. Note that if the lateral strain were not zero, some degree of particle rearrangement would be possible, resulting in an immediate increase in effective vertical stress and the increase in pore water pressure would be less than the increase in total vertical stress.

The increase in pore water pressure causes a pressure gradient in the pore water, resulting in a transient flow of pore water towards a free-draining boundary of the soil layer. This flow or *drainage* will continue until the pore water pressure again becomes equal to a value governed by a steady position of the water table. This final value is called the *steady-state pore water pressure*. In most situations the static and steady-state values of pore water pressure will be equal but it is possible for the position of the water table to change. The increase in pore water pressure above the final or steady-state value is called the *excess pore water pressure*. The reduction of the excess pore water pressure to the steady-state value is described as *dissipation* and when this has been completed the soil is said to be in a *drained* condition. Before dissipation of excess pore water pressure begins the condition of the soil is referred to as *undrained*.

As drainage of pore water takes place the solid particles become free to take up new positions with a resulting increase in the inter-particle forces. In other words, as the excess pore water pressure dissipates the effective vertical stress increases, accompanied by a corresponding reduction in volume. When dissipation of excess pore water pressure is complete the increment of total vertical stress will be carried entirely by the soil skeleton. Throughout the process the soil remains in a fully-saturated condition.

The time taken for drainage to be completed depends on the permeability of the soil. In soils of low permeability such as saturated clays, drainage will be slow and the whole process is referred to as *consolidation*. With deformation taking place in one direction only, consolidation is described as one-dimensional. In soils of high permeability such as saturated sands, drainage will be very rapid.

When a soil is subject to a *reduction* in total normal stress the scope for volume increase is limited because particle rearrangement due to total stress increase is largely irreversible. As a result of increase in the inter-particle forces there will be small elastic strains (normally ignored) in the solid particles especially around the contact areas and if clay mineral particles are present in the soil they may experience bending. In addition, the adsorbed water surrounding clay mineral particles will experience recoverable compression due to increase in inter-particle forces, especially if there is face-to-face orientation of the particles. When a decrease in total normal stress takes place in a soil there will thus be a tendency for the soil skeleton to expand to a limited extent, especially in soils containing an appreciable proportion of clay mineral particles. As a result the pore water pressure will be reduced and the excess pore water pressure will be negative. The pore water pressure will gradually increase to the steady-state value, flow taking place into the soil, accompanied by a corresponding reduction in effective normal stress and increase in volume. In soils of low permeability, this process, the reverse of consolidation, is called *swelling*.

Consolidation Analogy

The mechanics of the one-dimensional consolidation process can be represented by means of a simple analogy. Fig. 3.2a shows a spring inside a cylinder filled with water and a piston, fitted with a valve, on top of the spring. It is assumed that there can be no leakage between the piston and the cylinder and no friction. The spring represents the compressible soil skeleton, the water in the cylinder the pore water and the bore diameter of the valve the permeability of the soil. The cylinder itself simulates the condition of no lateral strain in the soil.

Suppose a load is now placed on the piston with the valve closed, as in Fig. 3.2b. Assuming water to be incompressible, the piston will not move as long as the valve is

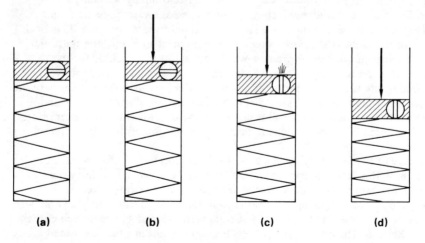

| (a) | (b) | (c) | (d) |

Figure 3.2   Consolidation analogy.

closed with the result that no load can be transmitted to the spring: the load will be carried by the water, the increase in pressure in the water being equal to the load divided by the piston area. This situation with the valve closed, corresponds to the undrained condition in the soil.

If the valve is now opened, water will be forced out through the valve at a rate governed by the bore diameter. This will allow the piston to move and the spring to be compressed as load is gradually transferred to it. This situation is shown in Fig. 3.2c. At any time the increase in load on the spring will correspond to the reduction in pressure in the water. Eventually, as shown in Fig. 3.2d, all the load will be carried by the spring and the piston will come to rest, this corresponding to the drained condition in the soil. At any time, the load carried by the spring represents the effective normal stress in the soil, the pressure of the water in the cylinder the pore water pressure and the load on the piston the total normal stress. The movement of the piston represents the change in volume of the soil and is governed by the compressibility of the spring (the equivalent of the compressibility of the soil skeleton). The piston and spring analogy represents only an element of soil since the stress conditions vary from point to point throughout a soil mass.

Example 3.1

A layer of saturated clay 4 m thick is overlain by sand 5 m deep, the water table being 3 m below the surface. The saturated unit weights of the clay and sand are 19 kN/m^3 and 20 kN/m^3 respectively: above the water table the unit weight of the sand is 17 kN/m^3. Plot the values of total vertical stress and effective vertical stress against depth. If sand to a height of 1 m above the water table is saturated with capillary water, how are the above stresses affected?

The total vertical stress is the weight of all material (solids + water) per unit area above the depth in question. Pore water pressure is the hydrostatic pressure corresponding to the depth below the water table. The effective vertical stress is the difference between the total vertical stress and the pore water pressure at the same depth. Alternatively, effective vertical stress may be calculated directly using the buoyant unit weight of the soil below the water table. The stresses need be calculated only at depths where there is a change in unit weight.

Depth (m)	σ_v (kN/m^2)		u (kN/m^2)	$\sigma_v' = \sigma_v - u$ (kN/m^2)
3	3×17	$= 51 \cdot 0$	0	$51 \cdot 0$
5	$(3 \times 17) + (2 \times 20)$	$= 91 \cdot 0$	$2 \times 9.8 = 19 \cdot 6$	$71 \cdot 4$
9	$(3 \times 17) + (2 \times 20) + (4 \times 19) = 167 \cdot 0$		$6 \times 9.8 = 58 \cdot 8$	$108 \cdot 2$

The alternative calculation of σ_v' at depths of 5 and 9 m is as follows:

Buoyant unit weight of sand = $20 - 9.8 = 10 \cdot 2 \text{ kN/m}^3$
Buoyant unit weight of clay = $19 - 9.8 = 9 \cdot 2 \text{ kN/m}^3$
At 5 m depth: $\sigma_v' = (3 \times 17) + (2 \times 10 \cdot 2) = 71 \cdot 4 \text{ kN/m}^2$
At 9 m depth: $\sigma_v' = (3 \times 17) + (2 \times 10 \cdot 2) + (4 \times 9 \cdot 2) = 108 \cdot 2 \text{ kN/m}^2$

The alternative method is recommended when only the effective stress is required. In all cases the stresses would normally be rounded off to the nearest whole number. The stresses are plotted against depth in Fig. 3.3.

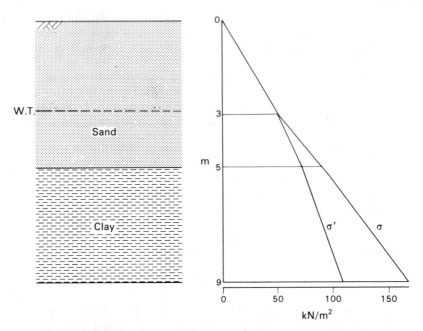

Figure 3.3   Example 3.1.

Effect of Capillary Rise

The water table is the level at which pore water pressure is atmospheric (i.e. $u = 0$).
Above the water table, water is held under negative pressure and, even if the soil is
saturated above the water table, does not contribute to hydrostatic pressure below the
water table. The only effect of the 1 m capillary rise, therefore, is to increase the total
unit weight of the sand between 2 m and 3 m depth from 17 kN/m^3 to 20 kN/m^3, an
increase of 3 kN/m^3. Both total and effective vertical stresses below 3 m depth are
therefore increased by the constant amount $3 \times 1 = 3.0$ kN/m^2, pore water pressures
being unchanged.

Example 3.2

A 5 m depth of sand overlies a 6 m layer of clay, the water table being at the surface;
the permeability of the clay is very low. The saturated unit weight of the sand is
19 kN/m^3 and that of the clay 20 kN/m^3. A 4 m depth of fill material of unit weight
20 kN/m^3 is placed on the surface over an extensive area. Determine the effective
vertical stress at the centre of the clay layer (a) immediately after the fill has been
placed, assuming this to take place rapidly, (b) many years after the fill has been
placed.

The soil profile is shown in Fig. 3.4. Since the fill covers an extensive area it can be
assumed that the condition of zero lateral strain applies. As the permeability of the
clay is very low, dissipation of excess pore water pressure will be very slow: immediately
after the rapid placing of the fill, no appreciable dissipation will have taken place.

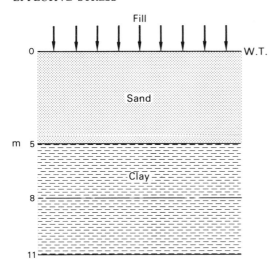

Figure 3.4 Example 3.2.

Therefore, the effective vertical stress at the centre of the clay layer immediately after placing will be virtually unchanged from the original value, i.e.:

$$\sigma'_v = (5 \times 9\cdot2) + (3 \times 10\cdot2) = 76\cdot6 \text{ kN/m}^2$$

(the buoyant unit weights of the sand and the clay respectively being $9\cdot2$ kN/m^3 and $10\cdot2$ kN/m^3).

Many years after the placing of the fill, dissipation of excess pore water pressure should be essentially complete and the effective vertical stress at the centre of the clay layer will be:

$$\sigma'_v = (4 \times 20) + (5 \times 9\cdot2) + (3 \times 10\cdot2) = 156\cdot6 \text{ kN/m}^2$$

Immediately after the fill has been placed, the total vertical stress at the centre of the clay increases by 80 kN/m^2 due to the weight of the fill. Since the clay is saturated and there is no lateral strain there will be a corresponding increase in pore water pressure of 80 kN/m^2. The static and steady-state pore water pressures are equal since there is no change in the level of the water table, the value being $(8 \times 9\cdot8) = 78\cdot4$ kN/m^2. Immediately after placing, the pore water pressure increases from $78\cdot4$ kN/m^2 to $158\cdot4$ kN/m^2 and then during subsequent consolidation gradually decreases again to $78\cdot4$ kN/m^2, accompanied by the gradual increase of effective vertical stress from $76\cdot6$ kN/m^2 to $156\cdot6$ kN/m^2.

3.4 Partially-Saturated Soils

In the case of partially-saturated soils part of the void space is occupied by water and part by air. The pore water pressure (u_w) must always be less than the pore air pressure (u_a) due to surface tension. Unless the degree of saturation is close to unity the pore air will form continuous channels through the soil and the pore water will be concentrated in the regions around the inter-particle contacts. The boundaries between pore water and pore air will be in the form of menisci whose radii will depend on the size of the pore spaces within the soil. Part of any wavy plane through the soil will therefore pass through water and part through air.

In 1955 Bishop proposed the following effective stress equation for partially-saturated soils:

$$\sigma = \sigma' + u_a - \chi(u_a - u_w) \tag{3.4}$$

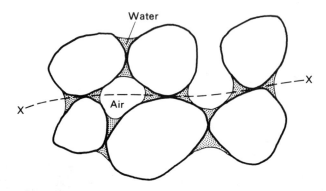

Figure 3.5   Partially-saturated soil.

where χ is a parameter, to be determined experimentally, related primarily to the degree of saturation of the soil. The term $(u_a - u_w)$ is a measure of the suction in the soil. For a fully-saturated soil $(S_r = 1)$, $\chi = 1$ and for a completely dry soil $(S_r = 0)$, $\chi = 0$. Equation 3.4 thus degenerates to equation 3.1 when $S_r = 1$. The value of χ is also influenced, to a lesser extent, by the soil structure and the way the particular degree of saturation was brought about. Equation 3.4 is not convenient for use in practice due to the presence of the parameter χ.

A physical model may be considered in which the parameter χ is interpreted as the average proportion of any cross-section which passes through water. Then across a given section of gross area A (Fig. 3.5) the total force is given by the equation:

$$\sigma A = \sigma' A + u_w \chi A + u_a (1 - \chi) A \tag{3.5}$$

which leads to equation 3.4.

If the degree of saturation of the soil is close to unity it is likely that the pore air will exist in the form of bubbles within the pore water and it is possible to draw a wavy plane through pore water only. The soil can then be considered as a fully-saturated soil but with the pore water having some degree of compressibility due to the presence of the air bubbles: equation 3.1 may then represent effective stress with sufficient accuracy for most practical purposes.

3.5   Influence of Seepage on Effective Stress

When water is seeping through the pores of a soil, total head is dissipated as viscous friction producing a frictional drag, acting in the direction of flow, on the solid particles. A transfer of energy thus takes place from the water to the solid particles and the force corresponding to this energy transfer is called *seepage force*. Seepage forces act on the particles of a soil in addition to gravitational forces and the combination of the forces on a soil mass due to gravity and seeping water is called the resultant body force. It is the resultant body force that governs the effective normal stress on a plane within a soil mass through which seepage is taking place.

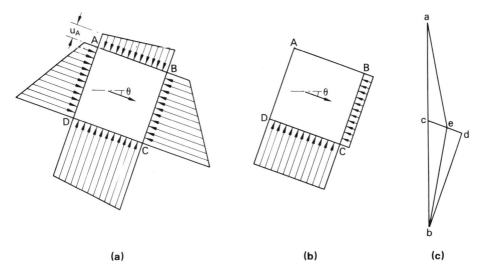

Figure 3.6   Forces under seepage conditions (After Taylor [3.2]).

Consider a point in a soil mass where the direction of seepage is at angle θ below the horizontal. A square element ABCD of dimension b (unit dimension normal to the paper) is centred at the above point with sides parallel and normal to the direction of seepage, as shown in Fig. 3.6a, i.e. the square element can be considered as a flow net field. Let the drop in total head between the sides AD and BC be Δh. Consider the pore water pressures on the boundaries of the element, taking the value of pore water pressure at point A as u_A. The difference in pore water pressure between A and D is due only to the difference in elevation head between A and D, the total head being the same at A and D. However the difference in pore water pressure between A and either B or C is due to the difference in elevation head *and* the difference in total head between A and either B or C. The pore water pressures at B, C and D are as follows:

$$u_B = u_A + \gamma_w \, (b \sin \theta - \Delta h)$$
$$u_C = u_A + \gamma_w \, (b \sin \theta + b \cos \theta - \Delta h)$$
$$u_D = u_A + \gamma_w b \cos \theta$$

The following pressure differences can now be established:

$$u_B - u_A = u_C - u_D = \gamma_w \, (b \sin \theta - \Delta h)$$
$$u_D - u_A = u_C - u_B = \gamma_w b \cos \theta$$

These values are plotted in Fig. 3.6b, giving the distribution diagrams of net pressure across the element in directions parallel and normal to the direction of flow.

Therefore the *force* on BC due to pore water pressure acting on the boundaries of the element, called the *boundary water force*, is given by:

$$\gamma_w \, (b \sin \theta - \Delta h)b$$

or,

$$\gamma_w b^2 \sin \theta - \Delta h \gamma_w b$$

and the boundary water force on CD by:

$$\gamma_w b^2 \cos \theta$$

If there were no seepage, i.e. if the pore water were static, the value of Δh would be zero, the forces on BC and CD would be $\gamma_w b^2 \sin \theta$ and $\gamma_w b^2 \cos \theta$ respectively and their resultant would be $\gamma_w b^2$ acting in the vertical direction. The force $\Delta h \gamma_w b$ represents the only difference between the static and seepage cases and is therefore called the seepage force (J), *acting in the direction of flow* (in this case normal to BC).

Now, the average hydraulic gradient across the element is given by:

$$i = \frac{\Delta h}{b}$$

hence,

$$J = \Delta h \gamma_w b = \frac{\Delta h}{b} \gamma_w b^2 = i \gamma_w b^2$$

or,

$$J = i \gamma_w V \tag{3.6}$$

where V is the volume of the soil element.

The *seepage pressure* (j) is defined as the seepage force per unit volume, i.e.

$$j = i \gamma_w \tag{3.7}$$

It should be noted that j (and hence J) depends only on the value of hydraulic gradient.

All the forces, both gravitational and due to seeping water, acting on the element ABCD may be represented in the vector diagram, Fig. 3.6c. The forces are summarised below:

> Total weight of element $= \gamma_{sat} b^2 =$ vector ab
>
> Boundary water force on CD (seepage and static cases)
> $\qquad = \gamma_w b^2 \cos \theta =$ vector bd
>
> Boundary water force on BC (seepage case)
> $\qquad = \gamma_w b^2 \sin \theta - \Delta h \gamma_w b =$ vector de
>
> Boundary water force on BC (static case)
> $\qquad = \gamma_w b^2 \sin \theta =$ vector dc
>
> Resultant boundary water force (seepage case)
> $\qquad =$ vector be
>
> Resultant boundary water force (static case)
> $\qquad = \gamma_w b^2 =$ vector bc
>
> Seepage force $\qquad = \Delta h \gamma_w b =$ vector ce

Resultant body force (seepage case)
= vector ae

Resultant body force (static case)
= vector $ac = \gamma'b^2$

The resultant body force can be obtained by one or other of the following force combinations:

(1) Total (saturated) weight + resultant boundary water force, i.e.
vector ab + vector be

(2) Effective (buoyant) weight + seepage force, i.e.
vector ac + vector ce

Only the resultant body force contributes to effective stress. A component of seepage force acting vertically upwards will therefore reduce a vertical effective stress component from the static value. A component of seepage force acting vertically downwards will increase a vertical effective stress component from the static value.

A problem may be solved using either force combination (1) or force combination (2) but it may be that one combination is more suitable than the other for a particular problem. Combination (1) involves consideration of the equilibrium of the whole soil mass (solids + water), while combination (2) involves consideration of the equilibrium of the soil skeleton only.

The Quick Condition

Consider the special case of seepage vertically upwards. The vector ce in Fig. 3.6c would then be vertically upwards and if the hydraulic gradient were high enough the resultant body force would be zero. The value of hydraulic gradient corresponding to zero resultant body force is called the *critical hydraulic gradient* (i_c). For an element of soil of volume V subject to upward seepage under the critical hydraulic gradient, the seepage force is therefore equal to the effective weight of the element, i.e.

$$i_c \gamma_w V = \gamma' V$$

$$\therefore \qquad i_c = \frac{\gamma'}{\gamma_w} = \frac{G_s - 1}{1 + e} \qquad (3.8)$$

The ratio γ'/γ_w, and hence the critical hydraulic gradient, is approximately $1\cdot0$ for most soils.

When the hydraulic gradient is i_c the effective normal stress on any plane will be zero, gravitational forces having been cancelled out by upward seepage forces. In the case of sands the contact forces between particles will be zero and the soil will have no strength. The soil is then said to be in a *quick* condition (quick meaning 'alive') and if the critical gradient is exceeded the surface will appear to be 'boiling' as the particles are moved around in the upward flow of water. It should be realised that 'quicksand' is not a special type of soil but simply sand through which there is an upward flow of water under a hydraulic gradient equal to or exceeding i_c. It is possible for clays to have strength at zero effective normal stress, so the quick condition may not necessarily result when the hydraulic gradient reaches the critical value given by equation 3.8.

Conditions Adjacent to Sheet Piling

High upward hydraulic gradients may be experienced in the soil adjacent to the down-stream face of a sheet pile wall. Fig. 3.7 shows part of the flow net for seepage under a sheet pile wall, the embedded length on the downstream side being d. A mass of

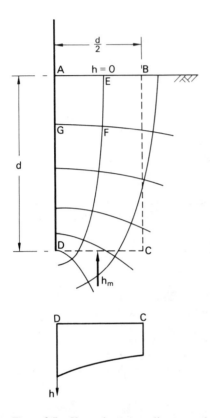

Figure 3.7   Upward seepage adjacent to sheet piling.

soil adjacent to the piling may become unstable and be unable to support the wall. Terzaghi has shown that failure is likely to occur within a soil mass of approximate dimensions $d \times d/2$ in section (ABCD in Fig. 3.7). Failure first shows in the form of a rise or *heave* at the surface, associated with an expansion of the soil which results in an increase in permeability. This in turn leads to increased flow, surface 'boiling' in the case of sands, and complete failure.

The variation of total head on the lower boundary CD of the soil mass can be obtained from the flow net equipotentials but for purposes of analysis it is sufficient to determine the average total head h_m by inspection. The total head on the upper boundary AB is zero.

The average hydraulic gradient is given by:

$$i_m = \frac{h_m}{d}$$

Since failure due to heaving may be expected when the hydraulic gradient becomes i_c the factor of safety (F) against heaving may be expressed as:

$$F = \frac{i_c}{i_m} \qquad (3.9)$$

In the case of sands, a factor of safety can also be obtained with respect to 'boiling' at the surface. The *exit* hydraulic gradient (i_e) can be determined by measuring the dimension Δs of the flow net field AEFG adjacent to the piling:

$$i_e = \frac{\Delta h}{\Delta s}$$

where Δh is the drop in total head between equipotentials GF and AE. Then the factor of safety is:

$$F = \frac{i_c}{i_e} \qquad (3.10)$$

There is unlikely to be any appreciable difference between the values of F given by equations 3.9 and 3.10.

The sheet pile wall problem shown in Fig. 3.7 can also be used to illustrate the two methods of combining gravitational and water forces.

(1) Total weight of mass ABCD = $\frac{1}{2}\gamma_{sat}d^2$

Average total head on CD = h_m

Elevation head on CD = $- d$

Average pore water pressure on CD = $(h_m + d)\gamma_w$

Boundary water force on CD = $\frac{d}{2}(h_m + d)\gamma_w$

Resultant body force of ABCD = $\frac{1}{2}\gamma_{sat}d^2 - \frac{d}{2}(h_m + d)\gamma_w$

$$= \frac{1}{2}(\gamma' + \gamma_w)d^2 - \frac{1}{2}(h_m d + d^2)\gamma_w$$
$$= \frac{1}{2}\gamma'd^2 - \frac{1}{2}h_m\gamma_w d$$

(2) Effective weight of mass ABCD = $\frac{1}{2}\gamma'd^2$

Average hydraulic gradient through ABCD = $\frac{h_m}{d}$

Seepage force on ABCD = $\frac{h_m}{d}\gamma_w\frac{d^2}{2} = \frac{1}{2}h_m\gamma_w d$

Resultant body force of ABCD = $\frac{1}{2}\gamma'd^2 - \frac{1}{2}h_m\gamma_w d$
as in (1) above.

The resultant body force will be zero, leading to heaving, when:

$$\tfrac{1}{2}h_m\gamma_w d = \tfrac{1}{2}\gamma'd^2$$

The factor of safety can then be expressed as:

$$F = \frac{\frac{1}{2}\gamma'd^2}{\frac{1}{2}h_m\gamma_w d} = \frac{\gamma'd}{h_m\gamma_w} = \frac{i_c}{i_m}$$

If the factor of safety against heaving is considered inadequate, the embedded length d may be increased or a surcharge load in the form of a filter may be placed on the surface AB, the filter being designed to prevent entry of soil particles. If the effective weight of the filter per unit area is w' then the factor of safety becomes:

$$F = \frac{\gamma' d + w'}{h_m \gamma_w}$$

Example 3.3

The flow net for seepage under a sheet pile wall is shown in Fig. 3.8a, the saturated unit weight of the soil being 20 kN/m³. Determine the values of effective vertical stress at A and B.

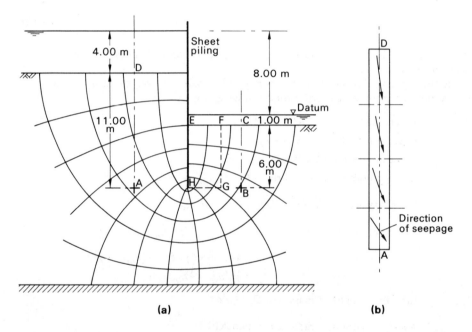

(a)   **(b)**

Figure 3.8   Example 3.8.

(1)   First consider the combination of total weight and resultant boundary water force. Consider the column of saturated soil of *unit area* between A and the soil surface at D. The total weight of the column is $11\gamma_{sat}$ (220 kN). Due to the change in level of the equipotentials across the column, the boundary water forces on the sides of the column will not be equal although in this case the difference will be small. There is thus a net horizontal boundary water force on the column. However as the effective *vertical* stress is to be calculated, only the vertical component of the resultant body force is required and the net horizontal boundary water force need not be considered. The boundary water force on the top surface of the column is due only to the depth of water above D and is $4\gamma_w$ (39 kN). The boundary water

force on the bottom surface of the column must be determined from the flow net, as follows:

Number of equipotential drops between the downstream soil surface and A = 8·2.

There are 12 equipotential drops between the upstream and downstream soil surfaces, representing a loss in total head of 8 m.

$$\therefore \text{ Total head at A, } h_A = \frac{8 \cdot 2}{12} \times 8 = 5 \cdot 5 \text{ m}$$

Elevation head at A, $z_A = -7 \cdot 0$ m

Pore water pressure at A, $u_A = \gamma_w (h_A - z_A)$

$$= 9 \cdot 8 (5 \cdot 5 + 7 \cdot 0) = 122 \text{ kN/m}^2$$

i.e. Boundary water force on bottom surface = 122 kN

Net vertical boundary water force = 122 − 39 = 83 kN

Now the total weight of the column = 220 kN

∴ Vertical component of resultant body force = 220 − 83 = 137 kN

i.e. Effective vertical stress at A = 137 kN/m².

It should be realised that the same result would be obtained by the direct application of the effective stress equation, the total vertical stress at A being the weight of saturated soil and water, per unit area, above A. Thus:

$$\sigma_A = 11\gamma_{sat} + 4\gamma_w = 220 + 39 = 259 \text{ kN/m}^2$$

$$u_A = 122 \text{ kN/m}^2$$

$$\sigma'_A = \sigma_A - u_A = 259 - 122 = 137 \text{ kN/m}^2$$

The only difference in concept is that the boundary water force per unit area on top of the column of saturated soil AD contributes to the total vertical stress at A. Similarly at B:

$$\sigma_B = 6\gamma_{sat} + 1\gamma_w = 120 + 9 \cdot 8 = 130 \text{ kN/m}^2$$

$$h_B = \frac{2 \cdot 4}{12} \times 8 = 1 \cdot 6 \text{ m}$$

$$z_B = -7 \cdot 0 \text{ m}$$

$$u_B = \gamma_w (h_B - z_B) = 9 \cdot 8(1 \cdot 6 + 7 \cdot 0) = 84 \text{ kN/m}^2$$

$$\sigma'_B = \sigma_B - u_B = 130 - 84 = 46 \text{ kN/m}^2$$

(2)   Now consider the combination of effective weight and seepage force. The direction of seepage alters over the depth of the column of soil AD as illustrated in Fig. 3.8b, the direction of seepage for any section of the column being determined from the flow net: the effective weight of the column must be combined with the vertical components of seepage force. More conveniently, the effective stress at A can be calculated using the algebraic sum of the buoyant unit weight of the soil and the average value of the vertical component of seepage pressure between A and D.

Between any two equipotentials the hydraulic gradient is $\Delta h/\Delta s$ (equation 2.15). Hence, if θ is the angle between the direction of flow and the horizontal, the vertical component of seepage pressure $(j \sin \theta)$ is;

$$\frac{\Delta h}{\Delta s}\gamma_w \sin \theta = \frac{\Delta h}{\Delta z}\gamma_w$$

where Δz $(= \Delta s/\sin \theta)$ is the vertical distance between the same equipotentials. The calculation is as follows.

Number of equipotential drops between D and A = 3·8

Loss in total head between D and A = $\dfrac{3·8}{12}$ x 8 = 2·5 m

Average value of vertical component of seepage pressure between D and A, acting in the same direction as gravity

$$= \frac{2·5}{11} \times 9·8 = 2·3 \text{ kN/m}^3$$

Buoyant unit weight of soil, $\gamma' = 20 - 9·8 = 10·2$ kN/m^3

For column AD, of unit area, resultant body force
$$= 11 (10·2 + 2·3) = 137 \text{kN}$$
i.e. Effective vertical stress at A = 137 kN/m^2

The calculation is now given for point B.

Loss in total head between B and C = $\dfrac{2·4}{12}$ x 8 = 1·6 m

Average value of vertical component of seepage pressure between B and C, acting in the opposite direction to gravity

$$= \frac{1·6}{6} \times 9·8 = 2·6 \text{ kN/m}^3$$

Hence, $\sigma'_B = 6(10·2 - 2·6) = 46$ kN/m^2

Example 3.4

Using the flow net in Fig. 3.8a, determine the factor of safety against failure by heaving adjacent to the downstream face of the piling. The saturated unit weight of the soil is 20 kN/m^3.

   The stability of the soil mass EFGH in Fig. 3.8a, 6 m by 3 m in section, will be analysed.

By inspection of the flow net, the average value of total head on the base GH is given by:

$$h_m = \frac{3·5}{12} \times 8 = 2·3 \text{ m}$$

The average hydraulic gradient between GH and the soil surface EF is:

$$i_m = \frac{2·3}{6} = 0·39$$

$$\text{Critical hydraulic gradient, } i_c = \frac{\gamma'}{\gamma_w} = \frac{10\cdot 2}{9\cdot 8} = 1\cdot 04$$

$$\text{Factor of safety, } F = \frac{i_c}{i_m} = \frac{1\cdot 04}{0\cdot 39} = 2\cdot 7$$

Problems

3.1   The bed of a river 5 m deep consists of sand of saturated unit weight 19·5 kN/m³. Calculate the effective vertical stress 5 m below the surface of the sand.

3.2   A layer of clay 4 m thick lies between two layers of sand each 4 m thick, the top of the upper layer of sand being ground level. The water table is 2 m below ground level but the lower layer of sand is under artesian pressure, the piezometric surface being 4 m above ground level. The saturated unit weight of the clay is 20 kN/m³ and that of the sand 19 kN/m³: above the water table the unit weight of the sand is 16·5 kN/m³. Calculate the effective vertical stresses at the top and bottom of the clay layer.

3.3   In a deposit of fine sand the water table is 3·5 m below the surface but sand to a height of 1·0 m above the water table is saturated by capillary water: above this height the sand may be assumed to be dry. The saturated and dry unit weights, respectively, are 20 kN/m³ and 16 kN/m³. Calculate the effective vertical stress in the sand 8 m below the surface.

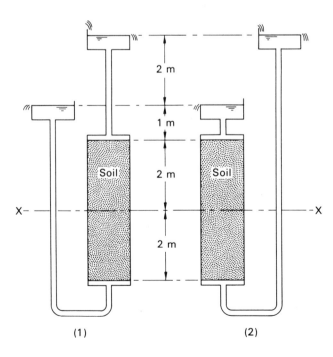

Figure 3.9   Problem 3.6.

3.4   A layer of sand extends from ground level to a depth of 9 m and overlies a layer of clay, of very low permeability, 6 m thick. The water table is 6 m below the surface of the sand. The saturated unit weight of the sand is 19 kN/m^3 and that of the clay 20 kN/m^3: the unit weight of the sand above the water table is 16 kN/m^3. Over a short period of time the water table rises by 3 m and is expected to remain permanently at this new level. Determine the effective vertical stress at depths of 8 m and 12 m below ground level (a) immediately after the rise of the water table, (b) several years after the rise of the water table.

3.5   An element of soil with sides horizontal and vertical measures 1 m in each direction. Water is seeping through the element in a direction inclined upwards at 30° above the horizontal under a hydraulic gradient of 0·35. The saturated unit weight of the soil is 21 kN/m^3. Draw a force diagram to scale showing the following: total and effective weights, resultant boundary water force, seepage force. What is the magnitude and direction of the resultant body force?

3.6   For the seepage situations shown in Fig. 3.9, determine the effective normal stress on plane XX in each case (a) by considering pore water pressure, (b) by considering seepage pressure. The saturated unit weight of the soil is 20 kN/m^3.

3.7   The section through a long cofferdam is shown in Fig. 2.24, the saturated unit weight of the soil being 20 kN/m^3. Determine the factor of safety against 'boiling' at the surface AB and the values of effective vertical stress at C and D.

3.8   The section through part of a cofferdam is shown in Fig. 2.25, the saturated unit weight of the soil being 19·5 kN/m^3. Determine the factor of safety against a heave failure in the excavation adjacent to the sheet piling. What depth of filter (unit weight 21 kN/m^3) would be required to ensure a factor of safety of 3·0?

References

3.1   Skempton, A. W. (1961): 'Effective Stress in Soils, Concrete and Rocks', *Proceedings of Conference on Pore Pressure and Suction in Soils*, Butterworths, London.

3.2   Taylor, D. W. (1948): *Fundamentals of Soil Mechanics*, John Wiley and Sons, New York.

3.3   Terzaghi, K. (1943): *Theoretical Soil Mechanics*, John Wiley and Sons, New York.

CHAPTER 4

Shear Strength

4.1 The Mohr–Coulomb Failure Criterion

This chapter is concerned with the resistance of a soil to failure in shear. A knowledge of shear strength is required in the solution of problems concerning the stability of soil masses. If at a point on any plane within a soil mass the shear stress becomes equal to the shear strength of the soil, failure will occur at that point. The shear strength (τ_f) of a soil at a point on a particular plane was originally expressed by Coulomb as a linear function of the normal stress (σ_f) on the plane at the same point:

$$\tau_f = c + \sigma_f \tan \phi \tag{4.1}$$

where c and ϕ are the *shear strength parameters*, now described as the *cohesion intercept* (or the apparent cohesion) and the *angle of shearing resistance*, respectively. In accordance with Terzaghi's fundamental concept that shear stress in a soil can be resisted only by the skeleton of solid particles, shear strength is expressed as a function of *effective* normal stress:

$$\tau_f = c' + \sigma'_f \tan \phi' \tag{4.2}$$

where c' and ϕ' are the shear strength parameters in terms of effective stress. Failure will thus occur at any point where a critical combination of shear stress and effective normal stress develops.

The shear strength of a soil can also be expressed in terms of the effective major and minor principal stresses σ'_1 and σ'_3 *at failure* at the point in question. At failure the straight line represented by equation 4.2 will be tangential to the Mohr circle representing the state of stress, as shown in Fig. 4.1, the coordinates of the tangent point being τ_f and σ'_f, where:

$$\tau_f = \tfrac{1}{2}(\sigma'_1 - \sigma'_3) \sin 2\theta \tag{4.3}$$

$$\sigma'_f = \tfrac{1}{2}(\sigma'_1 + \sigma'_3) + \tfrac{1}{2}(\sigma'_1 - \sigma'_3) \cos 2\theta \tag{4.4}$$

and θ is the theoretical angle between the major principal plane and the plane of failure. It is apparent that:

$$\theta = 45° + \frac{\phi'}{2} \qquad (4.5)$$

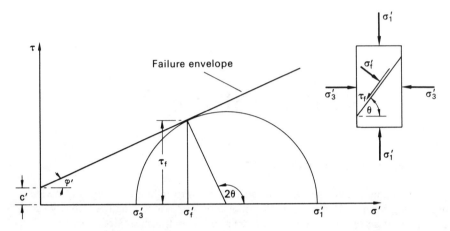

Figure 4.1   Stress conditions at failure.

From Fig. 4.1 the relationship between the effective principal stresses at failure and the shear strength parameters can also be obtained. Now:

$$\sin \phi' = \frac{\frac{1}{2}(\sigma_1' - \sigma_3')}{c' \cot \phi' + \frac{1}{2}(\sigma_1' + \sigma_3')}$$

$$\therefore \qquad (\sigma_1' - \sigma_3') = 2c' \cos \phi' + (\sigma_1' + \sigma_3') \sin \phi' \qquad (4.6)$$

Equation 4.6 is referred to as the Mohr-Coulomb failure criterion. If a number of states of stress are known, each producing shear failure in the soil, the criterion assumes that a common tangent, represented by equation 4.2, can be drawn to the Mohr circles representing the states of stress: the common tangent is called the *failure envelope* of the soil. The criterion implies that the effective intermediate principal stress σ_2' has no influence on the shear strength of the soil. The Mohr-Coulomb failure criterion, because of its simplicity, is widely used in practice although it is by no means the only possible failure criterion for soils. The failure envelope for a particular soil may not necessarily be a straight line but a straight line approximation can be taken over the stress range of interest and the shear strength parameters determined for that range.

By plotting $\frac{1}{2}(\sigma_1' - \sigma_3')$ against $\frac{1}{2}(\sigma_1' + \sigma_3')$ any state of stress can be represented by a *stress point* rather than by a Mohr circle, as shown in Fig. 4.2, and on this plot a modified failure envelope is obtained, represented by the equation:

$$\frac{1}{2}(\sigma_1' - \sigma_3') = a' + \frac{1}{2}(\sigma_1' + \sigma_3') \tan \alpha' \qquad (4.7)$$

where a' and α' are the modified shear strength parameters. The parameters c' and ϕ' are then given by:

$$\phi' = \sin^{-1} (\tan \alpha') \tag{4.8}$$

$$c' = \frac{a'}{\cos \phi'} \tag{4.9}$$

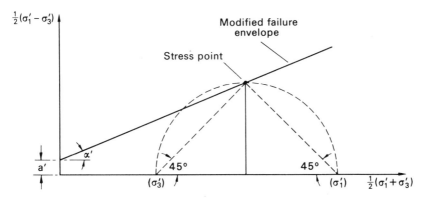

Figure 4.2   Alternative representation of stress conditions.

Lines drawn from the stress point at angles of $45°$ to the horizontal, as shown in Fig. 4.2, intersect the horizontal axis at points representing the values of the principal stresses σ_1' and σ_3'. It should be noted that $\frac{1}{2}(\sigma_1' - \sigma_3') = \frac{1}{2}(\sigma_1 - \sigma_3)$.

4.2   Shear Strength Tests

The shear strength parameters for a particular soil can be determined by means of laboratory tests on specimens taken from *representative* samples of the in-situ soil. Great care and judgement are required in the sampling operation and in the storage and handling of samples prior to testing, especially in the case of undisturbed samples where the object is to preserve the in-situ structure and water content of the soil. The effects of sample disturbance can be particularly serious in the case of clays. In general, samples may be obtained either from open pits or by means of some form of tube sampler; pit samples are normally subjected to least disturbance.

The Direct Shear Test

The specimen is confined in a metal box of square of circular cross-section split horizontally at mid-height, a small clearance being maintained between the two halves of the box. Porous plates are placed below and on top of the specimen if it is fully or partially saturated to allow free drainage: if the specimen is dry, solid metal plates may be used. The essential features of the apparatus are shown diagrammatically in Fig. 4.3. A vertical force (N) is applied to the specimen through a loading plate and shear stress is gradually applied on a horizontal plane by causing the two halves of the box to move relative to each other, the shear force (T) being measured together

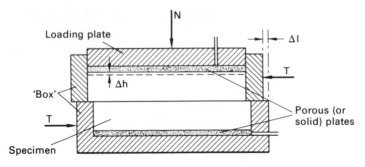

Figure 4.3   Direct shear apparatus.

with the corresponding shear displacement (Δl). Normally the change in thickness (Δh) of the specimen is also measured. A number of specimens of the soil are tested, each under a different vertical force, and the value of shear stress at failure is plotted against the normal stress for each test. The shear strength parameters are then obtained from the best line fitting the plotted points.

The test suffers from several disadvantages, the main one being that drainage conditions cannot be controlled. As pore water pressure cannot be measured, only the total normal stress can be determined, although this is equal to the effective

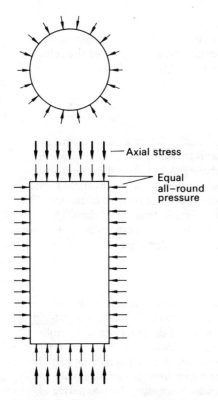

Figure 4.4   Stress system in triaxial test.

normal stress if the pore water pressure is zero. Only an approximation to the state of pure shear is produced in the specimen and shear stress on the failure plane is not uniform, failure occurring progressively from the edges towards the centre of the specimen. The area under the shear and vertical loads does not remain constant throughout the test. The advantages of the test are its simplicity and, in the case of sands, the ease of specimen preparation.

The Triaxial Test

This is the most widely used shear strength test and is suitable for all types of soil. The test has the advantages that drainage conditions can be controlled, enabling saturated soils of low permeability to be consolidated, if required, as part of the test procedure, and pore water pressure measurements can be made. A cylindrical specimen, generally having a length/diameter ratio of 2, is used in the test and is stressed under conditions of axial symmetry in the manner shown in Fig. 4.4. The main features of the apparatus are shown in Fig. 4.5. The circular base has a central pedestal on which the specimen is placed, there being access through the pedestal for drainage or for the measurement of pore water pressure. A perspex cylinder, sealed between a ring and a circular top cap, forms the body of the cell. The top cap has a central bush through which the loading ram passes. The cylinder and top cap clamp onto the base, a seal being made by means of an O-ring.

The specimen is placed on either a porous or a solid disc on the pedestal of the apparatus. A loading cap is placed on top of the specimen and the specimen is then sealed in a rubber membrane, O-rings under tension being used to seal the membrane to the pedestal and the loading cap. In the case of sands, the specimen must be prepared in a rubber membrane inside a rigid former which fits around the pedestal: a small negative pressure is applied to the pore water to maintain the stability of the specimen while the former is removed and prior to the application of the all-round pressure. A drainage connection may also be made through the loading cap to the top of the specimen, a flexible plastic tube leading from the loading cap to the base of the cell. The top of the loading cap and the lower end of the loading ram both have coned seatings, the load being transmitted through a steel ball. The specimen is subjected to an all-round fluid pressure in the cell, consolidation is allowed to take place if appropriate, then the axial stress is gradually increased by the application of compressive load through the ram until failure of the specimen takes place, usually on a diagonal plane. The system for applying the all-round pressure must be capable of compensating for pressure changes due to cell leakage or specimen volume change.

In the triaxial test, consolidation takes place under equal increments of total stress normal to the end and circumferential surfaces of the specimen. Lateral strain in the specimen is *not* equal to zero during consolidation under these conditions. Dissipation of excess pore water pressure takes place due to drainage through the porous disc at the bottom (or top) of the specimen. Drainage results in a flow of water which is collected in a burette, enabling the volume of water expelled from the specimen to be measured. The datum for excess pore water pressure is therefore atmospheric pressure, assuming the water level in the burette is at the same height as the centre of the specimen. Filter paper drains, in contact with the end porous disc, are sometimes placed around the circumference of the specimen: both vertical and radial drainage then take place and the rate of dissipation of excess pore water pressure is increased.

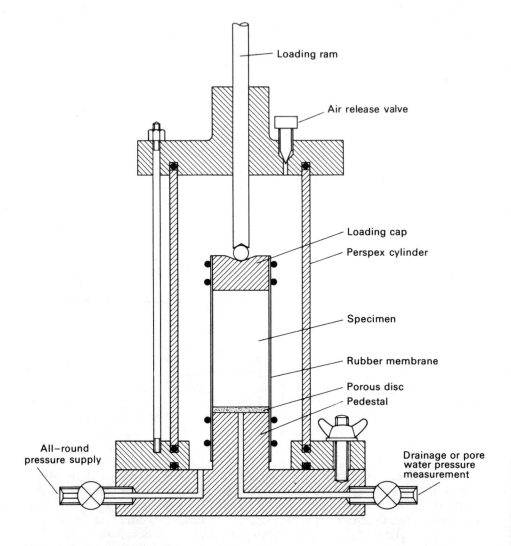

Figure 4.5   The triaxial apparatus.

The all-round pressure is taken to be the minor principal stress and the sum of the all-round pressure and the applied axial stress as the major principal stress, on the basis that there are no shear stresses on the surfaces of the specimen. The applied axial stress is thus referred to as the *principal stress difference*. The intermediate principal stress is taken as being equal to the minor principal stress. The stress conditions can be represented by a Mohr circle or a stress point at any stage of the test and in particular for the failure condition. If several specimens are tested, each under a different value of all-round pressure, the failure envelope can be drawn and the shear strength parameters for the soil determined. In calculating the principal stress difference, account must be taken of the fact that the average cross-sectional area (A) of the specimen does not remain constant throughout the test. If the original cross-sectional area of the specimen is A_0 then;

$$A = A_0 \, \frac{1 - \dfrac{\Delta V}{V_0}}{1 - \dfrac{\Delta l}{l_0}} \qquad (4.10)$$

where $\Delta V/V_0$ = volumetric strain, $\Delta l/l_0$ = axial strain. In the case of saturated soils the volume change ΔV is usually determined by measuring the volume of pore water

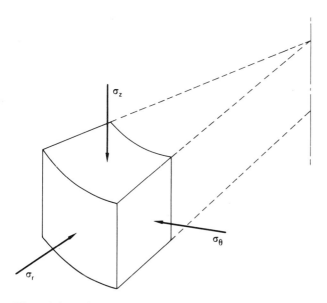

Figure 4.6   Axial, radial and circumferential stresses.

draining from the specimen. The change in axial length Δl corresponds to the movement of the loading ram, which can be measured by a dial gauge.

The above interpretation of the stress conditions in the triaxial test is approximate only. The principal stresses in a cylindrical specimen are in fact the axial, radial and circumferential stresses, σ_z, σ_r and σ_θ respectively, as shown in Fig. 4.6, and the state of stress throughout the specimen is statically indeterminate. In addition, the strain conditions in the specimen are not uniform due to frictional restraint produced by the loading cap and pedestal disc: this results in dead zones at each end of the specimen which becomes barrel-shaped as the test proceeds. Non-uniform deformation of the specimen can be largely eliminated by lubrication of the end surfaces. It has been shown, however, that non-uniform deformation has no significant effect on the measured strength of the soil provided the length/diameter ratio of the specimen is not less than 2.

A special case of the triaxial test is the *unconfined compression test* in which axial stress is applied to a specimen under zero (atmospheric) all-round pressure, no rubber membrane being required. The unconfined test, however, is applicable only for testing non-fissured, fully saturated clays.

A triaxial *extension* test can also be carried out in which an upward load is applied to a ram connected to the loading cap on the specimen. The all-round pressure then becomes the major principal stress and the net vertical stress the minor principal stress.

Pore Water Pressure Measurement

The pore water pressure in a triaxial specimen can be measured, enabling the results to be expressed in terms of effective stress. Pore water pressure must be measured under conditions of *no flow* either out of or into the specimen otherwise the correct pressure will be modified. It is, of course, possible to measure pore water pressure at one end of the specimen while drainage is taking place at the other end. The no flow condition is maintained by the use of a null indicator, essentially a U-tube partly filled with mercury. One limb of the indicator is connected through to the porous disc under the specimen. The other limb is connected to a pressure control cylinder

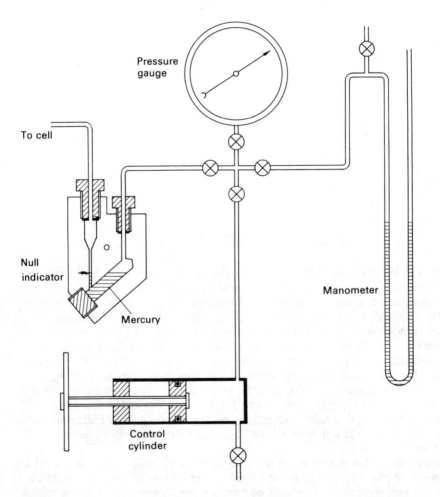

Figure 4.7   Pore water pressure measurement.

and a pressure gauge or manometer. The layout is illustrated in Fig. 4.7. The whole system is filled with de-aired water and it is important that the connection between the specimen and the null indicator should undergo negligible volume change under pressure.

Any change in pore water pressure in the specimen will tend to cause a movement of the mercury level in the indicator. The no flow condition is maintained by making a corresponding change in pressure in the other half of the system by means of the control cylinder so that the mercury level remains unaltered: at the same time the balancing pressure, which will equal the pore water pressure in the specimen, is recorded by the pressure gauge or the manometer.

Pore water pressure can also be measured by means of transducers which can be constructed with very low volume change characteristics and the null indicator system is not then required. A change in pressure produces a small deflection of the transducer diaphragm and the corresponding strain is calibrated against the pressure.

If the specimen is partially saturated a fine porous ceramic disc must be sealed into the pedestal of the cell if the correct pore water pressure is to be measured. Depending on the pore size of the ceramic, only pore water can flow through the disc provided the difference between the pore air and pore water pressures is below a certain value known as the *air entry value* of the disc. Under undrained conditions the ceramic disc will remain fully saturated with water provided the air entry value is high enough, enabling the correct pore water pressure to be measured. The use of a coarse porous disc, as normally used for a fully saturated soil, would result in the measurement of the pore air pressure in a partially saturated soil.

Types of Test

Many variations of test procedure are possible with the triaxial apparatus but the three principal types of test are as follows:

(1) *Unconsolidated-Undrained.**   The specimen is subjected to a specified all-round pressure then the principal stress difference is applied immediately with no drainage being permitted at any stage of the test.

(2) *Consolidated-Undrained.*   Drainage of the specimen is permitted under a specified all-round pressure until consolidation is complete: the principal stress difference is then applied with no drainage being permitted. Pore water pressure measurements may be made during the undrained part of the test.

(3) *Drained.*   Drainage of the specimen is permitted under a specified all-round pressure until consolidation is complete: with drainage still being permitted the principal stress difference is then applied at a rate slow enough to ensure that the excess pore water pressure is maintained at zero.

Shear strength parameters measured by means of the above test procedures are relevant only in cases where the field drainage conditions correspond to the test conditions. The strength of a soil under undrained conditions is different from that under drained conditions. Undrained conditions may be assumed in the field immediately after the application of total stress increases in soils of low permeability,

---

* The procedure for the unconsolidated-undrained triaxial test has been standardised in BS 1377 [4.5]. Details of the procedure for the unconfined compression test using a portable apparatus are also given in BS 1377.

before any significant consolidation has taken place. The drained condition is relevant in soils of low permeability only after consolidation under total stress increases is virtually complete. The shear strength of a soil of low permeability changes gradually from the undrained to the drained strength during the course of consolidation. In soils of high permeability the drained condition will be relevant at any time if it can be assumed that full dissipation of excess pore water pressure takes place within a negligibly short time after the application of total stress increases. The undrained strength of a soil is expressed in terms of total stress, the shear strength parameters being denoted by c_u and ϕ_u. The drained strength, on the other hand, is expressed in terms of effective stress, the shear strength parameters being c' and ϕ'.

Testing Under Back Pressure

Testing under back pressure involves raising the pore water pressure artificially by connecting a source of constant pressure through a porous disc to one end of a triaxial specimen. In a drained test this connection remains open throughout the test, drainage taking place against the back pressure: the back pressure is the datum for excess pore water pressure. In a consolidated-undrained test the connection to the back pressure source is closed at the end of the consolidation stage, before application of the principal stress difference is commenced.

   The object of applying a back pressure is to ensure full saturation of the specimen or to simulate in-situ pore water pressure conditions. During sampling the degree saturation of a clay may fall below 100% due to swelling on the release of in-situ stresses. Compacted specimens will have a degree of saturation below 100%. In both cases a back pressure is applied which is high enough to drive the pore air into solution in the pore water.

   It is essential to ensure that the back pressure does not by itself change the effective stresses in the specimen. It is necessary, therefore, to raise the all-round pressure simultaneously with the application of the back pressure and by an equal increment.

The Vane Shear Test

This test is used for the in-situ determination of the undrained strength of non-fissured, fully saturated clays: the test is not suitable for other types of soil. In particular the test is very suitable for soft clays, the shear strength of which may be significantly altered by the sampling process and subsequent handling. The test may not give reliable results if the clay contains sand or silt laminations.

   Details of the test are given in BS 1377. The equipment consists of a stainless steel vane (Fig. 4.8) of four thin rectangular blades, carried on the end of a high tensile steel rod: the rod is enclosed by a sleeve packed with grease. The length of the vane is equal to twice its overall width, typical dimensions being 150 mm by 75 mm and 100 mm by 50 mm. Preferably the diameter of the rod should not exceed 12·5 mm.

   The vane and rod are pushed into the clay below the bottom of a borehole to a depth of at least 3 times the borehole diameter: if care is taken this can be done without appreciable disturbance of the clay. Steady bearings are used to keep the rod and sleeve central in the borehole casing. The test can also be carried out in soft clays, without a borehole, by direct penetration of the vane from ground level: in this case a shoe is required to protect the vane during penetration.

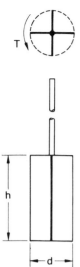

Figure 4.8   The vane test.

Torque is applied gradually to the upper end of the rod by means of suitable equipment until the clay fails in shear due to rotation of the vane. Shear failure takes place over the surface and ends of a cylinder having a diameter equal to the overall width of the vane. The rate of rotation of the vane should be within the range of 6° to 12° per minute. If desired the relationship between torque and angle of rotation may be recorded throughout the test. The shear strength is calculated from the expression:

$$T = \pi \tau_f \left(\frac{d^2 h}{2} + \frac{d^3}{6} \right)$$ (4.11)

where T = torque at failure, d = overall vane width, h = vane length. The shear strength is normally determined at intervals over the depth of interest. If, after the initial test, the vane is rotated rapidly through several revolutions the clay will become remoulded and the shear strength in this condition could then be determined if required.

4.3   Shear Strength of Sands

The shear strength characteristics of a sand can be determined from the results of either direct shear tests or drained triaxial tests. The characteristics of dry and saturated sands are the same provided all stress conditions are given in terms of effective stresses and there is zero excess pore water pressure in the case of saturated sands. Fig. 4.9a shows typical relationships between shear stress (τ) and shear displacement (Δl) in the direct shear test for dense and loose sand specimens. Similar relationships are obtained between principal stress difference and axial strain in drained triaxial tests.

With a dense sand there will be a considerable degree of *interlocking* between particles and before complete shear failure can take place this interlocking must be

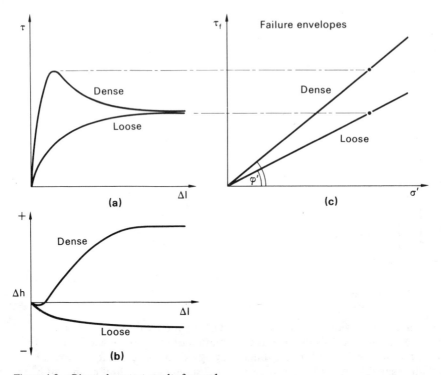

Figure 4.9   Direct shear test results for sand.

overcome in addition to the frictional resistance at the points of contact. After a
peak stress is reached at a low value of shear displacement the degree of interlocking
decreases and the shear stress necessary to continue shear displacement is correspond-
ingly reduced. The decrease in the degree of interlocking produces an increase in the
volume of the specimen during shear as is shown (Fig. 4.9b) by the relationship
between change in specimen thickness (Δh) and shear displacement in the direct
shear test (or between volume change and axial strain in the triaxial test). Eventually
the specimen becomes loose enough to allow particles to move over and around their
neighbours without any further net volume change and the shear stress becomes
constant at an ultimate or residual value. In most practical situations large strains
cannot be tolerated and the peak stress is used to define failure. The degree of interlocking will be greatest in the case of very dense, well-graded sands consisting of
angular particles.

    In the case of a loose sand there is no initial particle interlocking to be overcome and
the shear stress increases gradually to an ultimate value, there being no peak value.
The increase in shear stress is accompanied by a decrease in the volume of the
specimen. The ultimate values of shear stress and void ratio for loose and dense
specimens of the same soil tested under equal vertical stresses or all-round pressures
are approximately equal. A sand specimen is said to be at the *critical void ratio* if its
volume remains unchanged during the shearing process even although volume change
is otherwise possible.

    Only the drained strength of a sand is normally relevant in practice and typical
values of the shear strength parameter ϕ' (c' being zero) are given in Table 4.1.

Table 4.1

	(Loose)		(Dense)
Uniform sand, rounded particles	$27°$	–	$35°$
Well-graded sand, angular particles	$33°$	–	$45°$
Sandy gravel	$35°$	–	$50°$
Silty sand	$(27°-30°)$	–	$(30°-34°)$

In triaxial tests at very high all-round pressures (in excess of 500 kN/m^2) some fracturing or crushing of particles may occur, resulting in the failure envelope becoming curved: however in most practical situations the stresses are not high enough to produce this effect.

If, for some reason, expansion in a dense sand is prevented, interlocking can be overcome by the fracturing of particles if the applied stresses are high enough, resulting in the phenomenon of shear at constant volume.

4.4   Shear Strength of Saturated Clays

In addition to the drainage conditions, a factor influencing the shear strength characteristics of a saturated clay to a significant extent is the stress history of the clay. If the present effective stresses are the maximum values to which the clay has ever been subjected, the clay is said to be *normally-consolidated*. If, on the other hand, the effective stresses at some time in the past have been greater than the present values, the clay is said to be *overconsolidated*. The maximum value of effective stress in the past divided by the present value of the same stress is defined as the *over-consolidation ratio*. A normally-consolidated clay thus has an overconsolidation ratio of 1: an overconsolidated clay has an overconsolidation ratio greater than 1.

(1) Undrained Strength

In principle the *unconsolidated-undrained* triaxial test enables the undrained strength of the clay in its in-situ condition to be determined, the void ratio of the specimen at the start of the test being unchanged from the in-situ value at the depth of sampling. In practice, however, the effects of sampling and preparation result in a small increase in void ratio. There is also strong evidence that the undrained strength in-situ is significantly anisotropic, the strength depending on the direction of the major principal stress relative to the in-situ orientation of the specimen.

The effective stresses in the specimen remain unchanged after the application of the all-round pressure, regardless of its value, because for a fully saturated soil under undrained conditions any increase in all-round pressure results in an equal increase in pore water pressure (see section 4.6). Assuming all specimens to be identical, a number of unconsolidated-undrained tests, each at a different value of all-round pressure, should result, therefore, in equal values of principal stress difference at failure. The results are expressed in terms of total stress as shown in Fig. 4.10, the failure envelope being horizontal, i.e. $\phi_u = 0$ and the shear strength is given by $\tau_f = c_u$. It should be noted that if the values of pore water pressure at failure were measured in a series of tests only one effective stress circle (shown dotted in Fig. 4.10) would be obtained.

In the case of fissured clays the failure envelope at low values of all-round pressure is curved, as shown in Fig. 4.10. This is due to the fact that the fissures open to some extent on sampling, resulting in a lower strength: only when the all-round pressure becomes high enough to close the fissures again does the strength become constant. The unconfined compression test is not appropriate, therefore, in the case of fissured clays.

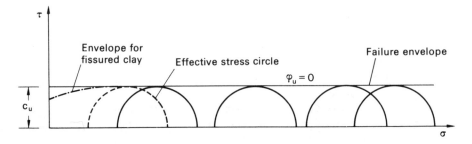

Figure 4.10   Unconsolidated-undrained triaxial test results for saturated clay.

The *consolidated-undrained* triaxial test enables the undrained strength of the clay to be determined after the void ratio has been changed from the in-situ value by consolidation. The undrained strength is thus a function of this void ratio or of the corresponding all-round pressure (p) under which consolidation took place. The all-round pressure during the undrained part of the test (i.e. when the principal stress difference is applied) has no influence on the strength of the clay, although it is normally the same pressure as that under which consolidation took place. The results of a series of tests, in terms of total stress, can be represented by plotting the value of c_u (ϕ_u being zero) against the corresponding consolidation pressure p, as shown in Fig. 4.11. For clays in the normally-consolidated state the relationship between c_u and p is linear, passing through the origin. For clays in the overconsolidated state the relationship is non-linear, as shown in Fig. 4.11.

The unconsolidated-undrained test and the undrained part of the consolidated-undrained test can be carried out rapidly (provided no pore water pressure measurements are to be made), failure normally being produced within a period of 5–10 minutes. Each test should be continued until the maximum value of principal stress difference has been passed or until an axial strain of 20% has been attained.

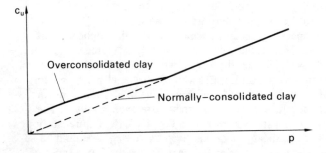

Figure 4.11   Consolidated-undrained triaxial test results for saturated clay.

The undrained strength of soft, non-fissured clays can be measured in-situ by means of the vane test, as previously described.

Clays may be classified on the basis of undrained shear strength as in Table 4.2 below.

Table 4.2
(CP 2004: 1972)

Consistency	Undrained strength (kN/m^2)
Very stiff or hard	> 150
Stiff	100–150
Firm to stiff	75–100
Firm	50–75
Soft to firm	40–50
Soft	20–40
Very soft	< 20

It should be realised that clays in-situ have been consolidated under conditions of zero lateral strain, the effective vertical and horizontal stresses being unequal, i.e. the clay has been consolidated anisotropically: a stress release then occurs on sampling. In the consolidated-undrained triaxial test the specimen is consolidated again under equal all-round pressure, normally equal to the value of the effective vertical stress in-situ, i.e. the specimen is consolidated isotropically. Isotropic consolidation in the triaxial test under a pressure equal to the in-situ effective vertical stress results in a void ratio lower than the in-situ value and therefore an undrained strength higher than the in-situ value. For this reason the consolidated-undrained test is not used extensively in the determination of undrained strength.

Sensitivity of Clays

Some clays are very sensitive to remoulding, suffering considerable loss of strength due to their natural structure being damaged or destroyed. The *sensitivity* of a clay is defined as the ratio of the undrained strength in the undisturbed state to the undrained strength, at the same water content, in the remoulded state. Remoulding for test purposes is normally brought about by the process of kneading. The sensitivity of most clays is between 1 and 4. Clays with sensitivities between 4 and 8 are referred to as *sensitive* and those with sensitivities between 8 and 16 as *extra-sensitive. Quick* clays are those having sensitivities greater than 16: the sensitivities of some quick clays may be of the order of 100.

(2) Strength in Terms of Effective Stress

The strength of a clay in terms of effective stress can be determined by means of either the consolidated-undrained triaxial test with pore water pressure measurement during the undrained part of the test, or the drained triaxial test. The undrained part of the consolidated-undrained test must be run at a rate of strain slow enough to allow equalisation of pore water pressure throughout the specimen, this rate being a function of the permeability of the clay. If the pore water pressure at failure is known, the effective principal stresses σ_1' and σ_3' can be calculated and the corresponding Mohr circle or stress point drawn. A number of tests, each performed at a different value of all-round pressure, enables the failure envelope to be drawn and the shear strength parameters c' and ϕ' determined. Typical results are illustrated in Fig. 4.12.

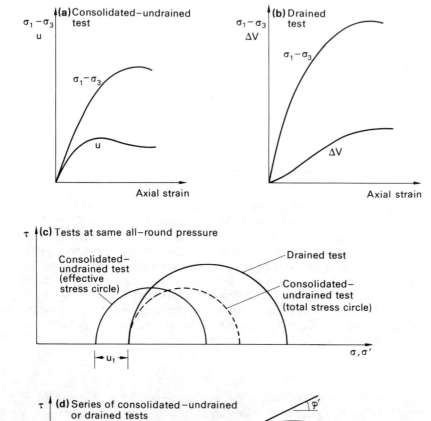

Figure 4.12   Strength of saturated clay in terms of effective stress.

For a normally-consolidated clay the value of c' is zero, whereas for an over-consolidated clay c' has a value not usually exceeding 30 kN/m². The value of ϕ' generally lies between 20° and 35°, lower values being associated with high plasticity index and vice versa.

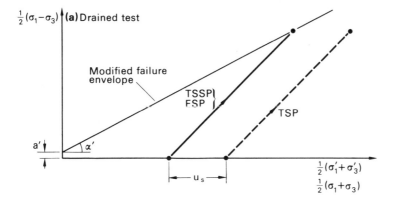

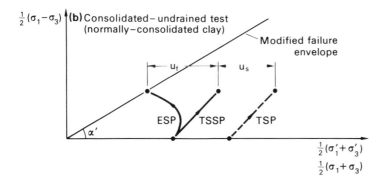

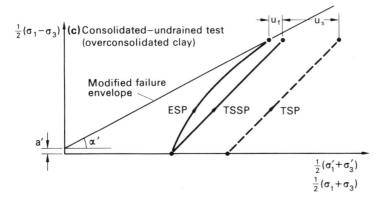

Figure 4.13   Stress paths for triaxial tests.

The parameters c' and ϕ' can also be obtained by means of drained triaxial tests (or direct shear tests). The rate of strain must be slow enough to ensure full dissipation of excess pore water pressure at any time during the application of the principal stress difference: total and effective stresses will thus be equal at any time. The rate of strain must again be related to the permeability of the soil. The volume change taking place during the application of the principal stress difference must be measured in the drained test so that the corrected cross-sectional area of the specimen can be calculated. Typical results are illustrated in Fig. 4.12.

Stress Paths

The successive states of stress in a test specimen or an in-situ element of soil can be represented by a series of Mohr circles or, in a less confusing way, by a series of stress points. The curve or straight line connecting the relevant stress points is called the *stress path*, giving a clear representation of the successive states of stress. Three possible stress paths may be drawn:

(1) the effective stress path (ESP),

(2) the total stress path (TSP),

(3) the path of total stress minus static pore water pressure (TSSP).

In the normal triaxial test procedure the static pore water pressure (u_s) is zero and the two total stress paths coincide. If a triaxial test is performed under a back pressure the static pore water pressure is equal to the back pressure. The static pore water pressure of an in-situ element is the pressure resulting from the water table level. Typical stress paths for a drained triaxial test and for consolidated-undrained tests with pore water pressure measurement on a normally-consolidated and an over-consolidated clay are shown in Fig. 4.13.

Residual Strength

After the peak shear strength in terms of effective stress has been reached, most clays show a decrease in strength with increasing strain until an ultimate or residual strength is reached at a large strain. A typical stress-deformation curve is shown in Fig. 4.14. Since a large displacement is necessary before the residual strength is reached, the most satisfactory method of measuring its value is by means of the specialised ring shear apparatus (an annular direct shear apparatus) in which an annular specimen is sheared by the rotation of one half of the apparatus relative to the other. Residual strength may also be measured by successive forward and reverse movements of the simple direct shear apparatus but the absence of a large continuous displacement in this test results in higher strengths than in the case of the ring shear test.

Peak strength is expressed by equation 4.2:

$$\tau_f = c' + \sigma'_f \tan \phi'$$

and residual strength as:

$$\tau_r = c'_r + \sigma'_f \tan \phi'_r \tag{4.12}$$

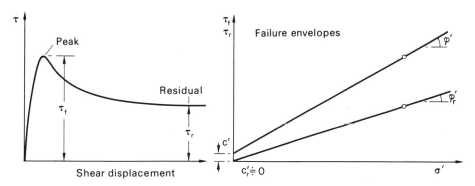

Figure 4.14   Residual strength.

Bishop defined the *brittleness index* as:

$$I_B = \frac{\tau_f - \tau_r}{\tau_f} \tag{4.13}$$

The brittleness index is dependent on stress level.

The decrease in strength from the peak to the residual value is considered to be due to the increase in water content accompanying volume increase during shear and to a reorientation of plate-like clay particles parallel to the failure plane. The difference between peak and residual strengths in silty clays is small but the difference increases with increasing clay content. The difference also tends to increase with increasing overconsolidation ratio.

4.5   Shear Strength of Partially Saturated Soils

The shear strength of a partially saturated soil is a function of the relevant effective stresses but it is extremely difficult to apply the principle of effective stress because of the parameter χ in equation 3.4. Effective stress parameters can be obtained from a series of consolidated-undrained tests with pore water pressure measurement or drained tests on specimens brought to a condition of full saturation by the application of back pressure. Total stress parameters may be determined from a series of unconsolidated-undrained tests on undisturbed specimens or on specimens compacted to

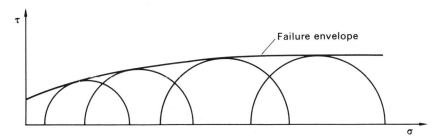

Figure 4.15   Undrained strength of partially-saturated soil.

the same density and water content as the in-situ soil. The undrained shear strength increases with increasing all-round pressure as shown in Fig. 4.15 but the strength increase becomes progressively smaller as the void ratio is reduced due to compression of the pore air. When the all-round pressure reaches a high enough value all the pore air will be driven into solution in the pore water and the failure envelope will become horizontal with $\phi_u = 0$. The curved failure envelope can be approximated to a straight line over the stress range of interest and values of c_u and ϕ_u obtained. The unconfined compression test cannot be used to determine the undrained strength of a partially saturated soil.

Example 4.1

The following results were obtained from direct shear tests on specimens of a sand compacted to the in-situ density. Determine the values of the shear strength parameters.

| Normal stress (kN/m²) | 50 | 100 | 200 | 300 |
| Shear stress at failure (kN/m²) | 36 | 80 | 154 | 235 |

Would failure occur on a plane within a mass of this sand at a point where the shear stress is $122\,kN/m^2$ and the effective normal stress $246\,kN/m^2$?

The values of shear stress at failure are plotted against the corresponding values of normal stress as shown in Fig. 4.16. The failure envelope is the line having the best fit

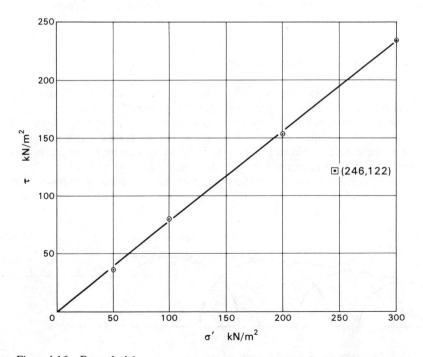

Figure 4.16   Example 4.1.

to the plotted points. In this case the envelope is a straight line through the origin, therefore the value of c' is zero. If the stress scales are the same, the value of ϕ' can be measured directly and is $38°$.

The stress state $\tau = 122$ kN/m^2, $\sigma' = 246$ kN/m^2 plots below the failure envelope and therefore would not produce failure.

Example 4.2

The following results were obtained at failure in a series of triaxial tests on specimens of a saturated clay initially 38 mm in diameter by 76 mm long. Determine the values of the shear strength parameters with respect to (a) total stress, (b) effective stress.

	Type of test	All-round pressure (kN/m^2)	Axial load (N)	Axial deformation (mm)	Volume change (ml)
(a)	Undrained	200	222	9·83	–
		400	215	10·06	–
		600	226	10·28	–
(b)	Drained	200	467	10·81	6·6
		400	848	12·26	8·2
		600	1265	14·17	9·5

The principal stress difference at failure in each test is obtained by dividing the axial load by the cross-sectional area of the specimen at failure. The corrected cross-sectional area is calculated from equation 4.10. There is, of course, no volume change during an undrained test on a saturated clay. The initial values of length, area and volume for each specimen are:

$$l_0 = 76 \text{ mm}; \quad A_0 = 1135 \text{ mm}^2; \quad V_0 = 86 \times 10^3 \text{ mm}^3$$

	σ_3 (kN/m^2)	$\Delta l/l_0$	$\Delta V/V_0$	Area (mm^2)	$\sigma_1 - \sigma_3$ (kN/m^2)	σ_1 (kN/m^2)
(a)	200	0·129	–	1304	170	370
	400	0·132	–	1309	164	564
	600	0·135	–	1312	172	772
(b)	200	0·142	0·077	1222	382	582
	400	0·161	0·095	1225	691	1091
	600	0·186	0·110	1240	1020	1620

The Mohr circles at failure and the corresponding failure envelopes for both series of tests are shown in Fig. 4.17. In both cases the failure envelope is the line nearest to a common tangent to the Mohr circles. The total stress parameters, representing the undrained strength of the clay, are:

$$c_u = 85 \text{ kN/m}^2; \quad \phi_u = 0$$

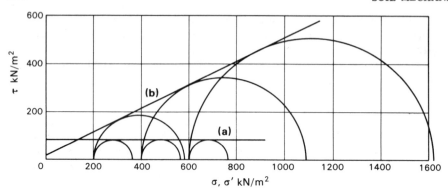

Figure 4.17   Example 4.2.

The effective stress parameters, representing the drained strength of the clay, are:

$$c' = 20 \text{ kN/m}^2; \quad \phi' = 26°$$

Example 4.3

The following results were obtained at failure in a series of consolidated-undrained tests, with pore water pressure measurement, on specimens of a saturated clay. Determine the values of the effective stress parameters c' and ϕ'.

All-round pressure (kN/m^2)	Principal stress difference (kN/m^2)	Pore water pressure (kN/m^2)
150	192	80
300	341	154
450	504	222

The values of the effective principal stresses σ_3' and σ_1' at failure are calculated by subtracting the pore water pressure at failure from the total principal stresses (all stresses kN/m^2):

σ_3	σ_1	σ_3'	σ_1'	$\frac{1}{2}(\sigma_1 - \sigma_3)$	$\frac{1}{2}(\sigma_1' + \sigma_3')$
150	342	70	262	96	166
300	641	146	487	170	316
450	954	228	732	252	480

The Mohr circles in terms of effective stress and the failure envelope are drawn in Fig. 4.18a. The shear strength parameters are measured as:

$$c' = 16 \text{ kN/m}^2; \quad \phi' = 29°$$

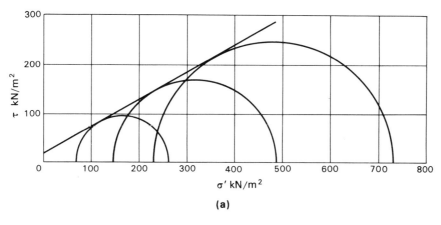

(a)

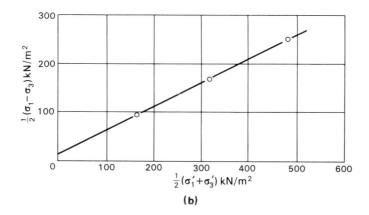

(b)

Figure 4.18   Example 4.3.

An alternative procedure is to represent the states of stress at failure by stress points, plotting $\frac{1}{2}(\sigma_1 - \sigma_3)$ against $\frac{1}{2}(\sigma_1' + \sigma_3')$ as shown in Fig. 4.18b, and drawing the line best fitting the points. The values of the modified parameters are:

$$a' = 13 \text{ kN/m}^2; \quad \alpha' = 26°$$

Then:

$$\phi' = \sin^{-1} (\tan 26°) = 29°$$

$$c' = \frac{13}{\cos 29°} = 16 \text{ kN/m}^2$$

4.6   Pore Pressure Coefficients

Pore pressure coefficients are used to express the response of pore pressure to *changes* in total stress *under undrained conditions*. Values of the coefficients may be determined in the laboratory and can be used to predict pore pressures in the field under similar stress conditions.

(1) Increment of Isotropic Stress

Consider an element of soil, of volume V and porosity n, in equilibrium under total principal stresses σ_1, σ_2 and σ_3, as shown in Fig. 4.19, the pore pressure being u_0. The element is subjected to equal increases in total stress $\Delta\sigma_3$ in each direction, resulting in an immediate increase Δu_3 in pore pressure.

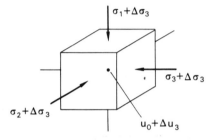

Figure 4.19   Soil element under isotropic stress increment.

The increase in effective stress in each direction = $\Delta\sigma_3 - \Delta u_3$
Reduction in volume of the soil skeleton = $C_s V(\Delta\sigma_3 - \Delta u_3)$

where, C_s = compressibility of soil skeleton under an isotropic effective stress increment.

Reduction in volume of the pore space = $C_v n V \Delta u_3$

where, C_v = compressibility of pore fluid under an isotropic pressure increment.

If the soil *particles* are assumed to be incompressible and if no drainage of pore fluid takes place then the reduction in volume of the soil skeleton must equal the reduction in volume of the pore space, i.e.:

$$C_s V(\Delta\sigma_3 - \Delta u_3) = C_v n V \Delta u_3$$

$$\therefore \qquad \Delta u_3 = \Delta\sigma_3 \left(\frac{1}{1 + n \dfrac{C_v}{C_s}} \right)$$

Writing $1/[1 + n(C_v/C_s)] = B$, defined as a pore pressure coefficient,

$$\Delta u_3 = B\Delta\sigma_3 \qquad\qquad (4.14)$$

In fully saturated soils the compressibility of the pore fluid (water only) is considered negligible compared with that of the soil skeleton, therefore $C_v/C_s \to 0$ and $B \to 1$. Equation 4.14 with $B = 1$ has already been assumed in the discussion on undrained strength earlier in the present chapter. In partially saturated soils the compressibility of the pore fluid is high due to the presence of pore air, therefore $C_v/C_s > 0$ and $B < 1$. The variation of B with degree of saturation for a particular soil is shown in Fig. 4.20.

The value of B can be measured in the triaxial apparatus. A specimen is set up under any value of all-round pressure and the pore water pressure measured (after

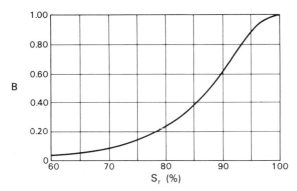

Figure 4.20 Typical relationship between B and degree of saturation.

consolidation if desired). Under undrained conditions the all-round pressure is then increased (or reduced) by an amount $\Delta\sigma_3$ and the *change* in pore water pressure (Δu) from the initial value is measured, enabling the value of B to be calculated from equation 4.14.

(2) *Major Principal Stress Increment*

Consider now an increase $\Delta\sigma_1$ in the total major principal stress only, as shown in Fig. 4.21, resulting in an immediate increase Δu_1 in pore pressure.

The increases in effective stress are:

$$\Delta\sigma_1' = \Delta\sigma_1 - \Delta u_1$$
$$\Delta\sigma_3' = \Delta\sigma_2' = -\Delta u_1$$

If the soil behaved as an elastic material then the reduction in volume of the soil skeleton would be:

$$\tfrac{1}{3}C_s V(\Delta\sigma_1 - 3\Delta u_1)$$

The reduction in volume of the pore space is:

$$C_v n V \Delta u_1$$

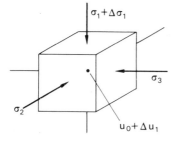

Figure 4.21 Soil element under major principal stress increment.

Again, these two volume changes will be equal for undrained conditions, i.e.:

$$\tfrac{1}{3} C_s V(\Delta\sigma_1 - 3\Delta u_1) = C_v n V \Delta u_1$$

$$\therefore \quad \Delta u_1 = \tfrac{1}{3}\left(\frac{1}{1 + n\dfrac{C_v}{C_s}}\right)\Delta\sigma_1$$

$$= \tfrac{1}{3} B \Delta\sigma_1$$

Soils, however, are not elastic and the above equation is re-written in the general form:

$$\Delta u_1 = AB\Delta\sigma_1 \tag{4.15}$$

where A is a pore pressure coefficient to be determined experimentally. AB may also be written as $\bar{A}$. In the case of fully saturated soils ($B = 1$):

$$\Delta u_1 = A\Delta\sigma_1 \tag{4.16}$$

The value of A for a fully saturated soil can be determined from measurements of pore water pressure during the application of principal stress difference under undrained conditions in a triaxial test. The *change* in total major principal stress is equal to the value of the principal stress difference applied and if the corresponding *change* in pore water pressure is measured the value of A can be calculated from equation 4.16. The value of the coefficient at any stage of the test can be obtained but the value at failure is of most interest. Typical variations of principal stress difference and pore water pressure with axial strain for different types of clay are shown in Fig. 4.22.

For highly compressible soils such as normally-consolidated clays the value of A is found to lie within the range 0·5 to 1·0. In the case of clays of high sensitivity the increase in major principal stress may cause collapse of the soil structure, resulting in very high pore water pressures and values of A greater than 1. For soils of lower compressibility such as lightly overconsolidated clays the value of A lies within the range 0 to 0·5. If the clay is heavily overconsolidated there is a tendency for the soil to dilate as the major principal stress is increased but under undrained conditions no water can be drawn into the element and a negative pore water pressure may result. The value of A for heavily overconsolidated soils may lie between $-0·5$ and 0. A typical relationship between the value of A at failure (A_f) and overconsolidation ratio (O.C.R.) for a fully saturated clay is shown in Fig. 4.23.

For the condition of zero lateral strain in the soil element, reduction in volume is possible in the direction of the major principal stress only. If C_{s0} is the uni-axial compressibility of the soil skeleton then under undrained conditions:

$$C_{s0} V(\Delta\sigma_1 - \Delta u_1) = C_v n V \Delta u_1$$

$$\therefore \quad \Delta u_1 = \Delta\sigma_1\left(\frac{1}{1 + n\dfrac{C_v}{C_{s0}}}\right)$$

$$= A\Delta\sigma_1$$

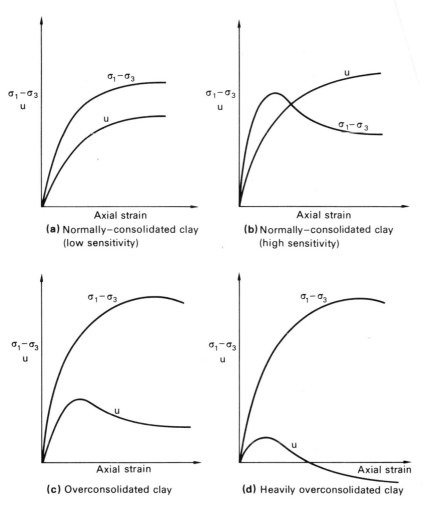

Figure 4.22 Typical variations of principal stress difference and pore pressure with axial strain for different types of clay.

where $A = 1/[1 + n(C_v/C_{s0})]$. For a fully saturated soil, $C_v/C_{s0} \rightarrow 0$ and $A \rightarrow 1$, for the condition of zero lateral strain only. This was assumed in the discussion on consolidation in Chapter 3.

(3) Combination of Increments

Cases (1) and (2) above may be combined to give the equation for the pore pressure response Δu to an isotropic stress increase $\Delta\sigma_3$ together with an axial stress increase $(\Delta\sigma_1 - \Delta\sigma_3)$ as occurs in the triaxial test. Combining equations 4.14 and 4.15:

$$\Delta u = \Delta u_3 + \Delta u_1$$
$$= B[\Delta\sigma_3 + A(\Delta\sigma_1 - \Delta\sigma_3)] \tag{4.17}$$

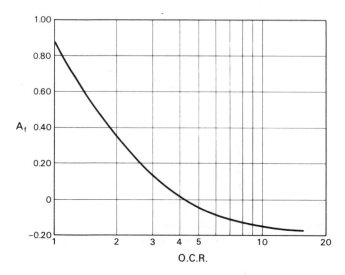

Figure 4.23   Typical relationship between A at failure and overconsolidation ratio.

An overall coefficient $\bar{B}$ can be obtained by dividing equation 4.17 by $\Delta\sigma_1$.

$$\frac{\Delta u}{\Delta\sigma_1} = B\left[\frac{\Delta\sigma_3}{\Delta\sigma_1} + A\left(1 - \frac{\Delta\sigma_3}{\Delta\sigma_1}\right)\right]$$

$\therefore$

$$\frac{\Delta u}{\Delta\sigma_1} = B\left[1 - (1 - A)\left(1 - \frac{\Delta\sigma_3}{\Delta\sigma_1}\right)\right]$$

or

$$\frac{\Delta u}{\Delta\sigma_1} = \bar{B} \tag{4.18}$$

Since soils are not elastic materials the pore pressure coefficients are not constants, their values depending on the stress levels over which they are determined.

Example 4.4

The following results refer to a consolidated-undrained triaxial test on a saturated clay specimen under an all-round pressure of 300 kN/m². Draw the total and effective stress paths and plot the variation of the pore pressure coefficient A during the test.

$\Delta l/l_0$	0	0·01	0·02	0·4	0·08	0·12
$\sigma_1 - \sigma_3$ (kN/m²)	0	138	240	312	368	410
u (kN/m²)	0	54	79	89	91	86

From the data the following values are calculated. For example when the strain is 0·01, $A = 54/138 = 0·39$. The stress paths and the variation of A are plotted in Fig. 4.24.

$\Delta l/l_0$	0	0·01	0·02	0·04	0·08	0·12
$\frac{1}{2}(\sigma_1 - \sigma_3)$	0	69	120	156	184	205
$\frac{1}{2}(\sigma_1 + \sigma_3)$	300	369	420	456	484	505
$\frac{1}{2}(\sigma_1' + \sigma_3')$	300	261	262	278	302	333
A	—	0·39	0·33	0·29	0·25	0·21

From the shape of the effective stress path and the value of A at failure it can be concluded that the clay is overconsolidated.

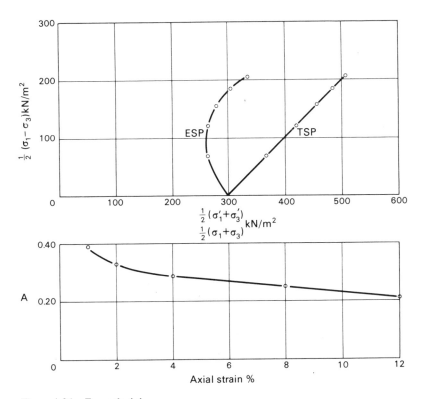

Figure 4.24   Example 4.4.

Example 4.5

In a triaxial test a soil specimen was consolidated under an all-round pressure of 800 kN/m² and a back pressure of 400 kN/m². Thereafter, under undrained conditions, the all-round pressure was raised to 900 kN/m², resulting in a pore water pressure reading of 495 kN/m²; then (with the all-round pressure remaining at 900 kN/m²) axial load was applied to give a principal stress difference of 585 kN/m² and a pore water pressure reading of 660 kN/m². Calculate the values of the pore pressure coefficients B, A and $\bar{B}$.

Corresponding to an increase in all-round pressure from 800 to 900 kN/m² the pore pressure increases from the value of the back pressure, 400 kN/m², to 495 kN/m².

$$\therefore \qquad B = \frac{\Delta u_3}{\Delta \sigma_3} = \frac{495 - 400}{900 - 800} = \frac{95}{100} = 0{\cdot}95$$

The total major principal stress increases from 900 kN/m² to (900 + 585) kN/m²: the corresponding increase in pore pressure is from 495 to 660 kN/m².

$$\therefore \qquad A = \frac{\Delta u_1}{\Delta \sigma_1} = \frac{660 - 495}{585} = \frac{165}{585} = 0{\cdot}28$$

The overall increase in pore pressure is from 400 to 660 kN/m², corresponding to an increase in total major principal stress from 800 kN/m² to (800 + 100 + 585) kN/m².

$$\therefore \qquad \bar{B} = \frac{\Delta u}{\Delta \sigma_1} = \frac{660 - 400}{100 + 585} = \frac{260}{685} = 0{\cdot}38$$

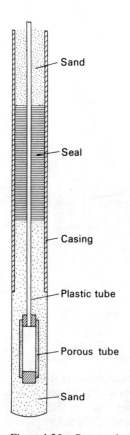

Figure 4.25   Casagrande piezometer.

4.7   In-situ Piezometer Measurements

Whenever there is a change in pore water pressure in-situ there will be corresponding changes, in the opposite sense, in the values of effective stress, resulting in a change in the shear strength of the soil. In-situ pore water pressures can be measured by means of piezometers.

If the soil has a relatively high permeability and is fully saturated, pore water pressure can be determined by measuring the water level in an open standpipe placed in a borehole (Fig. 4.25) since the water level will react almost immediately to any change in pressure. The lower end of the standpipe is either perforated or fitted with a porous element. Sand or fine gravel is packed around the lower end of the standpipe and the standpipe must be efficiently sealed in the borehole with clay or mortar immediately above the level of the stratum in which the pore water pressure is required. The remainder of the borehole is backfilled with sand except for a second seal near the surface to prevent the inflow of surface water. The top of the standpipe must remain accessible at all times and should be fitted with a cap.

If the soil has a relatively low permeability the pressure at the point of measurement will be altered if even a small flow of water is required to operate the measuring device and it will then take some time for the original pressure to be re-established. Thus in the case of soils of low permeability the piezometer is required to respond rapidly to a change in pore water pressure but without any significant flow of water: to achieve these requirements a closed hydraulic system is essential. The closed system employs a piezometer tip consisting of a plastic body into which a porous stone or ceramic is sealed: two types of tip are shown in Fig. 4.26. Two tubes lead from the tip to a Bourdon pressure gauge located as near as possible to the tip: the tubes are of nylon coated with polythene, nylon being impermeable to air and

(a) Embankment tip

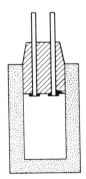

(b) Borehole Tip

Figure 4.26   Piezometer tips.

polythene to water. A change in pore water pressure in the soil adjacent to the tip will result in a small flow of water through the porous stone, continuing until an equal change has taken place in the closed measuring system. The time for this change to take place is called the response time of the piezometer and should be as short as possible. The hydraulic system should thus be as stiff as possible and no air should be tolerated in the system. The two tubes enable the system to be kept air free by the periodic circulation of de-aired water. The pressure recorded by the gauge must be corrected for the difference in elevation between the tip and the gauge, which should be sited below the level of the tip whenever possible.

4.8   States of Stress in Practice

In practice there are very few problems in which a state of axial symmetry exists as in the triaxial test. In practical states of stress the intermediate principal stress is not usually equal to the minor principal stress and the principal stress directions can undergo rotation as the failure condition is approached. A common condition is that of plane strain in which the strain in the direction of the intermediate principal stress is zero due to restraint imposed by virtue of the length of the structure in question. In the triaxial test, consolidation proceeds under equal all-round pressure (i.e. isotropic consolidation) whereas in-situ consolidation takes place under anisotropic stress conditions.

Tests of a more complex nature, generally employing adaptions of triaxial equipment, have been devised to simulate the more complex states of stress encountered in practice but these are used principally in research. The plane strain test uses a prismatic specimen in which strain in one direction (that of the intermediate principal stress) is maintained at zero throughout the test by means of two rigid side plates tied together. The all-round pressure is the minor principal stress and the sum of the applied axial stress and the all-round pressure the major principal stress. A more sophisticated test, also using a prismatic specimen, enables the values of all three principal stresses to be controlled independently, two side pressure bags or jacks being used to apply the intermediate principal stress. Independent control of the three principal stresses can also be achieved by means of tests on soil specimens in the form of hollow cylinders in which different values of external and internal fluid pressure can be applied in addition to axial stress. Torsion applied to the hollow cylinders results in the rotation of the principal stress directions.

Because of its relative simplicity it seems likely that the triaxial test will continue to be the main test for the determination of shear strength characteristics. If considered necessary, corrections can be applied to the results of triaxial tests to obtain the characteristics under more complex states of stress. For example, in the case of dense sands, it has been shown that the peak value of ϕ' in plane strain can be $4°$ to $5°$ higher than the corresponding value obtained by conventional triaxial tests: the increase in the case of loose sands is negligible.

Problems

4.1   What is the shear strength in terms of effective stress on a plane within a saturated soil mass at a point where the total normal stress is 295 kN/m^2 and the pore water pressure 120 kN/m^2? The effective stress parameters for the soil are $c' = 12$ kN/m^2 and $\phi' = 30°$.

4.2   A series of drained triaxial tests was carried out on specimens of a sand prepared at the same porosity and the following results were obtained at failure. Determine the value of the angle of shearing resistance ϕ'.

All-round pressure (kN/m^2)	100	200	400	800
Principal stress difference (kN/m^2)	452	908	1810	3624

4.3   In a series of unconsolidated-undrained triaxial tests on specimens of a fully saturated clay the following results were obtained at failure. Determine the values of the shear strength parameters c_u and ϕ_u.

All-round pressure (kN/m^2)	200	400	600
Principal stress difference (kN/m^2)	222	218	220

4.4   The effective stress parameters for a fully saturated clay are known to be $c' = 15$ kN/m^2 and $\phi' = 29°$. In an unconsolidated-undrained triaxial test on a specimen of the same clay the all-round pressure was 250 kN/m^2 and the principal stress difference at failure 134 kN/m^2. What was the value of pore water pressure in this specimen at failure?

4.5   In a series of unconsolidated-undrained triaxial tests on specimens of a partially saturated soil the following results were obtained at failure. What values of c_u and ϕ_u should be used for the stress range 150 to 250 kN/m^2?

All-round pressure (kN/m^2)	50	100	200	400
Principal stress difference (kN/m^2)	180	234	305	373

4.6   The following results were obtained at failure in a series of consolidated-undrained triaxial tests, with pore water pressure measurement, on specimens of a fully saturated clay. Determine the values of the shear strength parameters c' and ϕ'.

σ_3 (kN/m^2)	$\sigma_1 - \sigma_3$ (kN/m^2)	u (kN/m^2)
150	103	82
300	202	169
450	305	252
600	410	331

If a specimen of the same soil were consolidated under an all-round pressure of 250 kN/m^2 and the principal stress difference applied with the all-round pressure changed to 350 kN/m^2, what would be the expected value of principal stress difference at failure?

4.7   The following results were obtained at failure in a series of drained triaxial tests on fully saturated clay specimens originally 38 mm diameter by 76 mm long. Determine the values of the shear strength parameters c' and ϕ'.

All-round pressure (kN/m^2)	200	400	600
Axial compression (mm)	7·22	8·36	9·41
Axial load (N)	480	895	1300
Volume change (ml)	5·25	7·40	9·30

4.8   Derive equation 4.11.

In an in-situ vane test on a saturated clay a torque of 35 Nm is required to shear the soil. The vane is 50 mm wide by 100 mm long. What is the undrained strength of the clay?

4.9   A consolidated-undrained triaxial test on a specimen of saturated clay was carried out under an all-round pressure of 600 kN/m^2. Consolidation took place against a back pressure of 200 kN/m^2. The following results were recorded during the test:

$\sigma_1 - \sigma_3$ (kN/m^2)	0	80	158	214	279	319
u (kN/m^2)	200	229	277	318	388	433

Draw the three stress paths and give the value of the pore pressure coefficient A at failure.

4.10   In a triaxial test a soil specimen is allowed to consolidate fully under an all-round pressure of 200 kN/m^2. Under undrained conditions the all-round pressure is increased to 350 kN/m^2, the pore water pressure then being measured as 144 kN/m^2. Axial load is then applied under undrained conditions until failure takes place, the following results being obtained.

Axial strain (%)	0	2	4	6	8	10
Principal stress difference (kN/m^2)	0	201	252	275	282	283
Pore water pressure (kN/m^2)	144	244	240	222	212	209

Determine the value of the pore pressure coefficient B and plot the variation of coefficient A with axial strain, stating the value at failure.

References

4.1   Bishop, A. W. (1966): 'The Strength of Soils as Engineering Materials', *Geotechnique*, Vol. 16, No. 2.

4.2   Bishop, A. W., Alpan, I., Blight, G. E. and Donald, I. B. (1960): 'Factors Controlling the Strength of Partly Saturated Cohesive Soils', *Proc. A.S.C.E. Conference on Shear Strength of Cohesive Soils, Boulder, Colorado, U.S.A.*

4.3   Bishop, A. W., Green, G. E., Garga, V. K., Andresen, A. and Brown, J. D. (1971): 'A New Ring Shear Apparatus and its Application to the Measurement of Residual Strength', *Geotechnique*, Vol. 21, No. 4.

4.4   Bishop, A. W. and Henkel, D. J. (1962): *The Measurement of Soil Properties in the Triaxial Test* (2nd Edition), Edward Arnold Ltd., London.

4.5   British Standard 1377 (1967): *Methods of Testing Soils for Civil Engineering Purposes*, British Standards Institution, London.

4.6   Penman, A. D. M. (1956): 'A Field Piezometer Apparatus', *Geotechnique*, Vol. 6, No. 2.

4.7   Penman, A. D. M. (1961): 'A Study of the Response Time of Various Types of Piezometer', *Proceedings of Conference on Pore Pressure and Suction in Soils*, Butterworths, London.

4.8   Skempton, A. W. (1954): 'The Pore Pressure Coefficients A and B', *Geotechnique*, Vol. 4, No. 4.

4.9   Skempton, A. W. and Sowa, V. A. (1963): 'The Behaviour of Saturated Clays During Sampling and Testing', *Geotechnique*, Vol. 13, No. 4.

CHAPTER 5

Lateral Earth Pressure

5.1 Introduction

This chapter deals with the magnitude and distribution of lateral pressure between a soil mass and an adjoining earth-retaining structure. The complete solution of any problem would involve predictions of lateral pressures *and deformations* by considering the initial stress conditions in the soil, the stress–strain relationship for the soil and the boundary conditions describing soil-structure interaction. Such a solution would be extremely complex and in practice simplified methods are used. If the shape of the structure does not change as a result of lateral earth pressure, the structure experiencing only rotation or translation as a whole, it is said to be *rigid* and the problem may be solved by considering deformation in a very general way. If, however, the structure experiences distortion as a result of lateral earth pressure, the structural deformations influence the magnitude and distribution of pressure. Structures of this type are described as *flexible* and semi-empirical methods are normally used in their design.

The two classical theories of earth pressure are those due to Coulomb (1776) and Rankine (1857). Rankine's theory considers the stresses in a mass of soil when it reaches a state of *plastic equilibrium*, i.e. when shear failure is on the point of occurring throughout the soil mass. The stress conditions at failure in a two-dimensional element of soil are shown in Fig. 5.1, the relevant shear strength parameters being c and ϕ. Shear failure occurs along a plane at an angle of $(45° + \phi/2)$ to the major principal plane. If the soil mass as a whole is stressed such that the principal stresses at all points are in the same directions then, theoretically, there will be a network of failure planes equally inclined to the principal planes as shown in Fig. 5.1. It should be appreciated that the state of plastic equilibrium can be reached only if sufficient deformation of the soil can take place.

Coulomb's theory involves consideration of the stability as a whole of the wedge of soil between an earth-retaining structure and a trial failure plane. The *force* between the wedge and the structure is determined by considering, in an approximate way, the equilibrium of all the forces acting on the wedge when it is on the point of sliding either up or down the failure plane, i.e. when the wedge is in a condition of *limiting equilibrium*. Clearly, some lateral movement of the structure is implied to allow the condition of limiting equilibrium to develop. A series of trial failure planes is chosen so that the critical force can be determined.

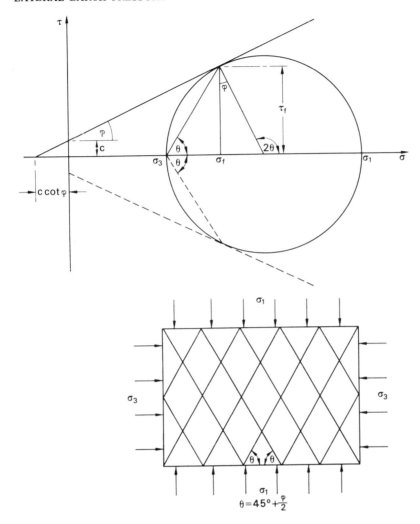

Figure 5.1   State of plastic equilibrium.

5.2   Rankine's Theory of Earth Pressure

Consider a semi-infinite mass of soil with a horizontal surface and having a vertical boundary formed by a *smooth* wall surface extending to semi-infinite depth, as represented in Fig. 5.2a. The soil is assumed to be homogeneous and isotropic. A soil element at any depth z is subjected to a vertical stress σ_z and a horizontal stress σ_x and, since there can be no lateral transfer of weight if the surface is horizontal, no shear stresses exist on horizontal and vertical planes. The vertical and horizontal stresses, therefore, are principal stresses.

If there is now a movement of the wall away from the soil, the value of σ_x decreases as the soil dilates or expands outwards, the decrease in σ_x being an unknown function of the lateral strain in the soil. If the expansion is large enough the value of σ_x decreases to a minimum value such that a state of plastic equilibrium develops.

Since this state is developed by a decrease in the horizontal stress σ_x, this must be the minor principal stress (σ_3). The vertical stress σ_z is then the major principal stress (σ_1).

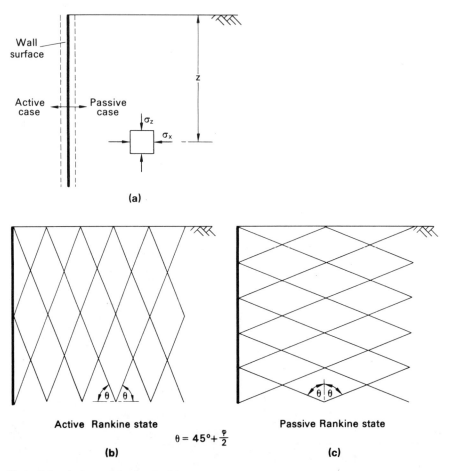

Figure 5.2   Active and passive Rankine states.

The stress σ_1 ($= \sigma_z$) is the total overburden pressure at depth z and is a fixed value for any depth. The value of σ_3 ($= \sigma_x$) is determined when a Mohr circle through the point representing σ_1 touches the failure envelope for the soil. The relationship between σ_1 and σ_3 when the soil reaches a state of plastic equilibrium can be derived from this Mohr circle. Rankine's original derivation assumed a zero value of the shear strength parameter c but a general derivation with c greater than zero is given below.

Referring to Fig. 5.1:

$$\sin \phi = \frac{\frac{1}{2}(\sigma_1 - \sigma_3)}{\frac{1}{2}(\sigma_1 + \sigma_3 + 2c \cot \phi)}$$

$\therefore$ $\qquad\sigma_3(1 + \sin\phi) = \sigma_1(1 - \sin\phi) - 2c\cos\phi$

$\therefore$ $\qquad\sigma_3 = \sigma_1\left(\dfrac{1 - \sin\phi}{1 + \sin\phi}\right) - 2c\,\dfrac{\sqrt{(1 - \sin^2\phi)}}{1 + \sin\phi}$

$\therefore$ $\qquad\sigma_3 = \sigma_1\left(\dfrac{1 - \sin\phi}{1 + \sin\phi}\right) - 2c\sqrt{\left(\dfrac{1 - \sin\phi}{1 + \sin\phi}\right)}$ $\qquad\qquad$ (5.1)

Alternatively, $\tan^2\left(45° - \dfrac{\phi}{2}\right)$ can be substituted for $\dfrac{1 - \sin\phi}{1 + \sin\phi}$.

As stated, σ_1 is the total overburden pressure at depth z, i.e.

$$\sigma_1 = \gamma z$$

The horizontal stress for the above condition is defined as the *active pressure* (p_A), being due directly to the self-weight of the soil. If:

$$K_A = \dfrac{1 - \sin\phi}{1 + \sin\phi}$$

is defined as the active pressure coefficient then equation 5.1 can be written as:

$$p_A = K_A\gamma z - 2c\sqrt{K_A} \qquad\qquad (5.2)$$

When the horizontal stress becomes equal to the active pressure the soil is said to be in the *active Rankine state*, there being two sets of failure planes each inclined at $(45° + \phi/2)$ to the *horizontal* (the direction of the major principal plane) as shown in Fig. 5.2b.

In the above derivation a movement of the wall away from the soil was considered. If, on the other hand, the wall is moved against the soil mass there will be lateral compression of the soil and the value of σ_x will increase until a state of plastic equilibrium is reached. For this condition σ_x becomes a maximum value and is the major principal stress σ_1. The stress σ_z, equal to the total overburden pressure, is then the minor principal stress, i.e.:

$$\sigma_3 = \gamma z$$

The maximum value σ_1 is reached when the Mohr circle through the point representing the fixed value σ_3 touches the failure envelope for the soil. In this case the horizontal stress is defined as the *passive pressure* (p_P), representing the maximum inherent resistance of the soil to lateral compression. Re-arranging equation 5.1:

$$\sigma_1 = \sigma_3\left(\dfrac{1 + \sin\phi}{1 - \sin\phi}\right) + 2c\sqrt{\left(\dfrac{1 + \sin\phi}{1 - \sin\phi}\right)} \qquad\qquad (5.3)$$

If:

$$K_P = \dfrac{1 + \sin\phi}{1 - \sin\phi}$$

is defined as the passive pressure coefficient then equation 5.3 can be written as:

$$p_P = K_P \gamma z + 2c\sqrt{K_P} \qquad (5.4)$$

When the horizontal stress becomes equal to the passive pressure the soil is said to be in the *passive Rankine state*, there being two sets of failure planes each inclined at $(45^\circ + \phi/2)$ to the *vertical* (the direction of the major principal plane) as shown in Fig. 5.2c.

Inspection of equations 5.2 and 5.4 shows that the active and passive pressures increase linearly with depth as represented in Fig. 5.3. When $c = 0$, triangular distributions are obtained in each case.

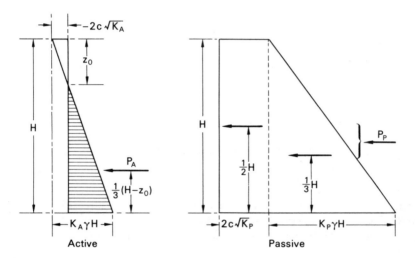

Figure 5.3   Active and passive pressure distributions.

When c is greater than zero the value of p_A is zero at a particular depth z_0. From equation 5.2 with $p_A = 0$:

$$z_0 = \frac{2c}{\gamma\sqrt{K_A}} \qquad (5.5)$$

This means that in the active case the soil is in a state of tension between the surface and depth z_0. In practice, however, this tension cannot be relied upon to act on the wall since cracks are likely to develop within the tension zone and the part of the pressure distribution diagram above depth z_0 should be neglected.

The force, per unit length of wall, due to the active pressure distribution is referred to as the *total active thrust* (P_A). For a vertical wall surface of height H:

$$P_A = \int_{z_0}^{H} p_A \, dz$$
$$= \tfrac{1}{2}K_A \gamma (H^2 - z_0^2) - 2c(\sqrt{K_A})(H - z_0) \qquad (5.6)$$

$$= \tfrac{1}{2}K_A \gamma (H - z_0)^2 \qquad (5.6a)$$

The force P_A acts at a distance of $\frac{1}{3}(H - z_0)$ above the bottom of the wall

The force due to the passive pressure distribution is referred to as the *t resistance* (P_P). For a vertical wall surface of height H:

$$P_P = \int_0^H p_P dz$$

$$= \tfrac{1}{2}K_P\gamma H^2 + 2c(\sqrt{K_P})H \tag{5.7}$$

The two components of P_P act at distances of $H/3$ and $H/2$ respectively above the bottom of the wall surface.

If a uniformly distributed surcharge pressure of q per unit area acts over the entire surface of the soil mass, the vertical stress σ_z at any depth is increased to $(\gamma z + q)$, resulting in an *additional* pressure of $K_A q$ in the active case or $K_P q$ in the passive case, both distributions being constant with depth as shown in Fig. 5.4. The corresponding forces on a vertical wall surface of height H are $K_A qH$ and $K_P qH$ respectively, each acting at mid-height. In the case of two layers of soil having different shear strengths the weight of the upper layer can be considered as a surcharge acting on the lower layer. There will be a discontinuity in the pressure diagram at the boundary between the two layers due to the different values of shear strength parameters.

Lateral Pressure Below the Water Table

If the soil below the water table is in the fully drained condition, the active and passive pressures must be expressed in terms of the effective weight of the soil and the effective stress parameters c' and ϕ'. For example, if the water table is at the surface and if no seepage is taking place, the active pressure at depth z is given by:

$$p_A = K_A \gamma' z - 2c'\sqrt{K_A}$$

where,

$$K_A = \frac{1 - \sin\phi'}{1 + \sin\phi'}$$

Corresponding equations apply in the passive case. The hydrostatic pressure $\gamma_w z$ due to the water in the soil pores must be considered *in addition* to the active or passive pressure.

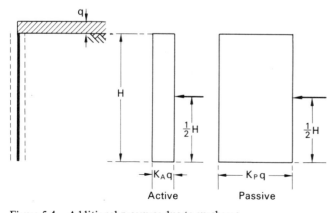

Figure 5.4   Additional pressures due to surcharge.

Example 5.1

(a) Calculate the total active thrust on a vertical wall 5 m high retaining a sand of unit weight 17 kN/m³ for which $\phi' = 35°$: the surface of the sand is horizontal and the water table is below the bottom of the wall. (b) Determine the thrust on the wall if the water table rises to a level 2 m below the surface of the sand. The saturated unit weight of the sand is 20 kN/m³.

(a) $$K_A = \frac{1 - \sin 35°}{1 + \sin 35°} = 0.27$$

$$P_A = \tfrac{1}{2}K_A\gamma H^2 = \tfrac{1}{2} \times 0.27 \times 17 \times 5^2 = 57.5 \text{ kN/m}$$

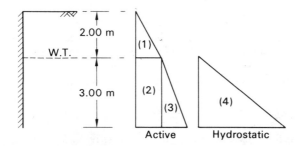

Figure 5.5   Example 5.1b.

(b)   The pressure distribution on the wall is now as shown in Fig. 5.5, including hydrostatic pressure on the lower 3 m of the wall. The components of the thrust are as follows:

(1) $\tfrac{1}{2} \times 0.27 \times 17 \times 2^2$ = 9.2 kN/m
(2) $0.27 \times 17 \times 2 \times 3$ = 27.6
(3) $\tfrac{1}{2} \times 0.27 \times (20 - 9.8) \times 3^2$ = 12.4
(4) $\tfrac{1}{2} \times 9.8 \times 3^2$ = 44.1
         Total thrust   93.3 kN/m

Example 5.2

The soil conditions adjacent to a sheet pile wall are given in Fig. 5.6, a surcharge pressure of 50 kN/m² being carried on the surface behind the wall. For soil (1), a sand above the water table, $c' = 0$, $\phi' = 38°$ and $\gamma = 18$ kN/m³. For soil (2), a saturated clay, $c' = 10$ kN/m², $\phi' = 28°$ and $\gamma_{sat} = 20$ kN/m³. Plot the distributions of active pressure behind the wall and passive pressure in front of the wall.

For soil (1),

$$K_A = \frac{1 - \sin 38°}{1 + \sin 38°} = 0.24; \quad K_P = \frac{1}{0.24} = 4.17$$

For soil (2),

$$K_A = \frac{1 - \sin 28°}{1 + \sin 28°} = 0.36; \quad K_P = \frac{1}{0.36} = 2.78$$

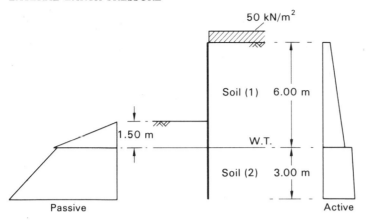

Figure 5.6 Example 5.2.

The pressures in soil (1) are calculated using $K_A = 0.24$, $K_P = 4.17$ and $\gamma = 18$ kN/m³. Soil (1) is then considered as a surcharge of (18×6) kN/m² on soil (2), in addition to the surface surcharge. The pressures in soil (2) are calculated using $K_A = 0.36$, $K_P = 2.78$ and $\gamma' = (20 - 9.8) = 10.2$ kN/m³.

Soil	Depth (m)	Active pressure (kN/m²)	
1	0	0.24 × 50	= 12.0
1	6	(0.24 × 50) + (0.24 × 18 × 6) = 12.0 + 25.9	= 37.9
2	6	0.36[50 + (18 × 6)] − (2 × 10 × √0.36) = 56.9 − 12.0	= 44.9
2	9	0.36[50 + (18 × 6)] − (2 × 10 × √0.36) + (0.36 × 10.2 × 3)	
		= 56.9 − 12.0 + 11.0	= 55.9

Soil	Depth (m)	Passive pressure (kN/m²)	
1	0	0	
1	1.5	4.17 × 18 × 1.5	= 112.6
2	1.5	(2.78 × 18 × 1.5) + (2 × 10 × √2.78) = 75.1 + 33.3	= 108.4
2	4.5	(2.78 × 18 × 1.5) + (2 × 10 × √2.78) + (2.78 × 10.2 × 3)	
		= 75.1 + 33.3 + 85.1	= 193.5

The active and passive pressure distributions are shown in Fig. 5.6. In addition there is equal hydrostatic pressure on each side of the wall below the water table.

Sloping Soil Surface

The Rankine theory will now be applied to cases in which the soil surface slopes at a constant angle β to the horizontal. It is assumed that the active and passive pressures act in a direction parallel to the sloping surface. Consider a rhombic element of soil, with sides vertical and at angle β to the horizontal, at depth z in a semi-infinite mass.

The vertical stress and the active or passive pressure are each inclined at β to the appropriate sides of the element, as shown in Fig. 5.7a. Since these stresses are not normal to their respective planes they are not principal stresses.

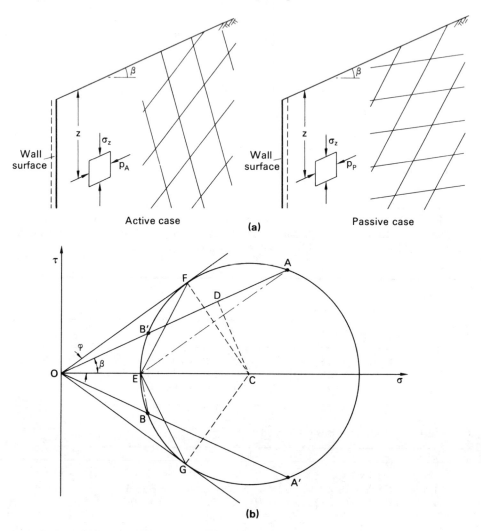

Figure 5.7   Active and passive states for sloping surface.

In the active case the vertical stress at depth z on a plane inclined at angle β to the horizontal is given by:

$$\sigma_z = \gamma z \cos \beta$$

and is represented by the distance OA on the stress diagram, Fig. 5.7b. If lateral expansion of the soil is sufficient to induce the state of plastic equilibrium, the Mohr circle representing the state of stress in the element must pass through point A (such that the greater part of the circle lies on the side of A towards the origin) and touch the failure envelope for the soil. The active pressure p_A is then represented by OB (numerically equal to OB$'$) on the diagram. When $c = 0$ the relationship between p_A and σ_z, giving the active pressure coefficient, can be derived from the diagram.

$$K_A = \frac{p_A}{\sigma_z} = \frac{OB}{OA} = \frac{OB'}{OA} = \frac{OD - AD}{OD + AD}$$

Now,

$$OD = OC \cos \beta$$
$$AD = \sqrt{(OC^2 \sin^2 \phi - OC^2 \sin^2 \beta)}$$

$$\therefore \qquad K_A = \frac{\cos \beta - \sqrt{(\cos^2 \beta - \cos^2 \phi)}}{\cos \beta + \sqrt{(\cos^2 \beta - \cos^2 \phi)}} \tag{5.8}$$

Thus the active pressure, acting parallel to the slope, is given by:

$$p_A = K_A \gamma z \cos \beta \tag{5.9}$$

and the total active thrust on a vertical wall surface of height H is:

$$P_A = \tfrac{1}{2} K_A \gamma H^2 \cos \beta \tag{5.10}$$

In the passive case the vertical stress σ_z is represented by the distance OB$'$ in Fig. 5.7b. The Mohr circle representing the state of stress in the element, after a state of plastic equilibrium has been induced by lateral compression of the soil, must pass through B$'$ (such that the greater part of the circle lies on the side of B$'$ away from the origin) and touch the failure envelope. The passive pressure p_P is then represented by OA$'$ (numerically equal to OA) and when $c = 0$ the passive pressure coefficient (equal to p_P/σ_z) is given by

$$K_P = \frac{\cos \beta + \sqrt{(\cos^2 \beta - \cos^2 \phi)}}{\cos \beta - \sqrt{(\cos^2 \beta - \cos^2 \phi)}} \tag{5.11}$$

Then the passive pressure, acting parallel to the slope, is given by:

$$p_P = K_P \gamma z \cos \beta \tag{5.12}$$

and the total passive resistance on a vertical wall surface of height H is:

$$P_P = \tfrac{1}{2} K_P \gamma H^2 \cos \beta. \tag{5.13}$$

The active and passive pressures can, of course, be obtained graphically from Fig. 5.7b. The above formulae apply only when the shear strength parameter c is zero: when c is greater than zero the graphical procedure should be used.

The directions of the two sets of failure planes can be obtained from Fig. 5.7b. In the active case EA and EB, respectively, represent the planes on which σ_z and p_A act. Thus EA represents a plane at angle β to the horizontal and EB represents a vertical plane. The failure planes are represented by the lines EF and EG and their directions relative to the horizontal or vertical can be determined. The two axes represent the principal planes. The directions of the various planes in the passive case are obtained in a similar way. The directions of the failure planes in the active and passive cases are shown in Fig. 5.7a: it can be shown that these directions are parallel to B$'$F and B$'$G (active case) or to AF and AG (passive case) in Fig. 5.7b.

Example 5.3

A vertical wall 6 m high, above the water table, retains a 20° soil slope, the retained soil having a unit weight of 18 kN/m³: the appropriate shear strength parameters are $c' = 0$ and $\phi' = 40°$. Determine the total active thrust on the wall and the directions of the two sets of failure planes relative to the horizontal.

In this case the total active thrust can be obtained by calculation. Using equation 5.8:

$$K_A = \frac{\cos 20° - \sqrt{(\cos^2 20° - \cos^2 40°)}}{\cos 20° + \sqrt{(\cos^2 20° - \cos^2 40°)}} = 0.265$$

Then:

$$P_A = \tfrac{1}{2} K_A \gamma H^2 \cos \beta$$
$$= \tfrac{1}{2} \times 0.265 \times 18 \times 6^2 \times 0.940 = 81 \text{ kN/m}$$

The result can also be determined using a stress diagram (Fig. 5.8). Draw the failure envelope on the τ/σ plot and a straight line through the origin at 20° to the horizontal. At a depth of 6 m:

$$\sigma_z = \gamma z \cos \beta = 18 \times 6 \times 0.940 = 102 \text{ kN/m}^2$$

and this stress is set off to scale (distance OA) along the 20° line. The Mohr circle is

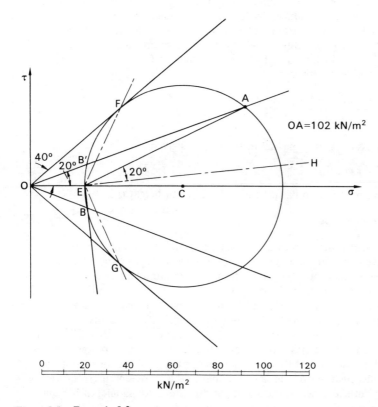

Figure 5.8   Example 5.3.

then drawn as in Fig. 5.8 and the active pressure (distance OB or OB') is scaled from the diagram, i.e.:

$$p_A = 27 \text{ kN/m}^2$$

Then:

$$P_A = \tfrac{1}{2} p_A H = \tfrac{1}{2} \times 27 \times 6 = 81 \text{ kN/m}$$

The complete Mohr circle should be drawn to obtain the directions of the failure planes. The stress σ_z acts on a plane at $20°$ above the horizontal, therefore the line EH, such that $A\hat{E}H = 20°$, represents the horizontal. The directions of the failure planes EF and EG relative to EH are then measured as $59°$ and $71°$ respectively (adding up to $90° + \phi$).

Earth Pressure At-Rest

It has been shown that active pressure is associated with lateral expansion of the soil and is a minimum value; passive pressure is associated with lateral compression of the soil and is a maximum value. If the lateral strain in the soil is zero the corresponding lateral pressure is called the *earth pressure at-rest* and is usually expressed in terms of effective stress by the equation:

$$p_0 = K_0 \gamma' z \tag{5.14}$$

where K_0 is defined as the coefficient of earth pressure at-rest, in terms of effective stress.

Since the at-rest condition does not involve failure of the soil (it represents a state of 'elastic' equilibrium) the Mohr circle representing the vertical and horizontal stresses does not touch the failure envelope and the horizontal stress cannot be evaluated. The value of K_0, however, can be determined experimentally by means

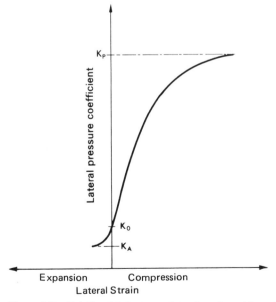

Figure 5.9   Relationship between lateral strain and lateral pressure coefficient.

of a triaxial test in which the axial stress and the all-round pressure are increased simultaneously such that the lateral strain in the specimen is maintained at zero. In the case of normally-consolidated clays a method of measuring K_0 in-situ by means of a hydraulic fracturing technique has been developed by Bjerrum and Andersen [5.2].

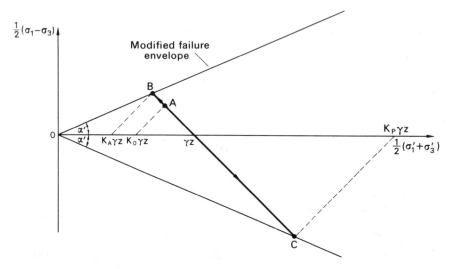

Figure 5.10   Effective stress paths for active and passive states.

Generally, for any condition intermediate to the active and passive states the value of the horizontal stress is unknown. The range of possible conditions can only be determined experimentally and Fig. 5.9 shows the form of the relationship between strain and the lateral pressure coefficient. The strain required to mobilise the passive pressure is considerably greater than that required to mobilise the active pressure. The effective stress paths for the development of the active and passive states from the K_0 condition (for $K_0 < 1$) are AB and AC respectively in Fig. 5.10.

For sands and normally-consolidated clays the value of K_0 can be related approximately to the effective stress parameter ϕ' by a formula proposed by Jaky:

$$K_0 = 1 - \sin \phi' \qquad\qquad (5.15)$$

For overconsolidated clays the value of K_0 depends on the stress history of the soil and can be greater than unity, a proportion of the at-rest pressure developed during initial consolidation being retained in the clay when the effective vertical stress

Table 5.1

Soil	K_0
Dense sand	0·35
Loose sand	0·6
Normally-consolidated clays (Norway)	0·5–0·6
Clay, O.C.R. = 3·5 (London)	1·0
Clay, O.C.R. = 20 (London)	2·8

is subsequently reduced. The value of K_0 increases as the overconsolidation ratio increases and values approaching 3 have been measured. The maximum possible value of K_0 for an overconsolidated clay is K_P.

Some typical values of K_0 are given in Table 5.1.

Application of Rankine Theory to Retaining Walls

In Rankine's theory the state of stress in a semi-infinite mass of soil is considered, the entire mass being subjected to lateral expansion or compression. The movement of

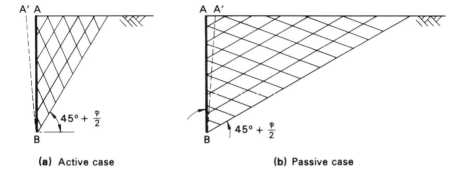

(a) Active case   (b) Passive case

Figure 5.11   Minimum deformation conditions.

a retaining wall of finite depth, however, cannot produce the active or passive state in the soil mass as a whole. The active state, for example, can be developed only within a wedge of soil between the wall and a failure plane passing through the lower end of the wall and at an angle of $(45° + \phi/2)$ to the horizontal, as shown in Fig. 5.11a: the remainder of the soil mass is in a state of 'elastic' equilibrium. A certain minimum value of lateral strain is necessary to develop the active state within the above wedge. A uniform strain within the wedge can be produced by a rotational movement $(A'B)$ of the wall, away from the soil, about its lower end and a deformation of this type, of sufficient magnitude, constitutes the minimum deformation condition for the development of the active state. If the deformation of the wall does not satisfy the minimum deformation condition the soil adjacent to the wall remains in a state of 'elastic' equilibrium and the lateral pressure will be between the at-rest and active values. If the wall deforms by rotation about its upper end the condition for the development of the active state is not satisfied since adequate strain in the soil near the surface cannot take place. In the passive case the minimum deformation condition is a rotational movement of the wall, about its lower end, into the soil. If this movement is of sufficient magnitude the passive state is developed within a wedge of soil between the wall and a failure plane at $(45° + \phi/2)$ to the vertical, as shown in Fig. 5.11b.

In practice the magnitude of wall deformation is unknown. The soil behind a wall is normally backfilled after the wall has been constructed and some degree of outward wall deformation will take place during backfilling. Since increased deformation results in a reduction of lateral pressure towards the active value, a retaining wall need be designed only to withstand the active pressure, provided free deformation is possible.

In the Rankine theory it is assumed that the wall surface is smooth whereas in practice considerable friction may be developed between the wall and the adjacent soil, depending on the wall material. Rankine's assumption results in an overestimation of the active pressure and an underestimation of the passive pressure (both being on the safe side) to an extent depending on the magnitude of wall friction.

Shear strength parameters in terms of either total stress or effective stress may be used in the theory, according to the drainage conditions of the problem. In practice, most backfills are of granular material, the shear strength parameter c' being zero.

5.3   Coulomb's Theory of Earth Pressure

Coulomb's theory takes into account the friction between the wall and the adjacent soil. The angle of friction between the soil and the wall material, denoted by δ, can be determined by means of a direct shear test. At any point on the wall surface a shearing resistance per unit area of $p_n \tan \delta$ will be developed, where p_n is the normal pressure on the wall at that point. A constant component of shearing resistance or 'wall adhesion' c_w can also be assumed if appropriate in the case of clays. In Coulomb's theory a minimum deformation condition for the wall, either away from or into the soil, is assumed, as in the Rankine theory, such that a state of shear failure develops in the wedge of soil between the wall and a failure surface ending at the heel of the wall. Due to wall friction the shape of the failure surface is curved near the bottom of the wall in both the active and passive cases, as shown in Fig. 5.12, but Coulomb simplified the analysis by assuming the failure surface to be plane. In the active case the curvature is slight and the error involved in assuming a plane surface is negligible. This is also true in the passive case for values of δ less than $\phi/3$ but for higher values of δ the error becomes large and the curvature of the failure surface cannot be ignored.

The analysis involves consideration of the stability of the soil wedge between the wall and a trial failure plane. The method is not exact as only force equilibrium is analysed, moment equilibrium not being considered. A number of trial failure planes must be selected in order that the critical force between the soil and the wall can be determined. The analysis is usually performed graphically and the procedure due to *Culmann* is convenient for soils having the shear strength parameter c equal to zero, as will be the case for most backfills. When $\delta = 0$ the Coulomb theory gives results identical to those from the Rankine theory for the case of a vertical wall and a horizontal soil surface.

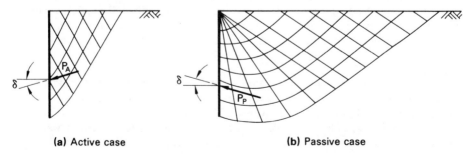

(a) Active case   (b) Passive case

Figure 5.12   Curvature due to wall friction.

Active Case

Fig. 5.13a shows the forces acting on the soil wedge between a wall surface AB, at angle α to the horizontal, and a trial failure plane BC, at angle θ to the horizontal: the soil surface AC may be of any form. For the failure condition the wedge is in equilibrium under its own weight (W), the *reaction* to the force (P) between the soil and the wall, and the reaction (R) on the failure plane. Since the soil wedge tends to move down the plane BC at failure the reaction P acts at angle δ below the normal to the wall. (In the unusual case of the wall settling more than the backfill the reaction P would act at angle δ above the normal.) At failure, when the shear strength of the soil has been fully mobilised, the direction of reaction R is at angle ϕ below the

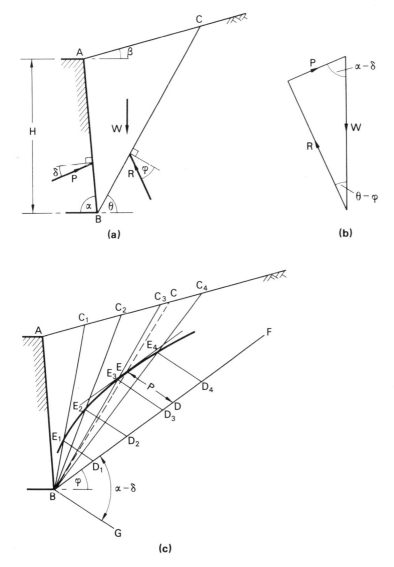

Figure 5.13   Coulomb theory: active case with $c = 0$.

normal to the failure plane (R being the resultant of the normal and shear forces on the failure plane). Since the directions of all three forces are known, together with the magnitude of W, the triangle of forces (Fig. 5.13b) can be drawn and the magnitude of P determined for the trial in question.

Culmann's procedure (Fig. 5.13c) involves constructing the force triangles corresponding to a series of trial failure surfaces. In the triangles the angle between W and P is $(\alpha - \delta)$ and the angle between W and R is $(\theta - \phi)$. Trial failure surfaces BC_1, BC_2, etc. are drawn and a line BF, known as the *weight line*, is drawn at angle ϕ to the horizontal: thus the angle between BF and any trial failure plane is $(\theta - \phi)$. A second line BG, known as the *pressure line*, is drawn at angle $(\alpha - \delta)$ to BF. The weights of the wedges ABC_1, ABC_2, etc. are calculated and are represented to scale by the distances BD_1, BD_2, etc. set off along the weight line BF. Lines are drawn through D_1, D_2, etc. parallel to the pressure line BG to intersect the corresponding failure surfaces at E_1, E_2, etc., BD_1E_1, BD_2E_2, etc. then being the triangles of forces for the trial wedges ABC_1, ABC_2, etc. The lengths D_1E_1, D_2E_2, etc. represent the values of the force P to scale. To determine the maximum value of P, which is the total active thrust on the wall, a curve known as the *Culmann curve* is drawn through the points E_1, E_2, etc. and a tangent parallel to BF is drawn to this curve. The line (DE) through the tangent point and parallel to BG represents the total active thrust to scale. The actual failure plane is BEC. Surcharge pressure on the soil surface is simply added to the weight of the appropriate wedge.

The point of application of the total active thrust is not given directly by the Coulomb theory but can be obtained from the pressure distribution on the wall. The pressure distribution can be deduced by determining the thrust over various depths, on the assumption that a network of shear planes is developed adjacent to the wall. A potential failure surface, therefore, can be considered to pass through any point on the back of the wall. If the thrust P_A is determined at two points at depths z and $(z + dz)$ then the increase in thrust with depth can be expressed as:

$$dP_A = p_A \, dz$$

where p_A is the average value of active pressure over the depth increment dz. Thus:

$$p_A = \frac{dP_A}{dz} \tag{5.16}$$

The pressure distribution diagram is obtained by evaluating equation 5.16 numerically for a series of depth increments between the top and bottom of the wall. The method, however, is cumbersome and is used only rarely in practice. If the ground surface is horizontal or slopes at a constant angle and carries no surcharge loading the pressure distribution diagram is triangular.

The Coulomb theory can be extended to soils for which the shear strength parameter c is greater than zero: a value is then assumed for the wall parameter c_w. It is assumed that tension cracks may extend to a depth of z_0 (equation 5.5), the trial failure planes extending from the heel of the wall to the bottom of the tension zone as in Fig. 5.14. The forces acting on the soil wedge at failure are:

(1) the weight of the wedge (W);

(2) the reaction (P) between the wall and the soil, acting at angle δ below the normal;

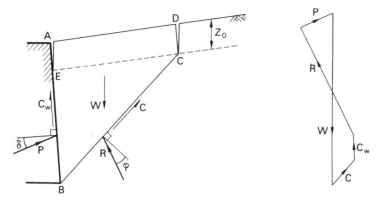

Figure 5.14   Coulomb theory: active case with $c > 0$.

(3) the force due to the constant component of shearing resistance on the wall
($C_w = c_w \times$ EB);

(4) the reaction (R) on the failure plane, acting at angle ϕ below the normal;

(5) the force on the failure plane due to the constant component of shear strength
($C = c \times$ BC).

The directions of all five forces are known together with the magnitudes of W, C_w
and C, therefore the polygon of forces can be drawn and the value of P determined.
The procedure must be repeated for a series of trial failure planes to obtain the
maximum value of P. If the tension crack fills with water, the hydrostatic pressure
due to this water imposes an additional force on the soil wedge.

Passive Case

The Culmann procedure can be adapted to the passive case if the failure surfaces are
assumed to be plane, i.e. when δ is less than $\phi/3$. In the passive case the reaction P
acts at angle δ above the normal to the wall surface (or δ below the normal if the wall
settles more than the backfill) and the reaction R at angle ϕ above the normal to the
failure plane. In the triangle of forces the angle between W and P is $(\alpha + \delta)$ and the
angle between W and R is $(\theta + \phi)$: these two angles locate the weight line and the
pressure line respectively in the Culmann construction. In the passive case the minimum
value of P must be determined.

When the value of δ is greater than $\phi/3$ the curvature of the failure surface should
be taken into account otherwise the total passive resistance will be significantly over-
estimated, representing an error on the unsafe side. An example of an analysis in
which curvature is considered is given in Fig. 5.15. The surface of the soil is
horizontal and the shear strength parameter c is equal to zero. In section the failure
surface is assumed to consist of a circular arc BC (centre 0, radius r) and a straight
line CE which is a tangent to the circular arc. When the wall deformation is such that
the total passive resistance is fully mobilised, the soil within the triangle ACE is in the
passive Rankine state, the angles EAC and AEC both being $(45° - \phi/2)$. The
horizontal force (Q) on the vertical plane DC, therefore, is the Rankine passive value
given by equation 5.7, acting horizontally at a distance of DC/3 above point C.

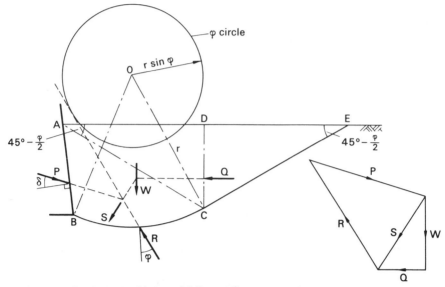

Figure 5.15 Passive case with curved failure surface.

It is necessary to analyse only the stability of the soil mass ABCD and the forces to be considered are:

(1) the weight (W) of ABCD acting through the centroid of the section;
(2) the force Q on DC;
(3) the reaction (P) to the force between the soil and the wall, acting at angle δ above the normal and at a distance of AB/3 above B;
(4) the reaction (R) on the failure surface BC.

When the shear strength along the circular arc BC is fully mobilised the reaction R is *assumed* to act at angle ϕ to the normal. The line of action of R is then tangential to a circle, centre 0, radius $r \sin \phi$: this circle is referred to as the *ϕ-circle*. It has been shown that the line of action of R is actually tangential to a circle, centre 0, of radius slightly greater than $r \sin \phi$ but the error in the value of force P due to the above assumption is on the safe side.

The values of forces W and Q are known and their resultant (S) is determined graphically as in Fig. 5.15. For equilibrium the lines of action of forces S, P and R must intersect. Therefore the line of action of R must pass through the inter-section of S and P and be tangential to the ϕ-circle: thus the direction of the force R is fixed. The polygon of forces can now be completed and the value of P determined. The analysis must be repeated for a number of failure surfaces to obtain the minimum value of P.

It is possible to introduce values of the parameters c and c_w into the analysis and to take into account the influence of a surcharge pressure q on the soil surface. In an alternative analysis the curve BC is assumed to be a logarithmic spiral.

Example 5.4

A retaining wall (above the water table) 6 m high, with a vertical back, retains a soil of unit weight 18 kN/m³, the soil surface sloping at an angle of 20° to the horizontal.

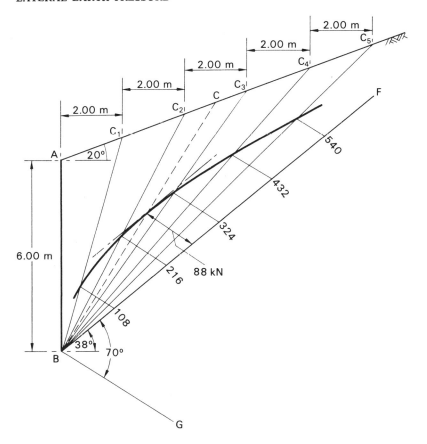

Figure 5.16   Example 5.4.

The appropriate shear strength parameters are $c' = 0$ and $\phi' = 38°$: the wall friction angle δ is $20°$. Determine the total active thrust on the wall according to Coulomb's theory using Culmann's procedure.

Trial planes are selected, as shown in Fig. 5.16, intersecting the surface at points C_1, C_2, etc., spaced at equal horizontal intervals of 2 m, giving a series of triangles ABC_1, $C_1 BC_2$, etc. having equal areas. The weights of wedges ABC_1 and ABC_2 are 108 kN/m and 216 kN/m, respectively: the weights of all the wedges are calculated.

Line BF is drawn at $38°$ (ϕ') to the horizontal and line BG at $70°$ ($\alpha - \delta$) to BF. The weights of the wedges are set off to scale along BF and the Culmann procedure completed as in Fig. 5.16, from which:

$$P_A = 88 \text{ kN/m}$$

Earth Pressure Coefficients

Tabulated values of earth pressure coefficients, based on the Coulomb theory, for the case of a vertical wall and a horizontal soil surface, are given in Civil Engineering Code of Practice No. 2 (*Earth Retaining Structures*) [5.4]. In general the *horizontal components* of total active thrust and total passive resistance can be expressed as:

$$P_{An} = \tfrac{1}{2}K_A\gamma H^2 - 2K_{Ac}cH \tag{5.17}$$

and

$$P_{Pn} = \tfrac{1}{2}K_P\gamma H^2 + 2K_{Pc}cH \tag{5.18}$$

where the coefficients K depend on the values of ϕ, c, δ and c_w. The coefficients published in the above Code appear in Table 5.2.

Table 5.2 Earth pressure coefficients

(a) Shear strength parameter $c = 0$

	δ	ϕ 25°	30°	35°	40°	45°
K_A	0°	0·41	0·33	0·27	0·22	0·17
	10°	0·37	0·31	0·25	0·20	0·16
	20°	0·34	0·28	0·23	0·19	0·15
	30°	—	0·26	0·21	0·17	0·14
K_p	0°	2·5	3·0	3·7	4·6	
	10°	3·1	4·0	4·8	6·5	
	20°	3·7	4·9	6·0	8·8	
	30°	—	5·8	7·3	11·4	

(b) Shear strength parameter $c > 0$

	δ	$\dfrac{c_w}{c}$	ϕ 0°	5°	10°	15°	20°	25°
K_A	0	all	1·00	0·85	0·70	0·59	0·48	0·40
	ϕ	values	1·00	0·78	0·64	0·50	0·40	0·32
K_{Ac}	0	0	2·00	1·83	1·68	1·54	1·40	1·29
	0	1·0	2·83	2·60	2·38	2·16	1·96	1·76
	ϕ	0·5	2·45	2·10	1·82	1·55	1·32	1·15
	ϕ	1·0	2·83	2·47	2·13	1·85	1·59	1·41
K_P	0	all	1·0	1·2	1·4	1·7	2·1	2·5
	ϕ	values	1·0	1·3	1·6	2·2	2·9	3·9
K_{Pc}	0	0	2·0	2·2	2·4	2·6	2·8	3·1
	0	0·5	2·4	2·6	2·9	3·2	3·5	3·8
	0	1·0	2·6	2·9	3·2	3·6	4·0	4·4
	ϕ	0·5	2·4	2·8	3·3	3·8	4·5	5·5
	ϕ	1·0	2·6	2·9	3·4	3·9	4·7	5·7

Active case: if $c < 50$ kN/m² then $c_w = c$;
                    if $c > 50$ kN/m² then $c_w = 50$ kN/m².
Passive case: if $c < 50$ kN/m² then $c_w = c/2$;
                    if $c > 50$ kN/m² then $c_w = 25$ kN/m².
(If wall tends to move downwards relative to ground then values of c_w may be taken as those for active case.)

Design of Earth-Retaining Structures

5.4 Gravity and Cantilever Walls

The stability of a gravity retaining wall (Fig. 5.17a) is due to the self-weight of the wall, perhaps aided by passive resistance developed in front of the wall. Walls of this type are uneconomic because the wall material (masonry or mass concrete) is used only for its dead weight. Cantilever walls of reinforced concrete (Fig. 5.17b) are more

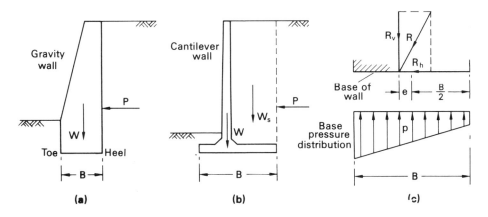

Figure 5.17   Gravity and cantilever retaining walls.

economic because the backfill itself is employed to provide most of the required dead weight. Both types of wall are liable to rotational or translational movements and the Rankine or Coulomb theories are used for the calculation of lateral pressure. For coarse-grained backfills, peak values of ϕ' are used: values of ϕ' obtained from triaxial tests will normally be an underestimate since plane strain conditions apply in retaining wall problems.

The retaining wall as a whole must satisfy two basic conditions: (1) the base pressure at the toe of the wall must not exceed the allowable bearing capacity of the soil (see Chapter 8); (2) the factor of safety against sliding between the base and the underlying soil must be adequate, a value of at least 1·5 usually being specified. Passive resistance in front of the wall should not be relied upon unless it is certain that the soil will always remain firm and undisturbed, an assumption that can seldom be made.

The first step in the design is to determine all the forces acting on the wall, from which the horizontal and vertical components (R_h and R_v respectively) of the resultant force R acting on the base of the wall are obtained. The position of the force R (Fig. 5.17c) is then determined by dividing the algebraic sum of the moments of all forces about any point on the base by the vertical component R_v. To ensure that the base pressure remains compressive over the entire base width, the resultant R must act within the middle third of the base, i.e. the eccentricity (e) of the base resultant must not exceed $B/6$, where B is the width of the base. If the middle third rule is observed, adequate safety against overturning of the wall will also be ensured.

If a linear distribution of pressure (p) under the base is assumed, the maximum and minimum base pressures can be calculated from the expression:

$$p = \frac{R_v}{B}\left(1 \pm \frac{6e}{B}\right) \tag{5.19}$$

The factor of safety against sliding (F_s), ignoring any passive resistance in front of the wall, is given by:

$$F_s = \frac{R_v \tan \delta}{R_h} \tag{5.20}$$

where δ is the angle of friction between the base and the underlying soil. If an adequate value of F_s cannot be achieved a key may be incorporated in the base.

If a wall is constructed on a compressible soil such as a fully saturated clay, non-uniform base pressure will result in progressive tilting of the wall due to consolidation of the soil. A wall constructed on compressible soil should be dimensioned so that the resultant R acts close to the mid-point of the base.

Clay backfills should be avoided if at all possible since climatic changes are likely to cause successive swelling and shrinkage of the soil. Swelling causes unpredictable pressures on, and movements of, the wall: subsequent shrinkage may result in the formation of cracks in the soil surface.

Some form of filter of coarse permeable material is desirable behind a retaining wall to prevent the development of high pore water pressures within the backfill, the water percolating into the filter draining out through weep-holes in the wall.

Certain categories of retaining walls are essentially unyielding, for example foundation walls supported by the floor system of the building and bridge abutments restrained by the deck structure. In such cases the at-rest value of lateral pressure, or pressures between the at-rest and active values, should be used in design. Sowers *et al.* [5.8] showed that compaction of a backfill against an unyielding wall can result in residual lateral pressures considerably higher than the corresponding values for uncompacted soil.

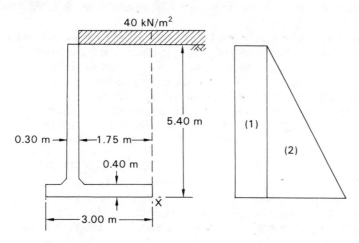

Figure 5.18   Example 5.5.

Example 5.5

Determine the maximum and minimum pressures under the base of the cantilever retaining wall detailed in Fig. 5.18 and the factor of safety against sliding. The appropriate shear strength parameters for the soil are $c' = 0$ and $\phi' = 40°$: the unit weight $\gamma = 17$ kN/m^3, the water table being below the base of the wall. Take $\delta = 30°$ on the base of the wall.

To determine the position of the base reaction, the moments of all forces about the heel of the wall (X) are calculated. The unit weight of concrete is taken to be 23·5 kN/m^3. The active pressure is calculated on the vertical through the heel of the wall. No shear stresses act on this vertical, therefore the Rankine theory ($\delta = 0$) is used to calculate the active pressure: the pressure distribution is shown in Fig. 5.18.

For $\phi' = 40°$ (and $\delta = 0$), $K_A = 0·22$.

	Force per m (kN)		Arm (m)	Moment per m (kNm)
(1)	0·22 x 40 x 5·40	= 47·5	2·70	128·2
(2)	$\frac{1}{2}$ x 0·22 x 17 x 5·40^2	= 54·6	1·80	98·3
		$R_h = 102·1$		
(Stem)	5·00 x 0·30 x 23·5	= 35·3	1·90	67·0
(Base)	3·00 x 0·40 x 23·5	= 28·2	1·50	42·3
(Soil)	5·00 x 1·75 x 17	= 148·8	0·875	130·2
(Load)	1·75 x 40	= 70·0	0·875	61·3
		$R_v = 282·3$		$M = 527·3$

Lever arm of base resultant:

$$\frac{M}{R_v} = \frac{527·3}{282·3} = 1·86 \text{ m}$$

i.e. the resultant acts within the middle third of the base.
Eccentricity of base reaction:

$$e = 1·86 - 1·50 = 0·36 \text{ m}$$

The maximum and minimum base pressures are given by:

$$p = \frac{R_v}{B}\left(1 \pm \frac{6e}{B}\right)$$

$$= \frac{282·3}{3}\left(1 \pm \frac{6 \times 0·36}{3}\right) = 94(1 \pm 0·72)$$

$$= 162 \text{ kN/m}^2 \text{ and } 26 \text{ kN/m}^2$$

The factor of safety against sliding is given by:

$$F = \frac{R_v \tan \delta}{R_h}$$

$$= \frac{282·3 \tan 30°}{102·1} = 1·6$$

Example 5.6

Fig. 5.19a gives details of a retaining wall with a vertical drain adjacent to the back surface. Determine the total thrust on the wall when the backfill becomes fully saturated due to continuous rainfall, with steady seepage towards the drain. Assume a failure plane at 55° to the horizontal. The relevant parameters for the backfill are $c' = 0$, $\phi' = 38°$, $\delta = 15°$ and $\gamma_{sat} = 20$ kN/m³.

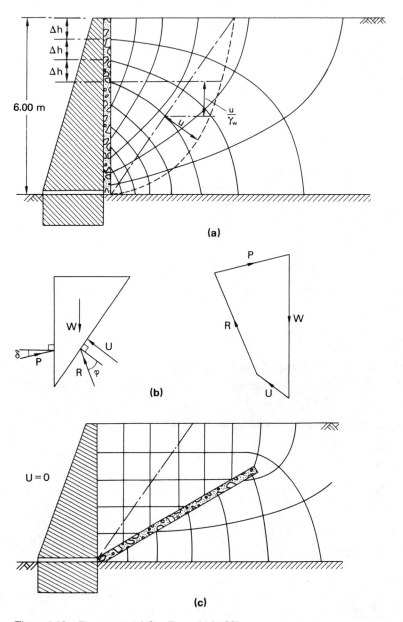

Figure 5.19   Example 5.6 (after Terzaghi [5.9]).

Determine also the thrust on the wall (a) if the vertical drain were replaced by an inclined drain below the failure plane, (b) if there were no drainage system behind the wall.

The flow net for seepage towards the vertical drain is shown in Fig. 5.19a. Since the permeability of the drain must be considerably greater than that of the backfill, the drain remains unsaturated and the pore pressure at every point within the drain is zero (atmospheric). Thus at every point on the boundary between the drain and the backfill total head is equal to elevation head. The equipotentials, therefore, must intersect this boundary at points spaced at equal vertical intervals Δh: the boundary itself is neither a flow line nor an equipotential.

The combination of total weight and boundary water force is used. The values of pore water pressure at the points of intersection of the equipotentials with the failure plane are evaluated and plotted normal to the plane. The boundary water force (U), acting normal to the plane, is equal to the area of the pressure diagram, thus:

$$U = 55 \text{ kN/m}$$

The water forces on the other two boundaries of the soil wedge are zero.

The total weight (W) of the soil wedge is now calculated, i.e.:

$$W = 252 \text{ kN/m}$$

The forces acting on the wedge are shown in Fig. 5.19b. Since the directions of the four forces are known, together with the values of W and U, the force polygon can be drawn, from which:

$$P_A = 108 \text{ kN/m}$$

or,

$$P_{An} = P_A \cos \delta = 105 \text{ kN/m}$$

Other failure surfaces would have to be chosen in order that the maximum value of total active thrust can be determined.

For the inclined drain shown in Fig. 5.19c the flow lines and equipotentials above the drain are vertical and horizontal, respectively. Thus at every point on the failure plane the pore water pressure is zero. This form of drain is preferable to the vertical drain. In this case:

$$P_{An} = \tfrac{1}{2} K_A \gamma_{sat} H^2$$

For $\phi' = 38°$ and $\delta = 15°$, $K_A = 0.21$.

$$\therefore \qquad P_{An} = \tfrac{1}{2} \times 0.21 \times 20 \times 6^2 = 76 \text{ kN/m}$$

For the case of no drainage system behind the wall, the pore water is static, therefore:

$$
\begin{aligned}
P_{An} &= \tfrac{1}{2} K_A \gamma' H^2 + \tfrac{1}{2} \gamma_w H^2 \\
&= (\tfrac{1}{2} \times 0.21 \times 10.2 \times 6^2) + (\tfrac{1}{2} \times 9.8 \times 6^2) \\
&= 39 + 176 = 215 \text{ kN/m}
\end{aligned}
$$

5.5   Cantilever Sheet Pile Walls

The stability of a cantilever sheet pile wall is due entirely to the passive resistance of the soil in front of the wall. Walls of this type are used only when the retained height of soil is relatively small. In sands and gravels they may be used to form permanent structures but in general they are used mainly as temporary structures. A cantilever sheet pile wall, especially in silt or clay, is liable to rotate about a point near its lower end: as a result, passive resistance is developed on the *back* of the wall below the point of rotation.

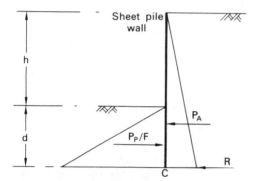

Figure 5.20   Cantilever sheet pile wall.

The pressure distribution assumed in design (for a soil having $c = 0$) is shown in Fig. 5.20, a point of rotation (C) being assumed at depth d below the surface in front of the wall. The force R is assumed to represent the passive resistance below the point of rotation. A factor of safety (F) must be applied to the passive resistance in front of the wall. The depth d can be calculated by equating moments about the point of rotation C to zero. This depth is then increased arbitrarily by 20% to allow for the development of passive resistance behind the wall.

5.6   Anchored Sheet Pile Walls

Anchored sheet pile walls (also called anchored bulkheads) are used extensively in waterfront construction. The wall is constructed by driving a row of sheet piling on the required line, followed by dredging to the required depth in front of the piling and/or backfilling behind the piling. The wall is supported near its upper end by tie rods anchored in the soil some distance behind the wall. Stability is due to the passive resistance developed in front of the wall together with the support due to the anchor system. The behaviour of anchored sheet pile walls is very complex due to soil-structure interaction resulting from the flexibility of the piling and considerable simplifications must be made in design.

Free Earth Support Method

In this method of analysis it is assumed that the depth of penetration below dredge level is insufficient to produce restraint at the lower end of the piling. The earth pressure distribution is assumed to be that given by the Rankine theory and since the wall is free to rotate about its lower end the bending moment diagram is of the form shown in Fig. 5.21. A factor of safety with respect to passive resistance must be incorporated in the design: the total passive resistance mobilised (P_{Pm}) is equal to the total passive resistance available (the Rankine value) divided by the chosen factor of safety which normally should not be less than 2. The distribution of the mobilised

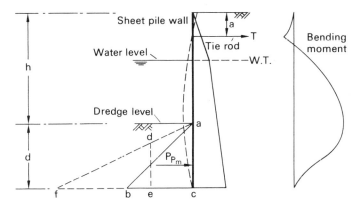

Figure 5.21   Anchored sheet pile wall: free earth support.

passive resistance is assumed to be triangular (abc in Fig. 5.21). Alternatively, the mobilised passive resistance can be represented by the trapezium adec, being part of the triangle afc representing the distribution of available passive resistance. The depth of penetration (d) then required for equilibrium can be determined from the condition that the algebraic sum of the moments about the anchor point must be zero, i.e. the sum of the moments on the active side must equal the sum of the moments on the passive side. This condition yields a cubic equation in d which can be solved by the substitution of trial values.

Having determined the penetration depth d, the tie rod force T, per unit length of wall, can be calculated from the condition that the algebraic sum of the horizontal forces must be zero. Finally, the bending moment diagram can be drawn, the maximum bending moment governing the pile section. It is recommended that the depth of penetration d be increased arbitrarily by 20% to guard against excess dredging, scour and the presence of pockets of weak soil.

Alternatively, the factor of safety with respect to passive resistance and the tie rod force for a wall having a known penetration depth can be determined by taking moments about the point of application of the passive resistance: the effective penetration depth is taken as the overall penetration depth divided by 1·2. The moment equation yields the value of T and the passive resistance which must be mobilised for equilibrium is then obtained by equating the horizontal forces to zero. The factor of safety is the ratio of the available to the mobilised passive resistance.

Example 5.7

The anchored sheet pile wall detailed in Fig. 5.22 is to be designed by the free earth support method. The saturated unit weight of the soil is 20 kN/m³; above the water table the unit weight is 18 kN/m³. The relevant shear strength parameters are $c' = 0$ and $\phi' = 35°$. For a factor of safety of 2 with respect to passive resistance, determine the required depth of penetration and the force in each tie rod if these are spaced at 2 m centres.

For $\phi' = 35°$ (and $\delta = 0$), $K_A = 0.27$ and $K_P = 3.7$.

Below the water table the effective unit weight of the soil is $(20 - 9.8) = 10.2$ kN/m³.

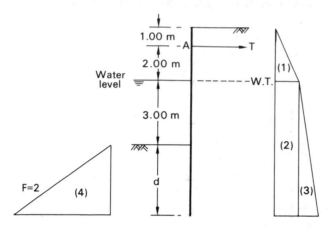

Figure 5.22   Example 5.7.

The earth pressure diagrams are shown in Fig. 5.22. The distributions of hydrostatic pressure on the two sides of the wall balance and can be eliminated from the calculations. The forces due to the pressure distributions and their lever arms about the anchor point A are set out below.

Force per m (kN)		Arm (m)
(1) $\frac{1}{2}$ x 0·27 x 18 x 3²	$= 21·8$	1
(2) 0·27 x 18 x 3 x $(d + 3)$	$= 14·6(d + 3)$	$\frac{d}{2} + 3·5$
(3) $\frac{1}{2}$ x 0·27 x 10·2 x $(d + 3)^2$	$= 1·38(d + 3)^2$	$\frac{2}{3}d + 4$
(4) $-\frac{1}{2}$ x 3·7 x 10·2 x d^2 x $\frac{1}{2}$	$= -9·45d^2$	$\frac{2}{3}d + 5$

For equilibrium the algebraic sum of the moments about A is equal to zero: this condition leads to the equation:

$$d^3 + 5·4d^2 - 21·3d - 41·7 = 0$$

By trial, the solution is:

$$d = 3·63$$

The required depth of penetration is $1·2d$, i.e. 4·36 m.

The algebraic sum of the forces in the above table, for $d = 3·63$, is:

$$21·8 + 96·8 + 60·7 - 124·5 = 54·8 \text{ kN/m}$$

For equilibrium the algebraic sum of the horizontal forces is zero, therefore the tie rod force T per unit length of wall is $(-)$ 54·8 kN. Since the tie rods are spaced at 2 m centres, the force carried by each rod is 2 x 54·8 = 109·6 kN.

Fixed Earth Support Method

This method is based on the assumption that penetration is deep enough to ensure that the soil below dredge level produces considerable restraint on the piling, preventing free rotation at its lower end. The deflected form of the wall is as shown in Fig. 5.23, the most significant feature being the presence of a point of contraflexure (C) near dredge level. The prevention of free rotation at the lower end of the piling

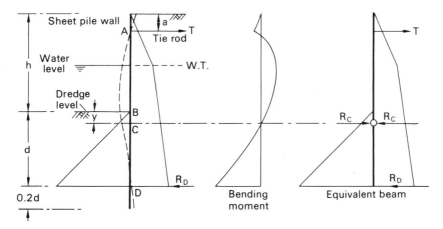

Figure 5.23   Anchored sheet pile wall: fixed earth support.

implies the development of passive resistance at the *back* of the wall for some distance above its lower end: this resistance is replaced arbitrarily by a concentrated force (R_D) acting at a distance $0\cdot2d$ above the end of the wall, the depth of penetration being $1\cdot2d$. There is no possibility of failure due to inadequate passive resistance, therefore a factor of safety of unity is assumed between dredge level and point D.

One method of analysis, known as the *Elastic Line Method*, involves assuming a trial value of d and determining from the pressure distribution diagram the deflection curve for the wall, using the methods of structural mechanics. For the correct value of d the deflection curve should give zero deflection at the anchor point A (assuming no anchor yield). Since the analysis must be repeated until the correct value of d is found, it is not used extensively in practice.

A much simpler method of analysis is the *Equivalent Beam Method*. Since the bending moment is zero at the point of contraflexure C, a hinge may be assumed at this point and the wall considered as two separate beams. For sand backfills, values of the distance (y) of the point of contraflexure below dredge level, in terms of the retained height (h), were obtained by Terzaghi using the elastic line method: these values are as follows:

ϕ	$20°$	$30°$	$40°$
y	$0\cdot25h$	$0\cdot08h$	$-0\cdot006h$

Alternatively, the point of contraflexure may be assumed to be *at* dredge level, i.e. $y = 0$.

In the case of the upper beam the only two unknowns are the tie rod force (T) and the shear force (R_C) at the hinge: both forces can be evaluated for conditions of equilibrium by equating moments about either A or C to zero, then equating horizontal forces to zero. In the case of the lower beam, assumed to be simply supported, the unknowns are the force R_D and the length CD, i.e. $(d - y)$. The length $(d - y)$ can be evaluated by equating moments about D to zero and the depth of penetration is then $1 \cdot 2d$. Compared with the free earth support method the fixed earth support method results in lower values of bending moments.

Earth Anchor

The tie rods are normally anchored in beams, plates or concrete blocks some distance behind the wall (Fig. 5.24). The tie rod force is resisted by the passive resistance mobilised by the anchor, reduced by the active pressure, a factor of safety of not less than 2 being employed to ensure that the anchor yield is not excessive. If the height (b) of the earth anchor is not less than half the depth (d_a) from the surface to the bottom of the anchor, the anchor can be assumed to develop passive resistance over the depth d_a. The anchor must be situated beyond the plane YZ (Fig. 5.24) to ensure that the passive wedge of the anchor does not encroach on the active wedge behind the wall: the lower end (X) of the active wedge should be taken at the bottom of the wall if the free earth support method is used in design or at 0·75 times the penetration depth if the fixed earth support method is used.

If: T = tie rod force per unit length of wall,
  s = spacing of tie rods,
  F = factor of safety,
  l = length of earth anchor per tie rod,

then:

$$Ts = \frac{\gamma d_a^2 l}{2F} (K_P - K_A)$$

(5.21)

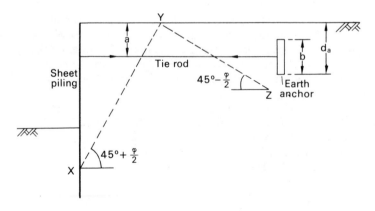

Figure 5.24   Earth anchor.

If an individual anchor is used for each tie rod the shearing resistance on the sides of the passive wedge produces additional anchor resistance. Anchors in clay should be avoided if at all possible.

Example 5.8

Re-design the anchored sheet pile wall detailed in Fig. 5.22 by the equivalent beam method. Design a continuous earth anchor to support the tie rods.

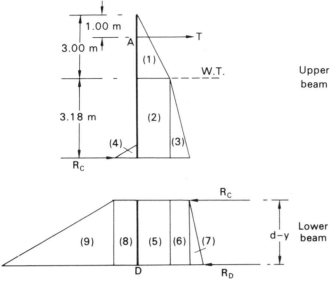

Figure 5.25   Example 5.8.

The equivalent beam is shown in Fig. 5.25, For $\phi' = 35°$, $y = 0.03h$ (by interpolation) $= 0.18$ m.

Consider the upper beam (length 6·18 m). For equilibrium the algebraic sum of the moments of the forces about A must be zero. The moments are calculated below.

Force per m (kN)			Arm (m)	Moment per m (kNm)
(1)	$\frac{1}{2}$ x 0·27 x 18 x 3^2	= 21·8	1·00	21·8
(2)	0·27 x 18 x 3 x 3·18	= 46·3	3·59	166·2
(3)	$\frac{1}{2}$ x 0·27 x 10·2 x 3·18^2	= 13·9	4·12	57·2
(4)	$-\frac{1}{2}$ x 3·7 x 10·2 x 0·18^2	= −0·6	5·12	− 3·1
		$-R_C$	5·18	− 5·18 R_C
		81·4 − R_C		242·1 − 5·18 R_C

Thus:

$$242·1 - 5·18 R_C = 0$$

∴ $$R_C = 46·7 \text{ kN/m}$$

Also, for equilibrium, the algebraic sum of the forces must be zero. Thus:

$$81·4 - R_C - T = 0$$

∴ $$T = 81·4 - 46·7 = 34·7 \text{ kN/m}$$

∴ Tie Rod Force = 2 x 34·7 = 69·4 kN

Consider, now, the lower beam: the length of the beam is $(d - y) = z$ (say). For equilibrium the algebraic sum of the moments of the forces about D must be zero.

Force per m (kN)			Arm (m)	Moment per m (kNm)
(5)	$0{\cdot}27 \times 18 \times 3 \times z$	$= 14{\cdot}6z$	$z/2$	$7{\cdot}3z^2$
(6)	$0{\cdot}27 \times 10{\cdot}2 \times 3{\cdot}18 \times z$	$= 8{\cdot}8z$	$z/2$	$4{\cdot}4z^2$
(7)	$\frac{1}{2} \times 0{\cdot}27 \times 10{\cdot}2 \times z^2$	$= 1{\cdot}4z^2$	$z/3$	$0{\cdot}47z^3$
(8)	$-3{\cdot}7 \times 10{\cdot}2 \times 0{\cdot}18 \times z$	$= -6{\cdot}8z$	$z/2$	$-3{\cdot}4z^2$
(9)	$-\frac{1}{2} \times 3{\cdot}7 \times 10{\cdot}2 \times z^2$	$= -18{\cdot}9z^2$	$z/3$	$-6{\cdot}3z^3$
	R_C	$= 46{\cdot}7$	z	$46{\cdot}7z$

Thus:

$$-5{\cdot}83z^3 + 8{\cdot}3z^2 + 46{\cdot}7z = 0$$

$$\therefore \qquad z^2 - 1{\cdot}42z - 8{\cdot}01 = 0$$

The solution is:

$$z = 3{\cdot}62$$

i.e. $\qquad d = 3{\cdot}62 + 0{\cdot}18 = 3{\cdot}80$

The required depth of penetration is $1{\cdot}2d$, i.e. $4{\cdot}56$ m.

For a continuous earth anchor, $s = l$ in equation 5.21. A factor of safety of 2 will be employed.

$$\therefore \qquad d_a^2 = \frac{2FT}{\gamma(K_P - K_A)}$$

$$= \frac{2 \times 2 \times 34{\cdot}7}{18(3{\cdot}7 - 0{\cdot}27)} = 2{\cdot}25 \text{ m}^2$$

$$\therefore \qquad d_a = 1{\cdot}50 \text{ m}$$

Hence $b = 1{\cdot}00$ m for an anchor centred $1{\cdot}00$ m below the surface.

Unbalanced Hydrostatic Pressure

The water level in front of an anchored sheet pile wall will fluctuate in tidal conditions, the maximum pressure on the back of the wall occurring at low tide. The hydrostatic pressures on the two sides of the wall will be unbalanced if the water table level at the back of the wall lags behind the tidal level in front of the wall and, due to the difference in the water table and tidal levels, seepage will take place under the wall. The distribution of unbalanced pressure can be determined from the flow net (see Example 2.1). For design purposes the unbalanced pressure distribution, for uniform soil conditions, can be approximated by the trapezium abcd in Fig. 5.26a, the actual distribution being represented by the dotted line. Fig. 5.26b shows the unbalanced pressure distribution in a case where the wall penetrates a stratum of low permeability, nearly all the total head loss occurring in this stratum.

Due to the upward flow of water, the soil in front of the wall will be subjected to upward seepage pressure, reducing the effective unit weight of the soil to $(\gamma' - i\gamma_w)$, where i is the average hydraulic gradient adjacent to the front of the wall. Consequently,

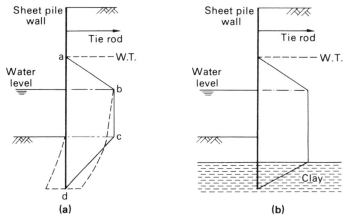

Figure 5.26   Unbalanced hydrostatic pressure.

the passive resistance of the soil in front of the wall will be reduced and this should be taken into account if i is appreciable. At the back of the wall the effective unit weight of the soil will be increased by downward seepage pressure but the increase will be very small and can be neglected.

Arching Effects

The above methods of analysis are highly simplified and involve very crude representations of the real behaviour of anchored sheet pile walls. Data from model tests and field measurements indicate that the earth pressure distributions differ from those predicted by the Rankine theory as illustrated in Fig. 5.27. The earth pressures on the most yielding parts of the wall (between dredge level and the anchor point) are reduced and those on the relatively unyielding parts of the wall (in the vicinity of the anchor and below dredge level) are increased with respect to the Rankine values. These redistributions of earth pressure are the result of the phenomenon known as *arching*.

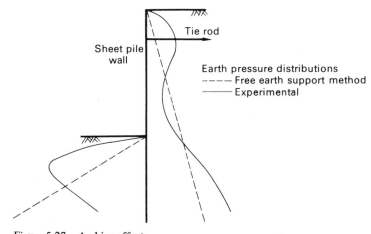

Figure 5.27   Arching effects.

Arching was defined by Terzaghi [5.9] in the following way. 'If one part of the support of a soil mass yields while the remainder stays in place, the soil adjoining the yielding part moves out of its original position between adjacent stationary soil masses. The relative movement within the soil is opposed by shearing resistance within the zone of contact between the yielding and stationary masses. Since the shearing resistance tends to keep the yielding mass in its original position, the pressure on the yielding part of the support is reduced and the pressure on the stationary parts is increased. This transfer of pressure from a yielding part to adjacent non-yielding parts of a soil mass is called the arching effect. Arching also occurs when one part of a support yields more than the adjacent parts.'

The conditions for arching are present in anchored sheet pile walls when they deflect. If yield of the anchor takes place, arching effects are reduced to an extent depending on the amount of yielding. On the passive side of the wall the pressure is increased just below dredge level as a result of larger deflections *into* the soil. In the case of backfilled walls, arching is only partly effective until the fill is above anchor level. Arching effects are much greater in sands than in silts or clays and are greater in dense sands than in loose sands.

Redistributions of earth pressure result in lower bending moments than those obtained from the free earth support of analysis using the Rankine earth pressure distributions, the greater the flexibility of the wall the greater the moment reduction. Rowe [5.6] proposed the use of moment reduction coefficients, to be applied to the results of free earth support analyses, based on the flexibility of the piling. These coefficients are for walls in sands only: no moment reduction should be applied in the cases of silts and clays.

5.7   Braced Excavations

Sheet piling or timbering is normally used to support the sides of deep, narrow excavations, stability being maintained by means of struts acting across the excavation, as shown in Fig. 5.28a. The piling is usually driven first, the struts being installed in stages as excavation proceeds. When the first row of struts is installed the depth of excavation is small and no significant yielding of the soil mass will have taken place. As the depth of excavation increases, yielding of the soil before strut installation becomes appreciable but the first row of struts prevents yielding near the surface. Deformation of the wall, therefore, will be of the form shown in Fig. 5.28a, being negligible at the top and increasing with depth. Thus the deformation condition of the Rankine theory is not satisfied and the theory cannot be used for this type of wall. Failure of the soil will take place along a surface of the form shown in Fig. 5.28a, only the lower part of the soil wedge within this surface reaching a state of plastic equilibrium, the upper part remaining in a state of elastic equilibrium.

Failure of a braced wall is normally due to the initial failure of one of the struts, resulting in the progressive failure of the whole system. The forces in the individual struts may differ widely because they depend on such random factors as the force with which the struts are wedged home and the time between excavation and installation of struts. The usual design procedure for braced walls is semi-empirical, being based on actual measurements of strut loads in excavations in sands and clays in a number of locations. For example, Fig. 5.28b shows the apparent distributions of earth pressure derived from load measurements in the struts at three sections of a braced excavation in a dense sand. Since it is essential that no individual strut should

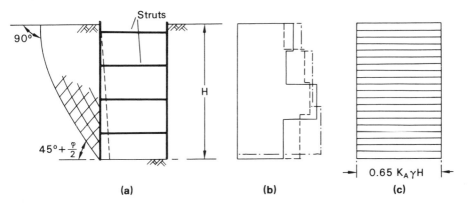

Figure 5.28   Braced excavation.

fail, the pressure distribution assumed in design is taken as the envelope covering all the random distributions obtained from field measurements. Such an envelope should not be thought of as representing the actual distribution of earth pressure with depth but as a hypothetical pressure diagram from which the strut loads can be obtained with some degree of confidence. The pressure envelope proposed by Terzaghi and Peck [5.11] for medium to dense sands is shown in Fig. 5.28c, being a uniform distribution of 0·65 times the Rankine active value. There is some uncertainty as to the pressure envelopes to be adopted for the different types of clays but an excellent review of the problem has been presented by Peck [5.5].

Problems

5.1   The backfill behind a retaining wall above the water table consists of a sand of unit weight 17 kN/m³, having shear strength parameters $c' = 0$ and $\phi' = 37°$. The height of the wall is 6 m and the surface of the backfill is horizontal. Determine the total active thrust on the wall according to the Rankine theory. If the wall is prevented from yielding, what is the approximate value of the thrust on the wall?

5.2   The depths of soil behind and in front of a retaining wall are 8 m and 3 m respectively, both soil surfaces being horizontal. The appropriate shear strength parameters for the soil are $c_u = 30$ kN/m² and $\phi_u = 22°$ and the unit weight is 18 kN/m³. Using the Rankine theory, determine the total active thrust behind the wall and the total passive resistance in front of the wall. Plot the pressure distributions in each case.

5.3   The back of a retaining wall is vertical and 9 m high. The backfill, of unit weight 20 kN/m³, slopes upwards at an angle of 15° to the horizontal: the relevant shear strength parameters are $c_u = 10$ kN/m² and $\phi_u = 25°$. By means of a Mohr diagram, determine the total active thrust on the wall. What are the directions of the Rankine failure planes and the principal planes relative to the horizontal?

5.4   Determine the total active thrust on the retaining wall (situated above the water table) shown in Fig. 5.29 according to the Coulomb theory (using Culmann's procedure). The unit weight of the soil is 20 kN/m³, the appropriate shear strength parameters are $c' = 0$ and $\phi' = 32°$ and the angle of friction between the soil and the wall is 20°.

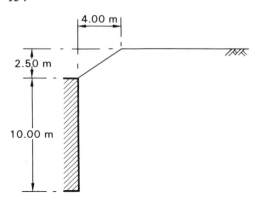

Figure 5.29   Problem 5.4.

5.5   By means of the ϕ-circle method, determine the total passive resistance in front of the wall shown in Fig. 5.30 for the specified failure surface. The area ABCD is 9·10 m^2 and its centroid is on the vertical 2·00 m horizontally from A. For the soil, $\gamma = 19$ kN/m^3, $c' = 0$, $\phi' = 30°$ and $\delta = 20°$. The wall is above water table level.

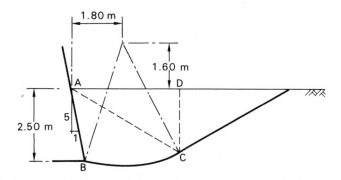

Figure 5.30   Problem 5.5.

5.6   Details of a cantilever retaining wall are given in Fig. 5.31. Calculate the maximum and minimum pressures under the base if the water table rises behind the wall to a level 3·90 m from the top of the wall. The shear strength parameters for the soil are $c' = 0$ and $\phi' = 38°$. The saturated unit weight of the soil is 20 kN/m^3 and above the water table the unit weight is 17 kN/m^3: the unit weight of the concrete is 23·5 kN/m^3. If $\delta = 25°$ on the base of the wall, what is the factor of safety against sliding?

5.7   The sides of an excavation 3·00 m deep in sand are to be supported by a cantilever sheet pile wall. The water table is 1·5 m below the bottom of the excavation. The sand has a saturated unit weight of 20 kN/m^3, a unit weight of 17 kN/m^3 above the water table and $\phi' = 36°$. Determine the depth of penetration of the piling below the bottom of the excavation to give a factor of safety of 2·0 with respect to passive resistance.

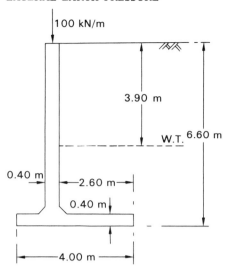

Figure 5.31   Problem 5.6.

5.8   An anchored sheet pile wall is constructed by driving a line of piling into a soil of saturated unit weight 21 kN/m³ and having shear strength parameters $c' = 10$ kN/m² and $\phi' = 27°$. Backfilling to a depth of 8 m is placed behind the piling, the backfill having a saturated unit weight of 20 kN/m³, a unit weight above the water table of 17 kN/m³ and shear strength parameters $c' = 0$ and $\phi' = 35°$. Tie rods are spaced at 2·5 m centres, 1·5 m below the surface of the backfill. The water level in front of the wall and the water table behind the wall are both 5 m below the surface of the backfill. Using the free earth support method, determine the depth of penetration required for a factor of safety of 2·0 with respect to passive resistance and the force in each tie rod.

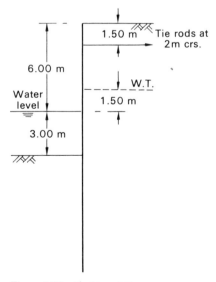

Figure 5.32   Problem 5.9.

5.9   The soil on both sides of the anchored sheet pile wall detailed in Fig. 5.32 has a saturated unit weight of 21 kN/m^3, a unit weight above the water table of 18 kN/m^3 and shear strength parameters $c' = 0$ and $\phi' = 36°$. There is a lag of 1·5 m between the water table behind the wall and the tidal level in front. The wall is to be designed by the equivalent beam method, assuming hinge at dredge level. Calculate the depth of penetration and the force in each tie rod.

5.10   The struts in a braced excavation 9 m deep in a dense sand are placed at 1·5 m centres vertically and 3·0 m centres horizontally: the bottom of the excavation is above the water table. The unit weight of the sand is 19 kN/m^3 and the shear strength parameters are $c' = 0$ and $\phi' = 40°$. What load should each strut be designed to carry?

References

5.1   Bishop, A. W. (1958): 'Test Requirements for Measuring the Coefficient of Earth Pressure at Rest', *Proc. Conference on Earth Pressure Problems, Brussels*, Vol. 1.

5.2   Bjerrum, L. and Andersen, K. (1972): 'In-situ Measurement of Lateral Pressures in Clay', *Proc. 5th European Conference S.M.F.E., Madrid*, Vol. 1.

5.3   Brooker, E. W. and Ireland, H. O. (1965): 'Earth Pressures at Rest Related to Stress History', *Canadian Geotechnical Journal*, Vol. 2.

5.4   Civil Engineering Code of Practice No. 2 (1951): *Earth Retaining Structures*, Institution of Structural Engineers, London.

5.5   Peck, R. B. (1969): 'Deep Excavations and Tunnelling in Soft Ground', *Proc. 7th International Conference S.M.F.E., Mexico* (State of the Art Volume).

5.6   Rowe, P. W. (1952): 'Anchored Sheet Pile Walls', *Proc. Institution of Civil Engineers*, Part 1.

5.7   Rowe, P. W. and Peaker, K. (1965): 'Passive Earth Pressure Measurements', *Geotechnique*, Vol. 15, No. 1.

5.8   Sowers, G. F., Robb, A. D., Mullis, C. H. and Glenn, A. J. (1957): 'The Residual Lateral Pressures Produced by Compacting Soils', *Proc. 4th International Conference S.M.F.E., London*, Vol. 2.

5.9   Terzaghi, K. (1943): *Theoretical Soil Mechanics*, John Wiley and Sons, New York.

5.10   Terzaghi, K. (1954): 'Anchored Bulkheads', *Transactions A.S.C.E.*, Vol. 119, p. 1243.

5.11   Terzaghi, K. and Peck, R. B. (1967): *Soil Mechanics in Engineering Practice* (2nd Edition), John Wiley and Sons, New York.

5.12   Tschebotarioff, G. P. (1962): 'Retaining Structures', Chapter 5 of *Foundation Engineering* (Ed. G. A. Leonards), McGraw-Hill, New York.

CHAPTER 6

Stresses and Displacements

6.1 Introduction

In many problems it is necessary to determine the stresses in a soil mass, in which the failure condition is not reached, due to loads applied near the surface. It may also be necessary to determine the vertical displacement of the soil surface (the 'immediate' settlement) due to such loads. The stresses and displacements depend on the stress-strain characteristics of the underlying soil and a realistic analysis is difficult because these characteristics are non-linear. Results from the theory of elasticity are generally used in practice, it being assumed that the soil is homogeneous and isotropic and that there is a linear relationship between stress and strain. A linear stress–strain relationship is approximately true when the stress levels are low relative to the failure values. The use of elastic theory clearly involves considerable simplification of real soil behaviour and it must be recognised that the results obtained are only approximations. At an advanced level, the finite element method, incorporating more realistic stress–strain characteristics, has been used successfully to determine the stresses and displacements in a soil mass.

Some of the results from elastic theory require knowledge of the values of Young's modulus (E) and Poisson's ratio (ν) for the soil. The modulus E can be estimated from the curve relating principal stress difference and axial strain in a triaxial test (an undrained test in the case of clays and a drained test in the case of sands). The value of E is usually determined as the secant modulus between the origin and one-third of the peak stress, i.e. within the normal range of working stress.

The volumetric strain of an element of elastic material under three principal stresses is given by:

$$\frac{\Delta V}{V} = \frac{1 - 2\nu}{E} (\sigma_1 + \sigma_2 + \sigma_3)$$

If this expression is assumed to apply to soils then for undrained conditions $\Delta V/V = 0$ and $\nu = 0.5$. If consolidation takes place then $\Delta V/V > 0$ and $\nu < 0.5$.

6.2   Stresses from Elastic Theory

The stresses within a semi-infinite, homogeneous, isotropic mass to which Hooke's law may be applied, due to a point load on the surface, were determined by Boussinesq in 1885. The vertical, radial, circumferential and shear stresses at a depth z and a horizontal distance r from the point of application of the load were given. The stresses due to surface loads distributed over a particular area can be obtained by integration from the point load solutions. The stresses at a point due to more than one surface load are obtained by superposition. In practice, loads are not usually applied directly on the surface but the results for surface loading can be applied conservatively in problems concerning loads at a shallow depth.

A range of solutions, suitable for determining the stresses below foundations, is given in the following sections. Negative values of loading can be used if the stresses due to excavation are required or in problems in which the principle of superposition is used. The stresses due to surface loading act in addition to the in-situ stresses due to the self-weight of the soil.

1. *Point Load*

Referring to Fig. 6.1, the stresses at point X due to a point load Q on the surface are as follows:

$$\sigma_z = \frac{3Q}{2\pi z^2} \left\{ \frac{1}{1 + (r/z)^2} \right\}^{5/2} \tag{6.1}$$

$$\sigma_r = \frac{Q}{2\pi} \left\{ \frac{3r^2 z}{(r^2 + z^2)^{5/2}} - \frac{1 - 2\nu}{r^2 + z^2 + z(r^2 + z^2)^{1/2}} \right\} \tag{6.2}$$

$$\sigma_\theta = -\frac{Q}{2\pi}(1 - 2\nu) \left\{ \frac{z}{(r^2 + z^2)^{3/2}} - \frac{1}{r^2 + z^2 + z(r^2 + z^2)^{1/2}} \right\} \tag{6.3}$$

$$\tau_{rz} = \frac{3Q}{2\pi} \left\{ \frac{rz^2}{(r^2 + z^2)^{5/2}} \right\} \tag{6.4}$$

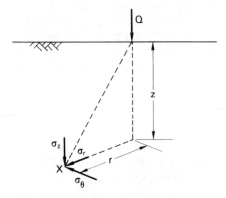

Figure 6.1   Stresses due to point load.

It should be noted that when $\nu = 0.5$ the second term in equation 6.2 vanishes and equation 6.3 gives $\sigma_\theta = 0$.

Equation 6.1 is used most frequently in practice and can be written in terms of an influence factor I_p, where:

$$I_p = \frac{3}{2\pi} \left\{ \frac{1}{1 + (r/z)^2} \right\}^{5/2}$$

Then:

$$\sigma_z = \frac{Q}{z^2} I_p$$

Values of I_p in terms of r/z are given in Table 6.1. The form of the variation of σ_z with z and r is illustrated in Fig. 6.2. The left-hand side of the figure shows the variation of σ_z with z on the vertical through the point of application of the load Q (i.e. for $r = 0$): the right-hand side of the figure shows the variation of σ_z with r for three different values of z.

Table 6.1   Influence factors for vertical stress due to point load

r/z	I_p	r/z	I_p	r/z	I_p
0·00	0·478	0·80	0·139	1·60	0·020
0·10	0·466	0·90	0·108	1·70	0·016
0·20	0·433	1·00	0·084	1·80	0·013
0·30	0·385	1·10	0·066	1·90	0·011
0·40	0·329	1·20	0·051	2·00	0·009
0·50	0·273	1·30	0·040	2·20	0·006
0·60	0·221	1·40	0·032	2·40	0·004
0·70	0·176	1·50	0·025	2·60	0·003

In another solution to the problem, due to Westergaard, the elastic mass is assumed to be reinforced laterally by horizontal inelastic sheets of negligible thickness, spaced at close intervals in the vertical direction, preventing lateral strain in the mass as a whole. The solution simulates an extreme condition of anisotropy and gives stresses less than the Boussinesq values. The conditions in most soil masses probably lie between the two extremes represented by the Boussinesq and Westergaard solutions. The Boussinesq solution is used more extensively in practice.

2. Line Load

Referring to Fig. 6.3, the stresses at point X due to a line load of Q per unit length on the surface are as follows:

$$\sigma_z = \frac{2Q}{\pi} \frac{z^3}{(x^2 + z^2)^2} \tag{6.5}$$

$$\sigma_x = \frac{2Q}{\pi} \frac{x^2 z}{(x^2 + z^2)^2} \tag{6.6}$$

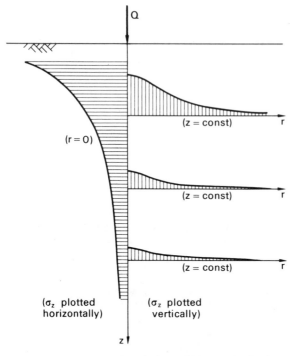

Figure 6.2   Variation of vertical stress due to point load.

$$\tau_{xz} = \frac{2Q}{\pi} \frac{xz^2}{(x^2 + z^2)^2} \tag{6.7}$$

Equation 6.6 can be used to estimate the lateral pressure on an earth-retaining structure due to a line load on the surface of the backfill. In terms of the dimensions

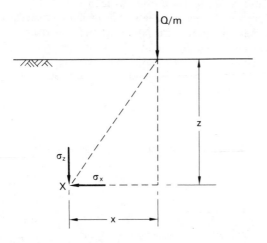

Figure 6.3   Stresses due to line load.

4. Circular Area Carrying Uniform Pressure

The vertical stress at depth z under the *centre* of a circular area of diameter $D = 2R$ carrying a uniform pressure q is given by:

$$\sigma_z = q\left[1 - \left\{\frac{1}{1 + (R/z)^2}\right\}^{3/2}\right]$$

(6.13)

$$= qI_c$$

Values of the influence factor I_c in terms of D/z are given in Table 6.2.

Table 6.2 Influence factors for vertical stress below centre of circular area (diameter D) carrying uniform pressure

D/z	I_c	D/z	I_c	D/z	I_c
0·00	0·000	1·20	0·370	2·40	0·738
0·20	0·015	1·40	0·450	2·60	0·773
0·40	0·057	1·60	0·524	2·80	0·804
0·60	0·121	1·80	0·589	3·00	0·829
0·80	0·200	2·00	0·647	4·00	0·911
1·00	0·285	2·20	0·696	6·00	0·968

5. Rectangular Area Carrying Uniform Pressure

A solution has been obtained for the vertical stress at depth z under a *corner* of a rectangular area of dimensions mz and nz (Fig. 6.7) carrying a uniform pressure q. The solution can be written in the form:

$$\sigma_z = qI_r$$

Values of the influence factor I_r in terms of m and n are given in the chart due to Fadum [6.1] shown in Fig. 6.7. The factors m and n are interchangeable. The chart can also be used for a strip area, considered as a rectangular area of infinite length. Superposition enables any area based on rectangles to be dealt with and enables the vertical stress under any point within or outside the area to be obtained.

Contours of equal vertical stress in the vicinity of a square area carrying a uniform pressure are plotted in Fig. 6.6b.

6. Influence Chart for Vertical Stress

Newmark [6.3] constructed an influence chart, based on the Boussinesq solution, enabling the vertical stress to be determined at any point below an area of any shape carrying a uniform pressure q. The chart (Fig. 6.8) consists of influence areas, the boundaries of which are two radial lines and two circular arcs. The loaded area is drawn on tracing paper to a scale such that the length of the scale line on the chart represents the depth z at which the vertical stress is required. The position of the loaded area on the chart is such that the point at which the vertical stress is required is at the centre of the chart. For the chart shown in Fig. 6.8 the influence value is 0·005, i.e. each influence area represents a vertical stress of 0·005q. Hence, if the number of

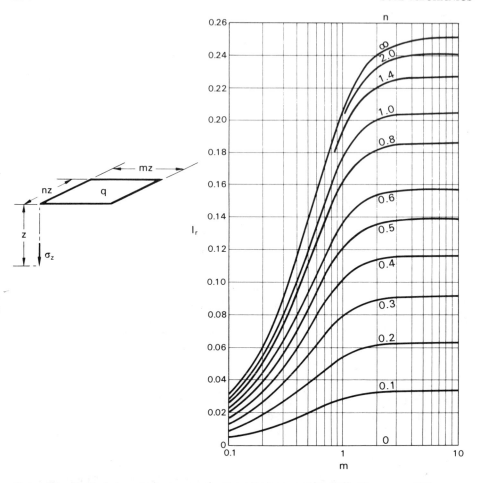

Figure 6.7   Vertical stress under corner of rectangular area carrying uniform pressure (After Fadum [6.1]).

influence areas covered by the scale drawing of the loaded area is N, the required vertical stress is given by:

$$\sigma_z = 0 \cdot 005 \; Nq$$

Example 6.1

A load of 1500 kN is carried on a foundation 2 m square at a shallow depth in a soil mass. Determine the vertical stress at a point 5 m below the centre of the foundation (a) assuming the load is uniformly distributed over the foundation, (b) assuming the load acts as a point load at the centre of the foundation.

(a) Uniform pressure,

$$q = \frac{1500}{2^2} = 375 \; \text{kN/m}^2$$

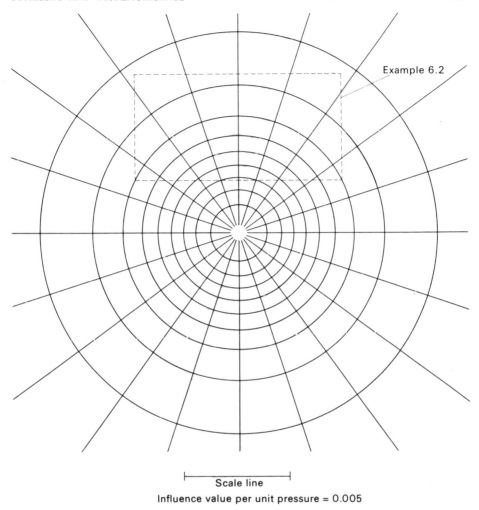

Scale line

Influence value per unit pressure = 0.005

Figure 6.8   Newmark's influence chart for vertical stress [6.3].

The area must be considered as four quarters to enable Fig. 6.7 to be used. In this case:

$$mz = nz = 1 \text{ m}$$

Then, for $z = 5$ m,

$$m = n = 0\cdot2$$

From Fig. 6.7,

$$I_r = 0\cdot018$$

Hence:

$$\sigma_z = 4qI_r = 4 \times 375 \times 0\cdot018 = 27 \text{ kN/m}^2$$

(b) From Table 6.1, $I_p = 0 \cdot 478$ since $r/z = 0$ vertically below a point load. Hence:

$$\sigma_z = \frac{Q}{z^2} I_p = \frac{1500}{5^2} \times 0 \cdot 478 = 29 \ \text{kN/m}^2$$

The point load assumption should not be used if the depth to the point X (Fig. 6.1) is less than 3 times the larger dimension of the foundation.

Example 6.2

A rectangular foundation 6 m x 3 m carries a uniform pressure of 300 kN/m² near the surface of a soil mass. Determine the vertical stress at a depth of 3 m below a point (A) on the centre line 1·5 m outside a long edge of the foundation, (a) using influence factors, (b) using Newmark's influence chart.

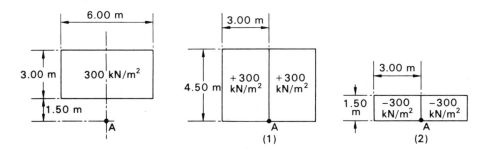

Figure 6.9   Example 6.2.

(a) Using the principle of superposition the problem is dealt with in the manner shown in Fig. 6.9. For the two rectangles (1) carrying a *positive* pressure of 300 kN/m²:

$$m = 1 \cdot 00 \ \text{and} \ n = 1 \cdot 50 \quad \therefore I_r = 0 \cdot 193$$

For the two rectangles (2) carrying a *negative* pressure of 300 kN/m²:

$$m = 1 \cdot 00 \ \text{and} \ n = 0 \cdot 50 \quad \therefore I_r = 0 \cdot 120$$

Hence:

$$\sigma_z = (2 \times 300 \times 0 \cdot 193) - (2 \times 300 \times 0 \cdot 120)$$
$$= 44 \ \text{kN/m}^2$$

(b) Using Newmark's influence chart (Fig. 6.8) the scale line represents 3 m, fixing the scale to which the rectangular area must be drawn. The area is positioned such that the point A is at the centre of the chart. The number of influence areas covered by the rectangle is approximately 30 (i.e. $N = 30$), hence:

$$\sigma_z = 0 \cdot 005 \times 30 \times 300$$
$$= 45 \ \text{kN/m}^2$$

Example 6.3

A strip footing 2 m wide carries a uniform pressure of 250 kN/m² on the surface of a deposit of sand. The water table is at the surface. The saturated unit weight of the sand is 20 kN/m³ and $K_0 = 0.40$. Determine the effective vertical and horizontal stresses at a point 3 m below the centre of the footing before and after the application of the pressure.

Before loading:

$$\sigma_z' = 3\gamma' = 3 \times 10 \cdot 2 = 30 \cdot 6 \text{ kN/m}^2$$

$$\sigma_x' = K_0 \sigma_z' = 0 \cdot 40 \times 30 \cdot 6 = 12 \cdot 2 \text{ kN/m}^2$$

After loading:

Referring to Fig. 6.5, for a point 3 m below the centre of the footing,

$$\alpha = 2 \tan^{-1}(\tfrac{1}{3}) = 36° \ 52' = 0 \cdot 643 \text{ radians}$$

$$\sin \alpha = 0 \cdot 600$$

$$\beta = 0$$

The increases in total stress due to the applied pressure are:

$$\Delta\sigma_z = \frac{q}{\pi}(\alpha + \sin \alpha) = \frac{250}{\pi}(0 \cdot 643 + 0 \cdot 600) = 99 \cdot 0 \text{ kN/m}^2$$

$$\Delta\sigma_x = \frac{q}{\pi}(\alpha - \sin \alpha) = \frac{250}{\pi}(0 \cdot 643 - 0 \cdot 600) = 3 \cdot 4 \text{ kN/m}^2$$

Hence,

$$\sigma_z' = 30 \cdot 6 + 99 \cdot 0 = 129 \cdot 6 \text{ kN/m}^2$$

$$\sigma_x' = 12 \cdot 2 + 3 \cdot 4 = 15 \cdot 6 \text{ kN/m}^2$$

6.3 Displacements from Elastic Theory

The vertical displacement (s_i) under an area carrying a uniform pressure q on the surface of a semi-infinite, homogeneous, isotropic mass to which Hooke's law may be applied, can be expressed as:

$$s_i = \frac{qB}{E}(1 - \nu^2)I_s \tag{6.14}$$

where I_s is an influence factor depending on the shape of the loaded area. In the case of a rectangular area, B is the lesser dimension (the greater dimension being L) and in the case of a circular area, B is the diameter. The loaded area is assumed to be flexible. Values of influence factors are given in Table 6.3 for displacements under the centre and a corner (the edge in the case of a circle) of the area and for the average displacement under the area as a whole. According to equation 6.14, vertical displacement increases in direct proportion to both the pressure and the width of the loaded area. The distribution of vertical displacement is of the form shown in Fig. 6.10a, extending beyond the edges of the area. The contact pressure between the loaded area and the supporting mass is uniform.

In the case of an extensive, homogeneous deposit of saturated clay, it is a reasonable approximation to assume that E is constant throughout the deposit and the distribution of Fig. 6.10a applies. In the case of sands, however, the value of E varies with confining pressure and, therefore, will increase with depth and vary across the width of the

Table 6.3   Influence factors for vertical displacement under flexible area carrying uniform pressure

Shape of area	I_s		
	Centre	Corner	Average
Square	1·12	0·56	0·95
Rectangle $L/B = 2$	1·52	0·76	1·30
Rectangle $L/B = 5$	2·10	1·05	1·83
Circle	1·00	0·64	0·85

loaded area, being greater under the centre of the area than at the edges. As a result, the distribution of vertical displacement will be of the form shown in Fig. 6.10b: the contact pressure will again be uniform if the area is flexible. Due to the variation of E, equation 6.14 is little used in practice in the case of sands.

(a)   (b)

Figure 6.10   Distributions of vertical displacement: (a) clay, (b) sand.

An approximate solution, due to Steinbrenner [6.5], is also available for the vertical displacement under a *corner* of a flexible rectangular area carrying a uniform pressure q on the surface of a mass of finite depth D resting on a rigid base. The displacement is given by:

$$s_i = \frac{qB}{E} \{ (1 - v^2)F_1 + (1 - v - 2v^2)F_2 \} \tag{6.15}$$

Values of F_1 and F_2 in terms of D/B and L/B are given in Fig. 6.11. This solution should be used in cases where rock level occurs at a relatively shallow depth.

If the loaded area is *rigid* the vertical displacement will be uniform across the width of the area and its magnitude will be only slightly less than the *average* displacement under a corresponding flexible area. The influence factors for average displacement in Table 6.3 can be used, therefore, as approximations in the case of a rigid area. The contact pressure under a rigid area is not uniform: for a circular area the forms of the distributions of contact pressure on clay and sand respectively are shown in Fig. 6.12a and Fig. 6.12b.

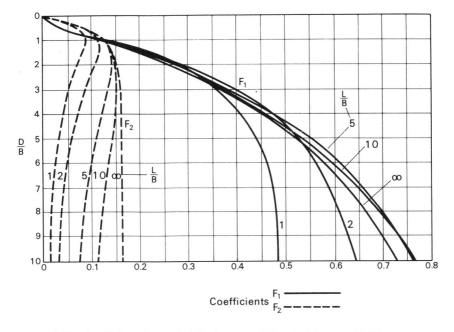

Figure 6.11   Coefficients for vertical displacement (After Steinbrenner [6.5]).

Example 6.4

A foundation 6 m x 4 m carries a uniform pressure of 200 kN/m² near the surface of a
deep deposit of saturated clay. If $E = 8.3 \times 10^4$ kN/m² for the clay, calculate the
immediate settlement under the centre and a corner of the foundation, assuming it to
be flexible.

For $L/B = 1.5$, the values of the influence factor I_s (Table 6.3) under the centre
and a corner of the area are 1.36 and 0.68, respectively. The value of Poisson's ratio
for undrained conditions is 0.5. The displacements are given by equation 6.14.

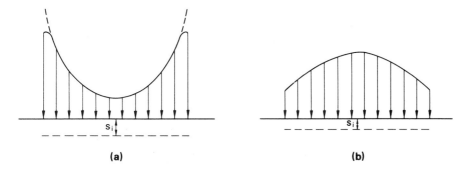

Figure 6.12   Contact pressure under rigid area: (a) clay, (b) sand.

Under the centre:

$$s_i = \frac{200 \times 4 \times 0.75 \times 1.36}{8.2 \times 10^4}$$

$$= 0.0098 \text{ m} = 10 \text{ mm}$$

Under a corner:

$$s_i = 5 \text{ mm}$$

Problems

6.1   Calculate the vertical stress in a soil mass at a depth of 5 m vertically below a point load of 5000 kN acting near the surface. Plot the variation of vertical stress with radial distance (up to 10 m) at a depth of 5 m.

6.2   Three point loads, 10,000 kN, 7500 kN and 9000 kN, act in line 5 m apart near the surface of a soil mass. Calculate the vertical stress at a depth of 4 m vertically below the centre (7500 kN) load.

6.3   Determine the vertical stress at a depth of 3 m below the centre of a shallow foundation 2 m x 2 m carrying a uniform pressure of 250 kN/m². Plot the variation of vertical stress with depth (up to 10 m) below the centre of the foundation.

6.4   A shallow foundation 25 m x 18 m carries a uniform pressure of 175 kN/m². Determine the vertical stress at a point 12 m below the mid-point of one of the longer sides (a) using influence factors, (b) by means of Newmark's chart.

6.5   A line load of 150 kN/m acts 2 m behind the back surface of an earth-retaining structure 4 m high. Calculate the total thrust, and plot the distribution of pressure, on the structure due to the line load.

6.6   A foundation 4 m x 4 m carries a uniform pressure of 200 kN/m² near the surface of a saturated clay layer: the layer extends to a depth of 8 m below the foundation and is underlain by a firm stratum. If $E = 8.3 \times 10^4$ kN/m² for the clay, determine the immediate settlement under the centre of the foundation (which is assumed to be flexible).

References

6.1   Fadum, R. E. (1948): 'Influence Values for Estimating Stresses in Elastic Foundations', *Proceedings 2nd International Conference S.M.F.E., Rotterdam*, Vol. 3.

6.2   Harr, M. E. (1966): *Foundations of Theoretical Soil Mechanics*, McGraw-Hill, New York.

6.3   Newmark, N. M. (1942): *Influence Charts for Computation of Stresses in Elastic Foundations*, University of Illinois Bulletin No. 338.

6.4   Scott, R. F. (1963): *Principles of Soil Mechanics*, Addison-Wesley, Reading, Massachusetts.

6.5   Steinbrenner, W. (1934): 'Tafeln zur Setzungsberechnung', *Die Strasse*, Vol. 1.

6.6   Terzaghi, K. (1943): *Theoretical Soil Mechanics*, John Wiley and Sons, New York.

CHAPTER 7

Consolidation Theory

7.1 Introduction

As explained in Chapter 3, consolidation is the gradual reduction in volume of a fully-saturated soil of low permeability due to drainage of some of the pore water, the process continuing until the excess pore water pressure set up by an increase in total stress has completely dissipated: the simplest case is that of one-dimensional consolidation to which certain practical problems may be approximated. The process of swelling, the reverse of consolidation, is the gradual increase in volume of a soil under negative excess pore water pressure.

Consolidation settlement is the vertical displacement of the surface corresponding to the volume change at any stage of the consolidation process. Consolidation settlement will result, for example, if a structure is built over a layer of saturated clay or if the water table is lowered permanently in a stratum overlying a clay layer. If, on the other hand, an excavation is made in a saturated clay, heaving (the reverse of settlement) will result in the bottom of the excavation due to swelling of the clay. In addition to consolidation settlement there will be an immediate settlement due to deformation of the soil under undrained conditions. Immediate settlement can be estimated using the results from elastic theory given in Chapter 6. This chapter is concerned with the prediction of both the magnitude and rate of consolidation settlement.

The progress of consolidation in-situ can be monitored by installing piezometers to record the change in pore water pressure with time. The magnitude of settlement can be measured by recording the levels of suitable reference points on a structure or in the ground: precise levelling is essential, working from a bench mark which is not subject to even the slightest settlement. Every opportunity should be taken of obtaining settlement data as it is only through such measurements that the adequacy of theoretical methods can be assessed.

7.2 The Oedometer Test

The characteristics of a soil during one-dimensional consolidation or swelling can be determined by means of the oedometer test. Fig. 7.1 shows diagrammatically a cross-

section through an oedometer. The test specimen is in the form of a disc, held inside
a metal ring and lying between two porous stones. The upper porous stone, which
can move inside the ring with a small clearance, is fixed below a metal loading cap
through which pressure can be applied to the specimen. The whole assembly sits in an

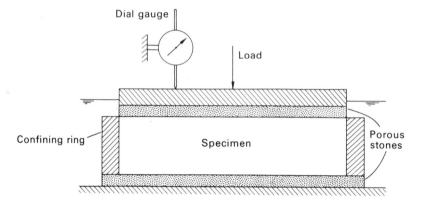

Figure 7.1   The oedometer test.

open cell of water to which the pore water in the specimen has free access. The ring
confining the specimen may be either fixed (clamped to the body of the cell) or
floating (being free to move vertically): the inside of the ring should have a smooth
polished surface to reduce side friction. The confining ring imposes a condition of
zero lateral strain on the specimen, the ratio of lateral to vertical effective stress being
K_0, the coefficient of earth pressure at rest. The compression of the specimen under
pressure is measured by means of a dial gauge operating on the loading cap.

The test procedure has been standardised in BS 1377 [7.2] which specifies that
the oedometer shall be of the fixed ring type. The initial pressure will depend on the
type of soil, then a sequence of pressures is applied to the specimen, each being
double the previous value. Each pressure is normally maintained for a period of
24 hours (in exceptional cases a period of 48 hours may be required), compression
readings being observed at suitable intervals during this period. At the end of the
increment period, when the excess pore water pressure has completely dissipated, the
applied pressure equals the effective vertical stress in the specimen. The results are

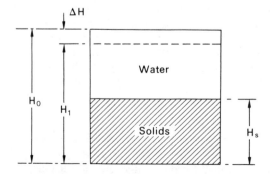

Figure 7.2   Phase diagram.

presented by plotting the thickness (or percentage change in thickness) of the specimen or the void ratio at the end of each increment period against the corresponding effective stress. The effective stress may be plotted to either a natural or a logarithmic scale. If desired, the expansion of the specimen can be measured under successive decreases in applied pressure. However, even if the swelling characteristics of the soil are not required, the expansion of the specimen due to the removal of the final pressure should be measured.

The void ratio at the end of each increment period can be calculated from the dial gauge readings and either the water content or dry weight of the specimen at the end of the test. Referring to the phase diagram in Fig. 7.2, the two methods of calculation are as follows.

(1)   Water content measured at end of test = w_1
Void ratio at end of test = $e_1 = w_1 G_s$ (assuming $S_r = 100\%$)
Thickness of specimen at start of test = H_0
Change in thickness during test = ΔH
Void ratio at start of test = $e_0 = e_1 + \Delta e$
where:

$$\frac{\Delta e}{\Delta H} = \frac{1 + e_0}{H_0} \tag{7.1}$$

In the same way Δe can be calculated up to the end of any increment period.

(2)   Dry weight measured at end of test = M_s (i.e. mass of solids)
Thickness at end of any increment period = H_1
Area of specimen = A

Equivalent thickness of solids = $H_s = \dfrac{M_s}{A G_s \rho_w}$

$$\text{Void ratio} = e_1 = \frac{H_1 - H_s}{H_s} = \frac{H_1}{H_s} - 1 \tag{7.2}$$

Compressibility Characteristics

Typical plots of void ratio (e) after consolidation, against effective stress (σ') for a saturated clay are shown in Fig. 7.3, the plots showing an initial compression followed by expansion and recompression. The shape of the curves is related to the stress history of the clay. The e–log σ' relationship for a normally-consolidated clay is linear (or very nearly so) and is called the virgin compression line. If a clay is over-consolidated its state will be represented by a point on the expansion or recompression parts of the e–log σ' plot. The recompression curve ultimately joins the virgin compression line: further compression then occurs along the virgin line. During compression, changes in soil structure continuously take place and the clay does not revert to the original structure during expansion. The plots show that a clay in the overconsolidated state will be much less compressible than the same clay in a normally-consolidated state.

The compressibility of the clay can be represented by one of the following coefficients.

(1) The *coefficient of volume change* (m_v), defined as the volume change per unit volume per unit increase in effective stress. The units of m_v are the inverse of pressure

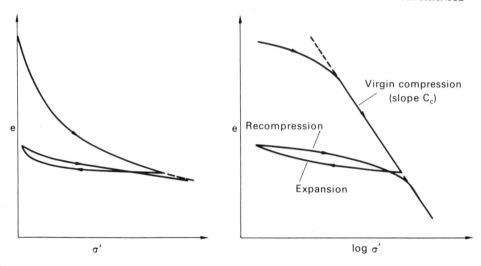

Figure 7.3   Void ratio–effective stress relationship.

(m^2/kN). The volume change may be expressed in terms of either void ratio or specimen thickness. If, for an increase in effective stress from σ_0' to σ_1' the void ratio decreases from e_0 to e_1, then:

$$m_v = \frac{1}{1 + e_0}\left(\frac{e_0 - e_1}{\sigma_1' - \sigma_0'}\right) \tag{7.3}$$

$$= \frac{1}{H_0}\left(\frac{H_0 - H_1}{\sigma_1' - \sigma_0'}\right) \tag{7.4}$$

The value of m_v for a particular soil is not constant but depends on the stress range over which it is calculated. BS 1377 specifies the use of the m_v coefficient calculated for a stress increment of $100\ kN/m^2$ in excess of the effective overburden pressure of the in-situ soil at the depth of interest, although the coefficient may also be calculated, if required, for any other stress range.

(2) The *compression index* (C_c) is the slope of the linear portion of the e-log σ' plot and is dimensionless. For any two points on the linear portion of the plot:

$$C_c = \frac{e_0 - e_1}{\log\dfrac{\sigma_1'}{\sigma_0'}} \tag{7.5}$$

The expansion part of the e-log σ' plot can be approximated to straight line the slope of which is referred to as the *expansion index* C_e.

Preconsolidation Pressure

Casagrande proposed an empirical construction to obtain from the e-log σ' curve for an overconsolidated clay the maximum effective vertical stress that has acted on the clay in the past, referred to as the *preconsolidation pressure* (σ_c'). Fig. 7.4 shows a

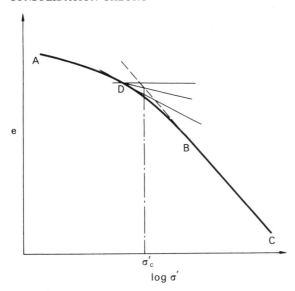

Figure 7.4   Determination of preconsolidation pressure.

typical e-log σ' curve for a specimen of clay, initially overconsolidated. The initial curve indicates that the clay is undergoing recompression in the oedometer, having at some stage in its history undergone expansion. Expansion of the clay in-situ may, for example, have been due to melting of ice sheets, erosion of overburden or a rise in water table level. The construction for estimating the preconsolidation pressure consists of the following steps.

(1) Produce back the straight line part (BC) of the curve.
(2) Determine the point (D) of maximum curvature on the recompression part (AB) of the curve.
(3) Draw the tangent to the curve at D and bisect the angle between the tangent and the horizontal through D.
(4) The vertical through the point of intersection of the bisector and CB produced gives the approximate value of the preconsolidation pressure.

Whenever possible the preconsolidation pressure for an overconsolidated clay should not be exceeded in construction. Compression will not usually be great if the effective vertical stress remains below σ'_c: only if σ'_c is exceeded will compression be large.

In-situ e–log σ' Curve

Due to the effects of sampling and preparation the specimen in an oedometer test will be slightly disturbed. It has been shown that an increase in the degree of specimen disturbance results in a slight decrease in the slope of the virgin compression line. It can therefore be expected that the slope of the line representing virgin compression of the in-situ soil will be slightly greater than the slope of the virgin line obtained in a laboratory test.

No appreciable error will be involved in taking the in-situ void ratio as being equal to the void ratio (e_0) at the start of the laboratory test. Schmertmann [7.11] pointed

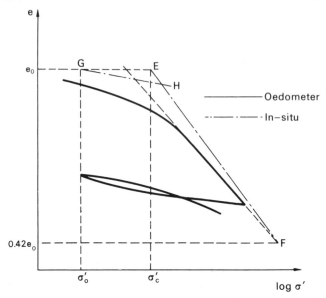

Figure 7.5   In-situ e–log σ' curve.

out that the laboratory virgin line may be expected to intersect the in-situ virgin line at a void ratio of approximately 0·42 times the initial void ratio. Thus the in-situ virgin line can be taken as the line EF in Fig. 7.5 where the coordinates of E are log σ_c' and e_0, and F is the point on the laboratory virgin line at a void ratio of 0·42 e_0.

In the case of overconsolidated clays the in-situ condition is represented by the point (G) having coordinates σ_0' and e_0, where σ_0' is the present effective overburden pressure. The in-situ recompression curve can be approximated to the straight line GH parallel to the mean slope of the laboratory recompression curve.

Example 7.1

The following compression readings were obtained in an oedometer test on a specimen of saturated clay (G_s = 2·73):

Pressure (kN/m²)	0	54	107	214	429	858	1716	3432	0
Dial gauge* (mm)	5·000	4·747	4·493	4·108	3·449	2·608	1·676	0·737	1·480

* After 24 hours.

The initial thickness of the specimen was 19·0 mm and at the end of the test the water content was 19·8%. Plot the e–log σ' curve and determine the preconsolidation pressure. Determine the values of m_v for the stress increments 100–200 kN/m² and 1000–1500 kN/m². What is the value of C_c for the latter increment?

Void ratio at end of test = $e_1 = w_1 G_s = 0.198 \times 2.73 = 0.541$
Void ratio at start of test = $e_0 = e_1 + \Delta e$
Now,

$$\frac{\Delta e}{\Delta H} = \frac{1 + e_0}{H_0} = \frac{1 + e_1 + \Delta e}{H_0}$$

i.e. $$\frac{\Delta e}{3.520} = \frac{1.541 + \Delta e}{19.0}$$

$$\Delta e = 0.350$$

$$e_0 = 0.541 + 0.350 = 0.891$$

In general the relationship between Δe and ΔH is given by:

$$\frac{\Delta e}{\Delta H} = \frac{1.891}{19.0}$$

i.e. $\Delta e = 0.0996 \, \Delta H$

and can be used to obtain the void ratio at the end of each increment period.

Pressure (kN/m^2)	ΔH (mm)	Δe	e
0	0	0	0.891
54	0.253	0.025	0.866
107	0.507	0.050	0.841
214	0.892	0.089	0.802
429	1.551	0.154	0.737
858	2.392	0.238	0.653
1716	3.324	0.331	0.560
3432	4.263	0.424	0.467
0	3.520	0.350	0.541

The e–log σ' curve using the above values is shown in Fig. 7.6. Using Casagrande's construction the value of the preconsolidation pressure is 325 kN/m^2.

$$m_v = \frac{1}{1 + e_0} \cdot \frac{e_0 - e_1}{\sigma_1' - \sigma_0'}$$

For $\sigma_0' = 100 \, kN/m^2$ and $\sigma_1' = 200 \, kN/m^2$,

$$e_0 = 0.845 \qquad \text{and } e_1 = 0.808$$

$\therefore$ $$m_v = \frac{1}{1.845} \times \frac{0.037}{100} = 2.0 \times 10^{-4} \, m^2/kN$$

For $\sigma_0' = 1000 \, kN/m^2$ and $\sigma_1' = 1500 \, kN/m^2$,

$$e_0 = 0.632 \qquad \text{and } e_1 = 0.577$$

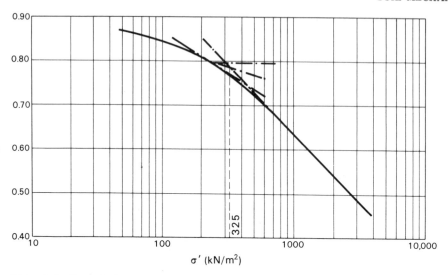

Figure 7.6   Example 7.1.

$$\therefore \quad m_v = \frac{1}{1 \cdot 632} \times \frac{0 \cdot 055}{500} = 6 \cdot 7 \times 10^{-5} \ \text{m}^2/\text{kN}$$

$$\text{and } C_c = \frac{0 \cdot 632 - 0 \cdot 577}{\log \dfrac{1500}{1000}} = \frac{0 \cdot 055}{0 \cdot 176} = 0 \cdot 31$$

Note that C_c will be the same for any stress range on the linear part of the e–log σ' curve; m_v will vary according to the stress range, even for ranges on the linear part of the curve.

7.3   Consolidation Settlement

In order to estimate consolidation settlement the value of either the coefficient of volume change or the compression index is required. Consider a layer of saturated clay of thickness H: due to construction the total vertical stress in an elemental layer of thickness dz at depth z is increased by $\Delta\sigma$ (Fig. 7.7). It is assumed that the condition of zero lateral strain applies within the clay layer. After the completion of consolidation an equal increase $\Delta\sigma'$ in effective vertical stress will have taken place corresponding to a stress increase from σ_0' to σ_1' and a reduction in void ratio from e_0 to e_1 on the e–σ' curve. The reduction in volume per unit volume of clay can be written in terms of void ratio:

$$\frac{\Delta V}{V_0} = \frac{e_0 - e_1}{1 + e_0}$$

Since the lateral strain is zero the reduction in volume per unit volume is equal to the reduction in thickness per unit thickness, i.e. the settlement per unit depth. Therefore,

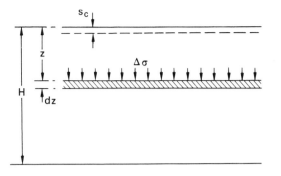 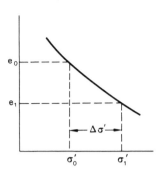

Figure 7.7   Consolidation settlement.

by proportion, the settlement of the layer of thickness dz will be given by:

$$ds_c = \frac{e_0 - e_1}{1 + e_0} \, dz$$

$$= \left(\frac{e_0 - e_1}{\sigma_1' - \sigma_0'}\right)\left(\frac{\sigma_1' - \sigma_0'}{1 + e_0}\right) dz$$

$$= m_v \Delta\sigma' dz$$

where, s_c = consolidation settlement.
The settlement of the layer of thickness H is given by:

$$s_c = \int_0^H m_v \Delta\sigma' dz$$

If m_v and $\Delta\sigma'$ are assumed constant with depth, then:

$$s_c = m_v \Delta\sigma' H \tag{7.6}$$

or,

$$s_c = \frac{e_0 - e_1}{1 + e_0} H \tag{7.7}$$

or, in the case of a normally-consolidated clay:

$$s_c + \frac{C_c \log \dfrac{\sigma_1'}{\sigma_0'}}{1 + e_0} H \tag{7.8}$$

In order to take into account the variation of m_v and/or $\Delta\sigma'$ with depth, the graphical procedure shown in Fig. 7.8 can be used to determine s_c. The variations of initial effective vertical stress (σ_0') and effective vertical stress increment $(\Delta\sigma')$ over the depth of the layer are represented in Fig. 7.8a: the variation of m_v is represented in Fig. 7.8b. The curve in Fig. 7.8c represents the variation with depth of the dimensionless product $m_v \Delta\sigma'$ and the area under this curve is the settlement of the layer. Alternatively the layer can be divided into a suitable number of sub-layers and the product $m_v \Delta\sigma'$ evaluated at the centre of each sub-layer: each product $m_v \Delta\sigma'$ is then

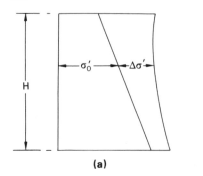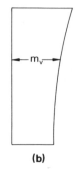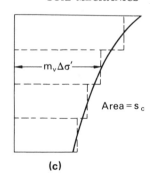

Figure 7.8   Consolidation settlement: graphical procedure.

multiplied by the appropriate sub-layer thickness to give the sub-layer settlement. The settlement of the whole layer is equal to the sum of the sub-layer settlements.

The calculation of consolidation settlement by the above procedures is referred to as the *one-dimensional* method.

7.4   Degree of Consolidation

For an element of soil at a particular depth z in a clay layer the progress of the consolidation process under a particular total stress increment can be expressed in terms of void ratio as follows:

$$U_z = \frac{e_0 - e}{e_0 - e_1}$$

where,

U_z is defined as the degree of consolidation, at a particular instant of time, at depth z $(0 \leqslant U_z \leqslant 1)$,

and

e_0 = void ratio before the start of consolidation,
e_1 = void ratio at the end of consolidation,
e = void ratio, at the time in question, during consolidation.

If the e–σ' curve is assumed to be linear over the stress range in question, as shown in Fig. 7.9, the degree of consolidation can be expressed in terms of σ':

$$U_z = \frac{\sigma' - \sigma'_0}{\sigma'_1 - \sigma'_0}$$

Suppose that the total vertical stress in the soil at the depth z is increased from σ_0 to σ_1 and there is *no lateral strain*. Immediately after the increase takes place, although the total stress has increased to σ_1, the effective vertical stress will still be σ'_0; only after the completion of consolidation will the effective stress become σ'_1. During consolidation $\Delta\sigma' = -\Delta u$.

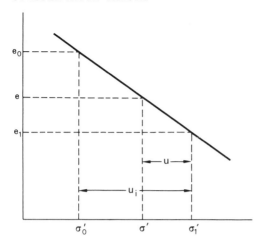

Figure 7.9   Assumed linear e-σ' relationship.

If:

> u_0 = pore water pressure *before* the increase in total stress;
> u_i (or Δu) = *increase* in pore water pressure above u_0 *immediately after* the increase in total stress;
> u = pore water pressure *in excess of* u_0 at a particular time during consolidation under the increase in total stress.

then,

$$\sigma_1' = \sigma_0' + u_i = \sigma' + u$$

The degree of consolidation can then be expressed as:

$$U_z = \frac{u_i - u}{u_i} = 1 - \frac{u}{u_i} \tag{7.9}$$

7.5   Terzaghi's Theory of One-Dimensional Consolidation

The assumptions made in the theory are listed below.

(1) The soil is homogeneous.
(2) The soil is fully-saturated.
(3) The solid particles and water are incompressible.
(4) Compression and flow are one-dimensional (vertical).
(5) Strains are small.
(6) Darcy's law is valid at all hydraulic gradients.
(7) The coefficient of permeability and the coefficient of volume change remain constant throughout the process.
(8) There is a unique relationship, independent of time, between void ratio and effective stress.

Regarding assumption (6) there is evidence of deviation from Darcy's law at low hydraulic gradients. Regarding assumption (7), the coefficient of permeability decreases as the void ratio decreases during consolidation. The coefficient of volume change also decreases during consolidation since the $e\text{-}\sigma'$ relationship is non-linear. However for small stress increments assumption (7) is reasonable. The main limitations of Terzaghi's theory (apart from its one-dimensional nature) arise from assumption (8). Experimental results show that the relationship between void ratio and effective stress is not independent of time.

The theory relates the following three quantities.

(1) The *excess* pore water pressure (u).

(2) The depth (z) below the top of the clay layer.

(3) The time (t) from the instantaneous application of a total stress increment.

Consider an element having dimensions dx, dy and dz within a clay layer of thickness $2d$, as shown in Fig. 7.10. An increment of total vertical stress $\Delta\sigma$ is applied to the element.

The flow velocity through the element is given by Darcy's law as:

$$v_z = ki_z = -k\frac{\partial h}{\partial z}$$

Since any change in total head (h) is due only to a change in pore water pressure:

$$v_z = -\frac{k}{\gamma_w}\frac{\partial u}{\partial z}$$

The condition of continuity (equation 2.7) can therefore be expressed as:

$$-\frac{k}{\gamma_w}\frac{\partial^2 u}{\partial z^2}\,dxdydz = \frac{dV}{dt} \tag{7.10}$$

The rate of volume change can be expressed in terms of m_v:

$$\frac{dV}{dt} = m_v\frac{\partial\sigma'}{\partial t}\,dxdydz$$

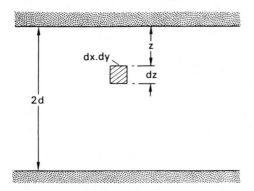

Figure 7.10   Element within a clay layer.

The total stress increment is gradually transferred to the soil skeleton, increasing effective stress, as the excess pore water pressure decreases. Hence the rate of volume change can be expressed as:

$$\frac{dV}{dt} = - m_v \frac{\partial u}{\partial t} \, dxdydz \tag{7.11}$$

Combining equations (7.10) and (7.11),

$$m_v \frac{\partial u}{\partial t} = \frac{k}{\gamma_w} \frac{\partial^2 u}{\partial z^2}$$

or,

$$\frac{\partial u}{\partial t} = c_v \frac{\partial^2 u}{\partial z^2} \tag{7.12}$$

This is the differential equation of consolidation, in which:

$$c_v = \frac{k}{m_v \gamma_w} \tag{7.13}$$

c_v being defined as the *coefficient of consolidation* and having units of m^2/s. Since k and m_v are assumed constant, c_v is constant during consolidation.

Solution of the Consolidation Equation

The total stress increment is assumed to be applied instantaneously and at zero time will be carried entirely by the pore water, i.e. the initial value of excess pore water pressure (u_i) is equal to $\Delta\sigma$ and the initial condition is:

$$u = u_i \quad \text{for } 0 \leqslant z \leqslant 2d \quad \text{when } t = 0.$$

The upper and lower boundaries of the clay layer are assumed to be free draining, the permeability of the soil adjacent to each boundary being very high compared to that of the clay. Thus the boundary conditions at any time after the application of $\Delta\sigma$ are:

$$u = 0 \quad \text{for } z = 0 \quad \text{and } z = 2d \quad \text{when } t > 0$$

The solution for the excess pore water pressure at depth z after time t is:

$$u = \sum_{n=1}^{n=\infty} \left(\frac{1}{d} \int_0^{2d} u_i \sin \frac{n\pi z}{2d} \, dz \right) \left(\sin \frac{n\pi z}{2d} \right) \exp \left(-\frac{n^2 \pi^2 c_v t}{4d^2} \right) \tag{7.14}$$

where,

d = length of longest drainage path
u_i = initial excess pore water pressure, in general a function of z.

For the particular case in which u_i is constant throughout the clay layer:

$$u = \sum_{n=1}^{n=\infty} \frac{2u_i}{n\pi} (1 - \cos n\pi) \left(\sin \frac{n\pi z}{2d} \right) \exp \left(-\frac{n^2 \pi^2 c_v t}{4d^2} \right) \tag{7.15}$$

When n is even $(1 - \cos n\pi) = 0$, and when n is odd $(1 - \cos n\pi) = 2$. Only odd values of n are therefore relevant and it is convenient to make the substitutions:

$$n = 2m + 1$$

and

$$M = \frac{\pi}{2}(2m + 1)$$

It is also convenient to substitute:

$$T_v = \frac{c_v t}{d^2} \tag{7.16}$$

a dimensionless number called the *time factor*.
Equation (7.15) then becomes:

$$u = \sum_{m=0}^{m=\infty} \frac{2u_i}{M}\left(\sin \frac{Mz}{d}\right) \exp\left(-M^2 T_v\right) \tag{7.17}$$

The progress of consolidation can be shown by plotting a series of curves of u against z for different values of t. Such curves are called *isochrones* and their form will depend on the initial distribution of excess pore water pressure and the drainage conditions at the boundaries of the clay layer. A layer for which both the upper and lower boundaries are free draining is described as an *open* layer: a layer for which only one boundary is free draining is a *half-closed* layer. Examples of isochrones are shown in Fig. 7.11. In part (a) of the figure the initial distribution of u_i is constant and for an open layer of thickness $2d$ the isochrones are symmetrical about the centre line. The upper half of this diagram also represents the case of a half-closed layer of thickness d. The slope of an isochrone at any depth gives the hydraulic gradient and also indicates the direction of flow. In parts (b) and (c) of the figure, with a triangular distribution of u_i, the direction of flow changes over certain parts of the layer. In part (c) the lower boundary is impermeable and for a time swelling takes place in the lower part of the layer.

The degree of consolidation at depth z and time t can be obtained by substituting the value of u (equation 7.17) in equation 7.9, giving:

$$U_z = 1 - \sum_{m=0}^{m=\infty} \frac{2}{M}\left(\sin \frac{Mz}{d}\right) \exp\left(-M^2 T_v\right) \tag{7.18}$$

In practical problems it is the *average* degree of consolidation (U) over the depth of the layer as a whole that is of interest, the consolidation settlement at time t being given by the product of U and the final settlement. The average degree of consolidation at time t for constant u_i is given by:

$$U = 1 - \frac{\dfrac{1}{2d}\displaystyle\int_0^{2d} u\, dz}{u_i}$$

$$= 1 - \sum_{m=0}^{m=\infty} \frac{2}{M^2} \exp\left(-M^2 T_v\right) \tag{7.19}$$

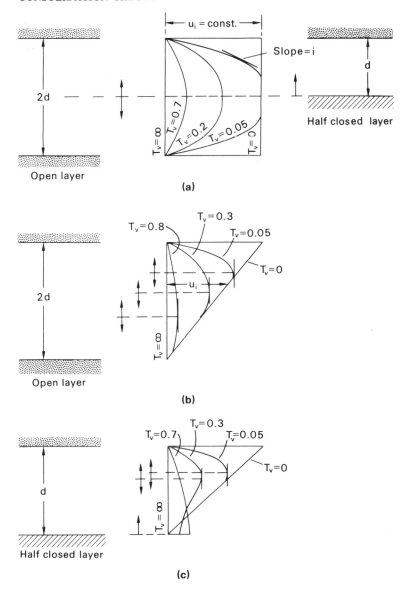

Figure 7.11   Isochrones.

The relationship between U and T_v given by equation 7.19 is represented by curve (1) in Fig. 7.12. Equation 7.19 can be represented almost exactly by the following empirical equations:

$$\text{for } U < 0\cdot60, \quad T_v = \frac{\pi}{4}\,U^2 \tag{7.20a}$$

$$\text{for } U > 0\cdot60, \quad T_v = -\,0\cdot933\,\log(1 - U) - 0\cdot085 \tag{7.20b}$$

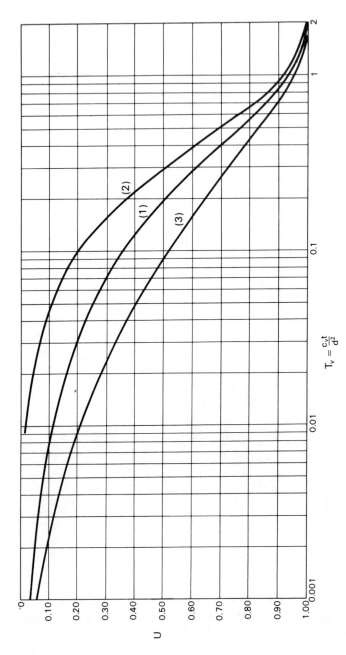

Figure 7.12   Relationships between average degree of consolidation and time factor.

If u_i is not constant the average degree of consolidation is given by:

$$U = 1 - \frac{\displaystyle\int_0^{2d} u\,dz}{\displaystyle\int_0^{2d} u_i\,dz} \qquad (7.21)$$

where,

$$\int_0^{2d} u\,dz = \text{area under isochrone at the time in question}$$

and

$$\int_0^{2d} u_i\,dz = \text{area under initial isochrone.}$$

(For a half-closed layer the limits of integration are 0 and d in the above equations.)

The initial variation of excess pore water pressure in a clay layer can usually be approximated in practice to a linear distribution. Curves (1), (2) and (3) in Fig. 7.12 represent the solution of the consolidation equation for the cases shown in Fig. 7.13.

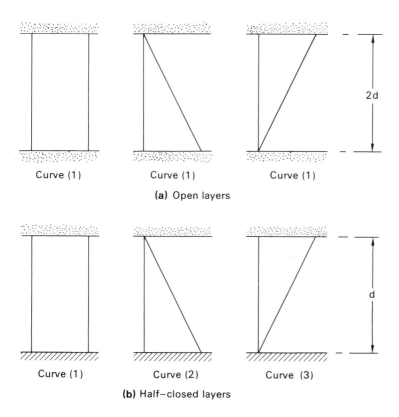

Curve (1)	Curve (1)	Curve (1)	

(a) Open layers

Curve (1)	Curve (2)	Curve (3)

(b) Half-closed layers

Figure 7.13   Initial variations of excess pore water pressure.

7.6   Determination of Coefficient of Consolidation

The value of c_v for a particular pressure increment in the oedometer test can be
determined by comparing the characteristics of the experimental and theoretical
consolidation curves, the procedure being referred to as *curve fitting*. The
characteristics of the curves are brought out clearly if time is plotted to a square root
or a logarithmic scale. Once the value of c_v has been determined, the coefficient of
permeability can be calculated from equation 7.13, the oedometer test being a useful
method for obtaining the permeability of a clay.

The Log Time Method (due to Casagrande)

The forms of the experimental and theoretical curves are shown in Fig. 7.14. The
experimental curve is obtained by plotting the dial gauge readings in the oedometer
test against the logarithm of time in minutes. The theoretical curve is given as the
plot of the average degree of consolidation against the logarithm of the time factor.
The theoretical curve consists of three parts: an initial curve which approximates
closely to a parabolic relationship, a part which is linear and a final curve to which
the horizontal axis is an asymptote at $U = 1 \cdot 0$ (or 100%). In the experimental
curve the point corresponding to $U = 0$ can be determined by using the fact that the
initial part of the curve represents an approximately parabolic relationship between
compression and time. Two points on the curve are selected (A and B in Fig. 7.14)
for which the values of t are in the ratio of 4:1, and the vertical distance between
them is measured. An equal distance set off above the first point fixes the point (a_s)
corresponding to $U = 0$. As a check the procedure should be repeated using different
pairs of points. The point corresponding to $U = 0$ will not generally correspond to
the point (a_0) representing the initial dial gauge reading, the difference being due
mainly to the compression of small quantities of air in the soil, the degree of
saturation being marginally below 100%: this compression is called *initial compression*.
The final part of the experimental curve is linear but not horizontal and the point
(a_{100}) corresponding to $U = 100\%$ is taken as the intersection of the two linear
parts of the curve. The compression between the a_s and a_{100} points is called *primary
consolidation* and represents that part of the process accounted for by Terzaghi's
theory. Beyond the point of intersection, compression of the soil continues at a very
slow rate for an indefinite period of time and is called *secondary compression*.
    The point corresponding to $U = 50\%$ can be located midway between the a_s and
a_{100} points and the corresponding time t_{50} obtained. The value of T_v corresponding
to $U = 50\%$ is $0 \cdot 196$ and the coefficient of consolidation is given by:

$$c_v = \frac{0 \cdot 196 \, d^2}{t_{50}}$$
(7.22)

the value of d being taken as half the average thickness of the specimen for the
particular pressure increment. BS 1377 states that if the average temperature of the
soil *in-situ* is known and differs from the average test temperature, a correction should
be applied to the value of c_v, correction factors being given in the standard.

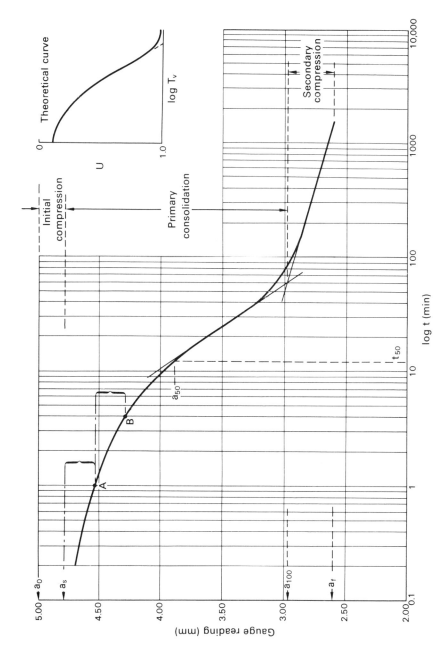

Figure 7.14 The log time method (Example 7.2).

The Root Time Method (*due to Taylor*)

Fig. 7.15 shows the forms of the experimental and theoretical curves, the dial gauge readings being plotted against the square root of time in minutes and the average degree of consolidation against the square root of time factor. The theoretical curve is linear up to about 60% consolidation and at 90% consolidation the abscissa (AC) is 1·15 times the abscissa (AB) of the production of the linear part of the curve. This characteristic is used to determine the point on the experimental curve corresponding to $U = 90\%$.

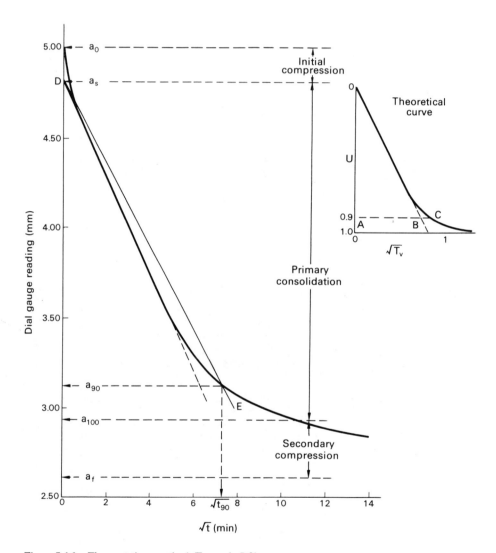

Figure 7.15   The root time method (Example 7.2).

The experimental curve usually consists of a short curve representing initial compression, a linear part and a second curve. The point (D) corresponding to $U = 0$

is obtained by producing back the linear part of the curve to the ordinate at zero time. A straight line (DE) is then drawn having abscissae 1·15 times the corresponding abscissae on the linear part of the experimental curve. The intersection of the line DE with the experimental curve locates the point (a_{90}) corresponding to $U = 90\%$ and the corresponding value $\sqrt{t_{90}}$ can be obtained. The value of T_v corresponding to $U = 90\%$ is 0·848 and the coefficient of consolidation is given by:

$$c_v = \frac{0·848d^2}{t_{90}} \tag{7.23}$$

If required, the point (a_{100}) on the experimental curve corresponding to $U = 100\%$, the limit of primary consolidation, can be obtained by proportion. As in the log time plot the curve extends beyond the 100% point into the secondary compression range. The root time method requires compression readings covering a much shorter period of time compared with the log time method which requires the accurate definition of the second linear part of the curve well into the secondary compression range. On the other hand, a straight line portion is not always obtained on the root time plot and in such cases the log time method should be used.

Other methods of determining c_v have been proposed by Naylor and Doran [7.10], Scott [7.12] and Cour [7.4].

The Compression Ratios

The relative magnitudes of the initial compression, the compression due to primary consolidation and the secondary compression can be expressed by the following ratios (reference Figs. 7.14 and 7.15).

$$\text{Initial compression ratio: } r_0 = \frac{a_0 - a_s}{a_0 - a_f} \tag{7.24}$$

$$\text{Primary compression ratio (log time): } r_p = \frac{a_s - a_{100}}{a_0 - a_f} \tag{7.25}$$

$$\text{Primary compression ratio (root time): } r_p = \frac{10(a_s - a_{90})}{9(a_0 - a_f)} \tag{7.26}$$

$$\text{Secondary compression ratio: } r_s = 1 - (r_0 + r_p) \tag{7.27}$$

In-situ Measurement of c_v

Piezometers can be used to determine the coefficient of consolidation (or swelling) of saturated clays in-situ, using the results of three-dimensional consolidation theory. The most satisfactory procedure is to maintain a constant head (above or below the ambient pore water pressure in the clay) at the piezometer tip and measure the rate of flow into or out of the system. If the rate of flow is measured at various times the value of c_v (and of the coefficient of permeability k) can be deduced. The reader is referred to the paper by Gibson [7.5] for details.

Secondary Compression

In the Terzaghi theory it is implied by assumption (8) that change in void ratio is due entirely to change in effective stress brought about by dissipation of excess pore water pressure, with permeability alone governing the time dependency of the process. However experimental results show that compression does not cease when the excess pore water pressure has dissipated to zero but continues at a very slow rate under constant effective stress. One hypothesis is that secondary compression is due to the gradual readjustment of the soil skeleton after the disturbance during primary consolidation. The rate of secondary compression is thought to be controlled by the highly-viscous adsorbed water surrounding the clay mineral particles in the soil.

The rate of secondary compression can be defined by the slope (C_α) of the final part of the compression/log time curve, measured as the unit compression over one decade on the log time scale. In highly plastic clays and organic soils the rate of secondary compression is usually high and in extreme cases the secondary compression part of the compression/log time curve may completely mask the primary part. For a particular soil the rate of secondary compression increases as the ratio of the pressure increment to the initial pressure decreases. The rate also increases with decrease in the thickness of specimen used in the oedometer test.

Example 7.2

The following compression readings were taken during an oedometer test on a saturated clay specimen $(G_s = 2·73)$ when the applied pressure was increased from 214 to 429 kN/m^2:

Time (min)	0	$\frac{1}{4}$	$\frac{1}{2}$	1	$2\frac{1}{4}$	4	9	16	25
Gauge (mm)	5·00	4·67	4·62	4·53	4·41	4·28	4·01	3·75	3·49

Time (min)	36	49	64	81	100	200	400	1440
Gauge (mm)	3·28	3·15	3·06	3·00	2·96	2·84	2·76	2·61

After 1440 min the thickness of the specimen was 13·60 mm and the water content 35·9%. Determine the coefficient of consolidation from both the log time and the root time plots and the values of the three compression ratios. Determine also the value of the coefficient of permeability.

Total change in thickness during increment = $5·00 - 2·61 = 2·39$ mm

Average thickness during increment = $13·60 + \dfrac{2·39}{2} = 14·80$ mm

Length of drainage path, $d = \dfrac{14·80}{2} = 7·40$ mm

From the log time plot (Fig. 7.14):

$t_{50} = 12·5$ minutes

$$c_v = \frac{0·196d^2}{t_{50}} = \frac{0·196 \times 7·40^2}{12·5 \times 60 \times 10^6} = 1·43 \times 10^{-8} \text{ m}^2/\text{s}$$

$$r_0 = \frac{5·00 - 4·79}{5·00 - 2·61} = 0·088$$

$$r_p = \frac{4 \cdot 79 - 2 \cdot 98}{5 \cdot 00 - 2 \cdot 61} = 0 \cdot 757$$

$$r_s = 1 - (0 \cdot 088 + 0 \cdot 757) = 0 \cdot 155$$

From the root time plot (Fig. 7.15):

$$\sqrt{t_{90}} = 7 \cdot 30 \quad \therefore \quad t_{90} = 53 \cdot 3 \text{ minutes}$$

$$c_v = \frac{0 \cdot 848 d^2}{t_{90}} = \frac{0 \cdot 848 \times 7 \cdot 40^2}{53 \cdot 3 \times 60 \times 10^6} = 1 \cdot 45 \times 10^{-8} \text{ m}^2/\text{s}$$

$$r_0 = \frac{5 \cdot 00 - 4 \cdot 81}{5 \cdot 00 - 2 \cdot 61} = 0 \cdot 080$$

$$r_p = \frac{10(4 \cdot 81 - 3 \cdot 12)}{9(5 \cdot 00 - 2 \cdot 61)} = 0 \cdot 785$$

$$r_s = 1 - (0 \cdot 080 + 0 \cdot 785) = 0 \cdot 135$$

In order to determine the permeability, the value of m_v must be calculated.

Final void ratio: $e_1 = w_1 G_s = 0 \cdot 359 \times 2 \cdot 73 = 0 \cdot 98$

Initial void ratio: $e_0 = e_1 + \Delta e$

Now, $\dfrac{\Delta e}{\Delta H} = \dfrac{1 + e_0}{H_0}$

i.e. $\dfrac{\Delta e}{2 \cdot 39} = \dfrac{1 \cdot 98 + \Delta e}{15 \cdot 99}$

$\therefore \quad \Delta e = 0 \cdot 35$

and $e_0 = 1 \cdot 33$

Now, $m_v = \dfrac{1}{1 + e_0} \cdot \dfrac{e_0 - e_1}{\sigma_1' - \sigma_0'}$

$$= \frac{1}{2 \cdot 33} \times \frac{0 \cdot 35}{215} = 7 \cdot 0 \times 10^{-4} \text{ m}^2/\text{kN}$$

Coefficient of permeability: $k = c_v m_v \gamma_w$

$$= 1 \cdot 44 \times 10^{-8} \times 7 \cdot 0 \times 10^{-4} \times 9 \cdot 8$$

$$= 1 \cdot 0 \times 10^{-10} \text{ m/s}$$

7.7 Correction for Construction Period

In practice, structural loads are applied to the soil not instantaneously but over a period of time. Initially there is usually a reduction in net load due to excavation, resulting in swelling of the clay: settlement will not begin until the applied load exceeds the weight of the excavated soil. Terzaghi proposed an empirical method of correcting the instantaneous time/settlement curve to allow for the construction period.

The net load (P') is the gross load less the weight of soil excavated and the effective construction period (t_c) is measured from the time when P' is zero. It is assumed that the net load is applied uniformly over the time t_c (Fig. 7.16) and that the degree of consolidation at time t_c is the same as if the load P' had been acting as a constant load for the period $t_c/2$. Thus the settlement at any time during the construction period is equal to that occurring for instantaneous loading at half that time; however, since the load acting is not the total load, the value of settlement so obtained must be reduced in the proportion of that load to the total load.

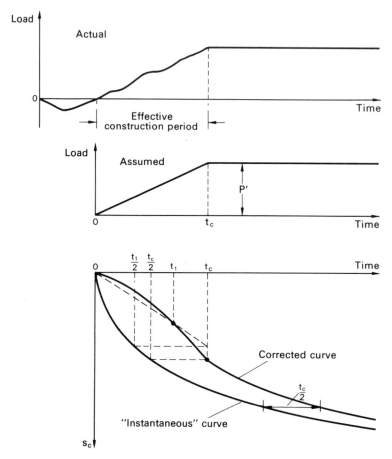

Figure 7.16   Correction for construction period.

For the period subsequent to the completion of construction, the settlement curve will be the instantaneous curve offset by half the effective construction period. Thus at any time after the end of construction the corrected time corresponding to any value of settlement is equal to the time from the start of loading less half the effective construction period. After a long period of time the magnitude of settlement is not appreciably affected by the construction time.

Example 7.3

A layer of clay 8 m thick lies between two layers of sand. The upper sand layer extends from ground level to a depth of 4 m, the water table being at a depth of 2 m. The lower sand layer is under artesian pressure, the piezometric level being

6 m above ground level. The saturated unit weights of the clay and sand respectively
are 20 kN/m^3 and 19 kN/m^3: the unit weight of the sand above the water table is
16 kN/m^3. For the clay $m_v = 9.4 \times 10^{-4}$ m^2/kN and $c_v = 4.5 \times 10^{-8}$ m^2/s. Due to
pumping from the artesian layer the piezometric level falls by 3 m over a period of
2 years. Draw the time/settlement curve due to consolidation of the clay for a
period of 5 years from the start of pumping.

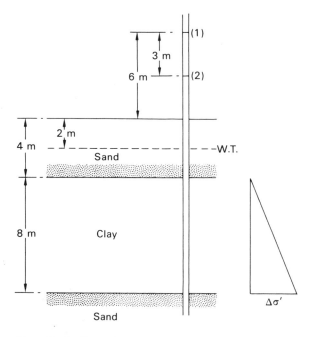

Figure 7.17   Example 7.3.

In this case, consolidation is due only to the difference in the static and steady-
state pore water pressures: there is no change in total vertical stress. The effective
vertical stress remains unchanged at the top of the clay layer but will be increased
by $3\gamma_w$ at the bottom of the layer due to the decrease in pore water pressure in the
adjacent artesian layer. The distribution of $\Delta\sigma'$ is shown in Fig. 7.17. The problem
is one-dimensional since the increase in effective vertical stress is the same over the
entire area in question. In calculating the consolidation settlement it is necessary to
consider only the value of $\Delta\sigma'$ at the centre of the layer. Note that in order to
obtain the value of m_v it would have been necessary to calculate the initial and final
values of effective vertical stress in the clay.

> At the centre of the clay layer, $\Delta\sigma' = 1.5\gamma_w = 14.7$ kN/m^2.
> The *final* consolidation settlement is given by:
>
> $$s_{cf} = m_v \Delta\sigma' H$$
> $$= 9.4 \times 10^{-4} \times 14.7 \times 8000$$
> $$= 110 \text{ mm}$$
>
> The clay layer is open, $\therefore$ $d = 4$ m

For $t = 5$ years, $T_v = \dfrac{c_v t}{d^2}$

$$= \frac{4 \cdot 5 \times 10^{-8} \times 5 \times 365 \times 24 \times 60^2}{4^2}$$

$$= 0 \cdot 443$$

From curve (1), Fig. 7.12, the corresponding value of U is $0 \cdot 73$. To obtain the time/settlement relationship a series of values of U is selected up to $0 \cdot 73$ and the corresponding times calculated from the time factor equation: the corresponding values of settlement (s_c) are given by the product of U and s_{cf}.

U	T_v	t (years)	s_c (mm)
$0 \cdot 10$	$0 \cdot 008$	$0 \cdot 09$	11
$0 \cdot 20$	$0 \cdot 031$	$0 \cdot 35$	22
$0 \cdot 30$	$0 \cdot 070$	$0 \cdot 79$	33
$0 \cdot 40$	$0 \cdot 126$	$1 \cdot 42$	44
$0 \cdot 50$	$0 \cdot 196$	$2 \cdot 21$	55
$0 \cdot 60$	$0 \cdot 285$	$3 \cdot 22$	66
$0 \cdot 73$	$0 \cdot 443$	$5 \cdot 00$	80

The plot of s_c against t gives the 'instantaneous' curve. Terzaghi's method of correction for the 2 year period over which pumping takes place is then carried out as shown in Fig. 7.18.

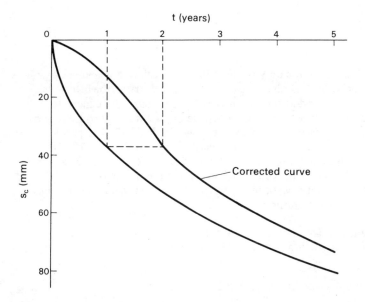

Figure 7.18   Example 7.3.

Example 7.4

An 8 m depth of sand overlies a 6 m layer of clay, below which is an impermeable stratum (Fig. 7.19); the water table is 2 m below the surface of the sand. Over a period of 1 year a 3 m depth of fill (unit weight 20 kN/m³) is to be dumped on the surface over an extensive area. The saturated unit weight of the sand is 19 kN/m³ and that of the clay 20 kN/m³; above the water table the unit weight of the sand is 17 kN/m³. For the clay, the relationship between void ratio and effective stress (units kN/m²) can be represented by the equation

$$e = 0.88 - 0.32 \log \frac{\sigma'}{100}$$

and the coefficient of consolidation is 4.0×10^{-8} m²/s.

(a) Calculate the final settlement of the area due to consolidation of the clay and the settlement after a period of 3 years from the start of dumping.

(b) If a very thin layer of sand, freely draining, existed 1.5 m above the bottom of the clay layer, what would be the values of the final and 3 year settlements?

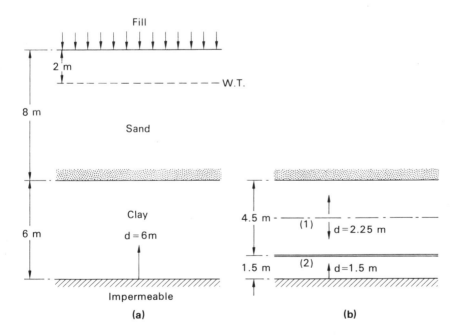

Figure 7.19   Example 7.4.

Since the fill covers a wide area, the problem can be considered to be one-dimensional. The consolidation settlement will be calculated in terms of C_c, considering the clay layer as a whole, therefore the initial and final values of effective vertical stress at the centre of the clay layer are required.

$$\sigma_0' = (17 \times 2) + (9 \cdot 2 \times 6) + (10 \cdot 2 \times 3) = 119 \cdot 8 \text{ kN/m}^2$$

$$e_0 = 0 \cdot 88 - 0 \cdot 32 \log 1 \cdot 198 = 0 \cdot 88 - 0 \cdot 025 = 0 \cdot 855$$

$$\sigma_1' = 119 \cdot 8 + (3 \times 20) = 179 \cdot 8 \text{ kN/m}^2$$

$$\log \frac{179 \cdot 8}{119 \cdot 8} = 0 \cdot 176$$

The final settlement is calculated from equation 7.8:

$$s_{cf} = \frac{0 \cdot 32 \times 0 \cdot 176 \times 6000}{1 \cdot 855} = 182 \text{ mm}$$

In the calculation of the degree of consolidation 3 years after the start of dumping, the corrected value of time to allow for the 1 year dumping period is

$$t = 3 - \tfrac{1}{2} = 2 \cdot 5 \text{ years}$$

The layer is half-closed, $\therefore \quad d = 6$ m

Then, $\quad T_v = \dfrac{c_v t}{d^2} = \dfrac{4 \cdot 0 \times 10^{-8} \times 2 \cdot 5 \times 365 \times 24 \times 60^2}{6^2}$

$$= 0 \cdot 0875$$

From curve (1), Fig. (7.12): $\quad U = 0 \cdot 335$

Settlement after 3 years: $\quad s_c = 0 \cdot 335 \times 182 = 61$ mm

(b) The final settlement will still be 182 mm (ignoring the thickness of the drainage layer): only the rate of settlement will be affected. From the point of view of drainage there is now an open layer of thickness 4·5 m ($d = 2 \cdot 25$ m) above a half-closed layer of thickness 1·5 m ($d = 1 \cdot 5$ m): these layers are numbered (1) and (2) respectively.

By proportion, $T_{v_1} = 0 \cdot 0875 \times \dfrac{6^2}{2 \cdot 25^2} = 0 \cdot 622$

$$\therefore \quad U_1 = 0 \cdot 825$$

and, $\quad T_{v_2} = 0 \cdot 0875 \times \dfrac{6^2}{1 \cdot 5^2} = 1 \cdot 40$

$$\therefore \quad U_2 = 0 \cdot 97$$

Now for each layer, $s_c = U s_{cf}$, which is proportional to UH. Hence if $\bar{U}$ is the overall degree of consolidation for the two layers combined:

$$4 \cdot 5 U_1 + 1 \cdot 5 U_2 = 6 \cdot 0 \bar{U}$$

i.e. $\quad (4 \cdot 5 \times 0 \cdot 825) + (1 \cdot 5 \times 0 \cdot 97) = 6 \cdot 0 \bar{U}$

Hence, $\quad \bar{U} = 0 \cdot 86$

and the 3 year settlement is:

$$s_c = 0 \cdot 86 \times 182 = 157 \text{ mm}$$

7.8   Numerical Solution

The one-dimensional consolidation equation can be solved numerically by the method of finite differences. The method has the advantage that any pattern of initial excess pore water pressure can be adopted and it is possible to consider problems in which the load is applied gradually over a period of time. The errors associated with the method are negligible and the solution is easily programmed for the computer.

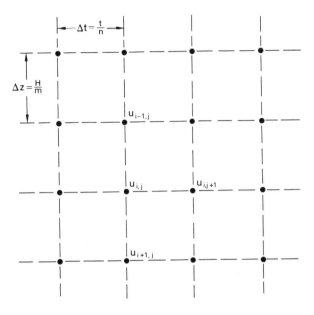

Figure 7.20   Depth-time grid.

The method is based on a depth-time grid as shown in Fig. 7.20. The depth of the clay layer is divided into m equal parts of thickness Δz and any specified period of time is divided into n equal intervals Δt. Any point on the grid can be identified by the subscripts i and j, the depth position of the point being denoted by i ($0 \leqslant i \leqslant m$) and the elapsed time by j ($0 \leqslant j \leqslant n$). The value of excess pore water pressure at any depth after any time is therefore denoted by $u_{i,j}$.

The following finite difference approximations can be derived from Taylor's theorem:

$$\frac{\partial u}{\partial t} = \frac{1}{\Delta t}(u_{i,j+1} - u_{i,j})$$

$$\frac{\partial^2 u}{\partial z^2} = \frac{1}{(\Delta z)^2}(u_{i-1,j} + u_{i+1,j} - 2u_{i,j})$$

Substituting these values in equation 7.12 yields the finite difference approximation of the one-dimensional consolidation equation:

$$u_{i,j+1} = u_{i,j} + \frac{c_v \Delta t}{(\Delta z)^2}(u_{i-1,j} + u_{i+1,j} - 2u_{i,j}) \qquad (7.28)$$

It is convenient to write:

$$\beta = \frac{c_v \Delta t}{(\Delta z)^2} \tag{7.29}$$

this term being called the *operator* of equation 7.28. It has been shown that for convergence the value of the operator must not exceed $\frac{1}{2}$. The errors due to neglecting higher order derivatives in Taylor's theorem are reduced to a minimum when the value of the operator is $\frac{1}{6}$.

It is usual to specify the number of equal parts m into which the depth of the layer is to be divided and as the value of β is limited a restriction is thus placed on the value of Δt. For any specified period of time t in the case of an *open* layer:

$$T_v = \frac{c_v(n\Delta t)}{(\frac{1}{2}m\Delta z)^2}$$

$$= 4\frac{n}{m^2}\beta \tag{7.30}$$

In the case of a *half-closed* layer the denominator becomes $(m\Delta z)^2$ and:

$$T_v = \frac{n}{m^2}\beta \tag{7.31}$$

A value of n must therefore be chosen such that the value of β in equation 7.30 or 7.31 does not exceed $\frac{1}{2}$.

Equation 7.28 does not apply to points on an impermeable boundary. There can be no flow across an impermeable boundary, a condition represented by the equation:

$$\frac{\partial u}{\partial z} = 0$$

which can be represented by the finite difference approximation:

$$\frac{1}{2\Delta z}(u_{i-1,j} - u_{i+1,j}) = 0$$

the impermeable boundary being at a depth position denoted by subscript i

i.e. $u_{i-1,j} = u_{i+1,j}$

For all points *on* an impermeable boundary, equation 7.28 then becomes:

$$u_{i,j+1} = u_{i,j} + \frac{c_v \Delta t}{(\Delta z)^2}(2u_{i-1,j} - 2u_{i,j}) \tag{7.32}$$

The degree of consolidation at any time t can be obtained by determining the areas under the initial isochrone and the isochrone at time t as in equation 7.21.

Example 7.5

A half-closed clay layer (free-draining at the upper boundary) is 10 m thick and the value of c_v is $2 \cdot 5 \times 10^{-7}$ m²/s. The initial distribution of excess pore water pressure is as follows:

Depth (m)	0	2	4	6	8	10
Pressure (kN/m²)	60	54	41	29	19	15

Obtain the values of excess pore water pressure after consolidation has been in progress for 1 year.

The layer is half-closed, $\therefore$ $d = 10$ m

For $t = 1$ year, $T_v = \dfrac{c_v t}{d^2} = \dfrac{2 \cdot 5 \times 10^{-7} \times 365 \times 24 \times 60^2}{10^2} = 0 \cdot 079$

The layer is divided into 5 equal parts, i.e. $m = 5$

Now, $T_v = \dfrac{n}{m^2} \beta$

$\therefore$ $n\beta = 0 \cdot 079 \times 5^5 = 1 \cdot 98$, say $2 \cdot 0$

(This makes the actual value of $T_v = 0 \cdot 080$ and $t = 1 \cdot 01$ years)
The value of n will be taken as 10 (i.e. $\Delta t = 1/10$ year), making $\beta = 0 \cdot 2$.
The finite difference equation then becomes:

$u_{i,j+1} = u_{i,j} + 0 \cdot 2 \, (u_{i-1,j} + u_{i+1,j} - 2u_{i,j})$

but on the impermeable boundary:

$u_{i,j+1} = u_{i,j} + 0 \cdot 2 \, (2u_{i-1,j} - 2u_{i,j})$

On the permeable boundary, $u = 0$ for all values of t, assuming the initial pressure of 60 kN/m² instantaneously becomes zero.
    The computation is set out below, all pressures having been multiplied by 10.

i \\ j	0	1	2	3	4	5	6	7	8	9	10
0	0	0	0	0	0	0	0	0	0	0	0
1	540	406	326	273	235	207	185	167	153	141	131
2	410	412	387	357	329	304	282	263	246	232	219
3	290	294	299	300	296	290	283	275	267	260	253
4	190	202	213	224	233	240	245	249	251	252	252
5	150	166	180	194	206	217	226	234	240	244	247

7.9   Consolidation Settlement: Skempton-Bjerrum Method

Predictions of in-situ consolidation settlement are normally based on the results of one-dimensional oedometer tests using representative samples of the clay. Due to the confining ring the net lateral strain in the test specimen is zero and for this condition the initial excess pore water pressure is equal theoretically to the increase in total vertical stress, i.e. the pore pressure coefficient A is equal to unity. In practice the condition of zero lateral strain is satisfied approximately in the case of thin clay layers and for layers under loaded areas which are large compared with the thickness of the layer. In many practical situations, however, appreciable lateral strain will occur and the initial excess pore water pressure will depend on the in-situ stress conditions and the value of the pore pressure coefficient A (which will not be equal to unity): Skempton and Bjerrum [7.13] developed a method of taking this into account.

Due to surface loading, total principal stress increases $\Delta\sigma_1$ and $\Delta\sigma_3$ will result at any point in the clay layer and the initial excess pore water pressure at the point is given by equation 4.17, i.e.:

$$u_i = \Delta\sigma_3 + A(\Delta\sigma_1 - \Delta\sigma_3)$$

$$= \Delta\sigma_1 \left[A + \frac{\Delta\sigma_3}{\Delta\sigma_1}(1 - A) \right] \tag{7.33}$$

the value of the pore pressure coefficient B being unity for a fully-saturated soil. From equation 7.33 it is seen that:

$$u_i > \Delta\sigma_3$$

and

$$u_i = \Delta\sigma_1 \text{ if } A = 1$$

The value of A depends on the type of clay and the values of the stresses. The in-situ effective stresses (A) before loading, (B) immediately after loading and (C) after consolidation, are represented in Fig. 7.21 and the corresponding Mohr circles in Fig. 7.22. In Fig. 7.22, abc is the effective stress path for in-situ loading and consolidation, ab representing an immediate change of stress (assuming loading to be immediate) and bc a gradual change of stress as the excess pore water pressure dissipates. Immediately after loading there is a reduction in σ_3' due to u_i being greater than $\Delta\sigma_3$. Consolidation will therefore involve lateral recompression. Circle (D) in Fig. 7.22 represents the corresponding stresses in the oedometer test after consolidation and ad is the corresponding effective stress path for the oedometer test.

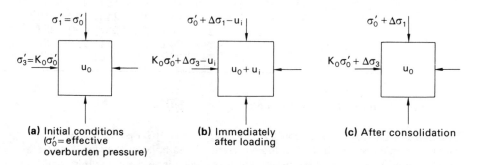

Figure 7.21   In-situ effective stresses.

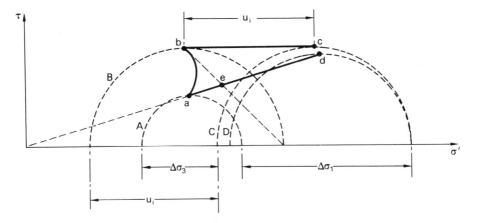

Figure 7.22   Stress paths.

Skempton and Bjerrum proposed that the effect of lateral strains be neglected, thus enabling the oedometer test to be maintained as the basis of the method, although it was admitted that this simplification could involve errors not exceeding 20% in vertical consolidation settlements. However, the value of excess pore water pressure given by equation 7.33 should be used.

By the one-dimensional method, consolidation settlement is given as:

$$s_{\text{oed}} = \int_0^H m_v \Delta\sigma_1 \, dz$$

and by the Skempton-Bjerrum method as:

$$s_s = \int_0^H m_v u_i \, dz$$

$$= \int_0^H m_v \Delta\sigma_1 \left[A + \frac{\Delta\sigma_3}{\Delta\sigma_1}(1 - A) \right] dz$$

A coefficient μ is introduced, such that:

$$s_s = \mu s_{\text{oed}} \tag{7.34}$$

where,

$$\mu = \frac{\int_0^H m_v \Delta\sigma_1 \left[A + \frac{\Delta\sigma_3}{\Delta\sigma_1}(1 - A) \right] dz}{\int_0^H m_v \Delta\sigma_1 \, dz}$$

If it can be assumed that m_v and A are constant with depth then μ can be expressed as:

$$\mu = A + (1 - A)\alpha \tag{7.35}$$

where,

$$\alpha = \frac{\displaystyle\int_0^H \Delta\sigma_3 \, dz}{\displaystyle\int_0^H \Delta\sigma_1 \, dz} \tag{7.36}$$

Taking Poisson's ratio (ν) as 0·5 for a saturated clay during loading under undrained conditions, the value of α depends only on the shape of the loaded area and the thickness of the clay layer in relation to the dimensions of the loaded area: thus α can be estimated using elastic theory.

Equation 7.36 implies axial symmetry and is strictly applicable only for a circular footing (Fig. 7.23). It will serve, however, as a reasonable approximation for a square footing (using a circular footing of the same area). Under a strip footing the stress conditions will not be symmetrical and the longitudinal horizontal stress increment will be $\Delta\sigma_2$, where σ_2 is the intermediate principal stress, and this should be taken into account in evaluating α (Muir Wood [7.9]).

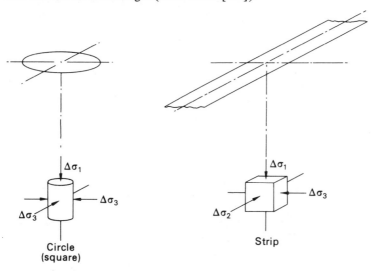

Figure 7.23   Circular and strip footings.

Values of α in terms of depth/breadth ratio are given in Table 7.1.

Table 7.1

z/B	0	0·25	0·50	1	2	4	10	∞
Circular footing*	1·00	0·67	0·50	0·38	0·30	0·28	0·26	0·25
Strip footing†	1·00	0·80	0·63	0·53	0·45	0·40	0·36	0·25

* Reference 7.13.   † Reference 7.9.

The appropriate value of α and the value of the pore pressure coefficient A are substituted in equation 7.35. Values of μ are typically within the following ranges.

Soft, sensitive clays:	1·0 to 1·2
Normally-consolidated clays:	0·6 to 1·0
Overconsolidated clays:	0·4 to 0·7
Heavily overconsolidated clays:	0·25 to 0·4

The Skempton–Bjerrum method is an improvement in principle over the one-dimensional method but requires a knowledge of the appropriate value of A.

Example 7.6

A building is supported on a raft 30 m square, the net foundation pressure, assumed uniformly distributed, being 135 kN/m². The soil profile is shown in Fig. 7.24. From oedometer tests on the clay $m_v = 2·5 \times 10^{-4}$ m²/kN and from triaxial tests $A = 0·32$. Determine the final differential settlement between the centre and a corner of the raft (assuming it to be flexible) due to consolidation of the clay.

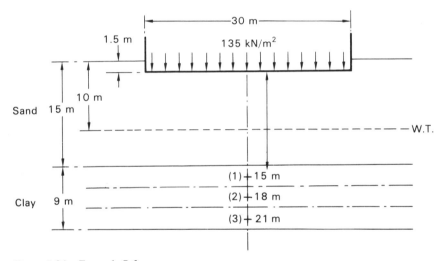

Figure 7.24   Example 7.6.

The clay will be divided into three sub-layers each 3 m thick. Since the settlement is to be calculated in terms of m_v, only the total stress *increments* at the centre of each sub-layer are required. Using Fig. 6.7 the values of $\Delta\sigma$ (kN/m²) below the centre and a corner of the raft are calculated below. $\Delta\sigma$ (= $\Delta\sigma'$ for one-dimensional consolidation) is assumed to be constant over the depth of each sub-layer.

Layer	z(m)	Centre			Corner		
		m,n	I_r^*	$\Delta\sigma$	m,n	I_r	$\Delta\sigma$
1	15	1·00	0·176	95	2·00	0·232	31
2	18	0·83	0·150	81	1·67	0·221	30
3	21	0·72	0·131	71	1·43	0·211	28

* To be multiplied by 4.

Below centre: $s_{oed} = 2 \cdot 5 \times 10^{-4} \times 3000 \times (95 + 81 + 71)$
                            $= 185$ mm

Below corner: $s_{oed} = 2 \cdot 5 \times 10^{-4} \times 3000 \times (31 + 30 + 28)$
                            $= 67$ mm

(In this particular case, no appreciable error would arise if the clay layer had been considered as a whole.)

Diameter of circle of same area as raft = 33·8 m

Ratio $\dfrac{z}{B} = \dfrac{18}{33 \cdot 8} = 0 \cdot 53$ (at centre of clay layer)

From Table 7.1: $\alpha = 0 \cdot 49$

$\therefore \quad \mu = A + (1 - A) \alpha$

$\quad = 0 \cdot 32 + (0 \cdot 68 \times 0 \cdot 49) = 0 \cdot 65$

Final differential settlement = $0 \cdot 65 (185 - 67) = 77$ mm.

7.10   The Stress Path Method

This is a comparatively recent development and although its possible application in practice lies in the future it recognises the fact that soil behaviour is influenced to a considerable extent by the stress path followed by the soil in reaching its final condition. The actual stress path for an average soil element subject to undrained loading followed by consolidation is *abc* in Fig. 7.22, while the stress paths for consolidation only according to the one-dimensional and Skempton–Bjerrum methods are *ad* and *ed* respectively.

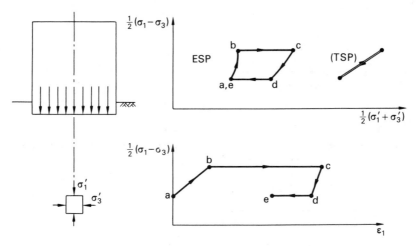

Figure 7.25   The stress path method (After Lambe [7.8]).

In the proposed stress path method, due to Lambe [7.7], the actual stress paths for a number of 'average' in-situ elements are estimated and laboratory triaxial tests are run as nearly as possible along the same stress paths, the measured vertical strains during the test then being used to obtain the settlements. In-situ pore water pressure conditions and partial drainage during the construction period can be simulated. Fig. 7.25 shows a soil element under a storage tank and the effective stress path and vertical strains for a triaxial specimen in which undrained loading (*ab*), consolidation (*bc*), undrained unloading (*cd*) and swelling (*de*) are simulated.

The method depends on the test specimens being truly representative. The triaxial techniques involved in running correct stress paths may be very complex. The weakness of the method lies in the use of elastic theory to determine the principal stress increments due to loading.

7.11   Vertical Sand Drains

The slow rate of consolidation in saturated clays of low permeability may be accelerated by means of vertical sand drains which shorten the drainage path within the clay. Consolidation is then due mainly to horizontal radial drainage, resulting in the faster dissipation of excess pore water pressure; vertical drainage becomes of minor importance. In theory the final magnitude of consolidation settlement is the same, only the *rate* of settlement being affected.

In the case of an embankment constructed over a highly compressible clay layer (Fig. 7.26), sand drains installed in the clay would enable the embankment to be brought into service much sooner and there would be a quicker increase in the shear strength of the clay. A degree of consolidation of the order of 80% would be desirable at the end of construction. Any advantages, of course, must be set against the additional cost of the sand drain installation.

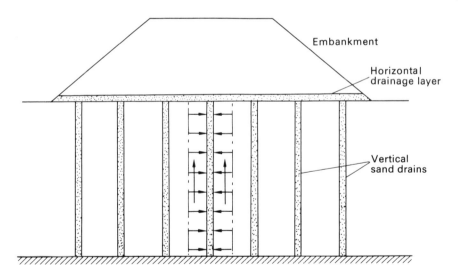

Figure 7.26   Vertical sand drains.

Sand drains are installed by driving vertical boreholes through the clay layer and backfilling with a suitably-graded sand. The sand should be capable of allowing the efficient flow of water without permitting fine clay particles to be washed in. Sand drains have been installed to depths of over 30 m. As the object is to reduce the length of drainage path the spacing of the drains is the most important design consideration. The drains may be spaced in square, rectangular or triangular patterns. The spacing of the drains must obviously be less than the thickness of the clay layer; there is no question of using sand drains in thin clay layers. The diameter of the drains is not very important. A successful design depends basically on the correct selection of soil parameters, therefore the coefficients of consolidation in both the horizontal and vertical directions (c_h and c_v respectively) must be known fairly accurately. The ratio c_h/c_v is normally between 1 and 2, the higher the ratio the more beneficial a sand drain installation will be. The values of the coefficients for the clay adjacent to the drains may be reduced due to remoulding during installation, an effect known as *smear*. Another design complication is that the sand drains tend to act as weak piles, reducing the stress increment in the clay to an unknown degree and resulting in lower values of excess pore water pressure and consolidation settlement. Secondary compression is not taken into account and cannot be controlled by sand drains. Experience has shown that sand drains are not successful in soils having a high secondary compression ratio, such as highly plastic clays and peat.

In polar coordinates the three-dimensional form of the consolidation equation, with different soil properties in the horizontal and vertical directions, is:

$$\frac{\partial u}{\partial t} = c_h \left(\frac{\partial^2 u}{\partial r^2} + \frac{1}{r} \frac{\partial u}{\partial r} \right) + c_v \frac{\partial^2 u}{\partial z^2} \tag{7.37}$$

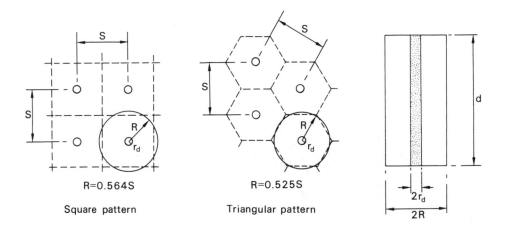

R=0.564S   R=0.525S

Square pattern   Triangular pattern

Figure 7.27   Cylindrical blocks.

The vertical prismatic blocks of soil surrounding the sand drains are replaced by cylindrical blocks, of radius R, having the same cross-sectional area (Fig. 7.27). The solution to equation 7.37 can be written in two parts:

$$U_v = f(T_v)$$

and

$$U_r = f(T_r)$$

where:

U_v = average degree of consolidation due to vertical drainage only;

U_r = average degree of consolidation due to horizontal (radial) drainage only;

$$T_v = \frac{c_v t}{d^2} = \text{time factor for consolidation due to vertical drainage only;}$$
(7.38)

$$T_r = \frac{c_h t}{4R^2} = \text{time factor for consolidation due to radial drainage only.}$$
(7.39)

The expression for T_r confirms the fact that the closer the spacing of the drains the quicker the consolidation process due to radial drainage proceeds. The solution for radial drainage, due to Barron, is given in Fig. 7.28, the U_r/T_r relationship depending on the ratio $n = R/r_d$, where R is the radius of the equivalent cylindrical block and r_d is the radius of the sand drain. It can also be shown that:

$$(1 - U) = (1 - U_v)(1 - U_r)$$
(7.40)

where U is the average degree of consolidation under combined vertical and radial drainage.

Example 7.7

An embankment is to be constructed over a layer of clay 10 m thick, with an impermeable lower boundary. Construction of the embankment will increase the total vertical stress in the clay by 65 kN/m². For the clay $c_v = 1.5 \times 10^{-7}$ m²/s, $c_h = 2.5 \times 10^{-7}$ m²/s and $m_v = 2.5 \times 10^{-4}$ m²/kN. The design requirement is that all but 25 mm of the settlement due to consolidation of the clay layer will have taken place after 6 months. Determine the spacing, in a square pattern, of 400 mm diameter sand drains to achieve the above requirement.

Final settlement = $m_v \Delta\sigma' H = 2.5 \times 10^{-4} \times 65 \times 10{,}000$
$= 162$ mm

For $t = 6$ months (183 days), $U = \dfrac{162 - 25}{162} = 0.85$

Diameter of sand drains is 0.4 m, i.e. $r_d = 0.2$ m

Radius of cylindrical block: $R = n r_d = 0.2n$

The layer is half-closed, $\therefore\quad d = 10$ m

$$T_v = \frac{c_v t}{d^2} = \frac{1.5 \times 10^{-7} \times 183 \times 24 \times 60^2}{10^2} = 0.0237$$

From curve (1), Fig. 7.12: $U_v = 0.17$

$$T_r = \frac{c_h t}{4R^2} = \frac{2.5 \times 10^{-7} \times 183 \times 24 \times 60^2}{4 \times 0.2^2 \times n^2} = \frac{24.7}{n^2}$$

i.e. $\quad n = \sqrt{\left(\dfrac{24.7}{T_r}\right)}$

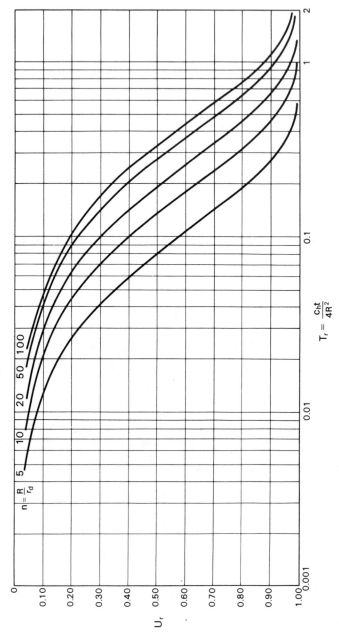

$$T_r = \frac{c_h t}{4R^2}$$

Figure 7.28   Solution for radial consolidation.

Now $(1 - U) = (1 - U_v)(1 - U_r)$

$\therefore \qquad 0 \cdot 15 = 0 \cdot 83 (1 - U_r)$

$\therefore \qquad \qquad U_r = 0 \cdot 82$

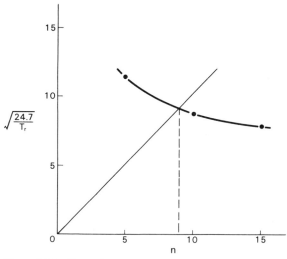

Figure 7.29   Example 7.7.

A trial and error solution is necessary to obtain the value of n. Starting with a value of n corresponding to one of the curves in Fig. 7.28 the value of T_r for $U_r = 0 \cdot 82$ is obtained from that curve. Using this value of T_r the value of $\sqrt{(24 \cdot 7/T_r)}$ is calculated and plotted against the selected value of n.

n	T_r	$\sqrt{(24 \cdot 7/T_r)}$
5	0·20	11·1
10	0·33	8·6
15	0·42	7·7

From Fig. 7.29 it is seen that $n = 9$.

$\therefore \qquad R = 0 \cdot 2 \times 9 = 1 \cdot 8 \text{ m}$

Spacing of drains in a square pattern is given by:

$$S = \frac{R}{0 \cdot 564} = \frac{1 \cdot 8}{0 \cdot 564} = 3 \cdot 2 \text{ m}$$

Problems

7.1   In an oedometer test on a specimen of saturated clay ($G_s = 2 \cdot 72$) the applied pressure was increased from 107 to 214 kN/m^2 and the following compression readings recorded:

Time (min)	0	$\frac{1}{4}$	$\frac{1}{2}$	1	$2\frac{1}{4}$	4	$6\frac{1}{4}$	9	16
Gauge (mm)	7·82	7·42	7·32	7·21	6·99	6·78	6·61	6·49	6·37

Time (min)	25	36	49	64	81	100	300	1440
Gauge (mm)	6·29	6·24	6·21	6·18	6·16	6·15	6·10	6·02

After 1440 minutes the thickness of the specimen was 15·30 mm and the water content 23·2%. Determine the values of the coefficient of consolidation and the compression ratios from (a) the root time plot and (b) the log time plot. Determine also the values of the coefficient of volume change and the coefficient of permeability.

7.2   The following results were obtained from an oedometer test on a specimen of saturated clay:

Pressure (kN/m^2)	27	54	107	214	429	214	107	54
Void ratio		1·243	1·217	1·144	1·068	0·994	1·001	1·012	1·024

A layer of this clay 8 m thick lies below a 4 m depth of sand, the water table being at the surface. The saturated unit weight for both soils is 19 kN/m^3. A 4 m depth of fill of unit weight 21 kN/m^3 is placed on the sand over an extensive area. Determine the final settlement due to consolidation of the clay. If the fill were to be removed some time after the completion of consolidation, what heave would eventually take place due to swelling of the clay?

7.3   In an oedometer test a specimen of saturated clay 19 mm thick reaches 50% consolidation in 20 minutes. How long would it take a layer of this clay 5 m thick to reach the same degree of consolidation under the same stress and drainage conditions? How long would it take the layer to reach 30% consolidation?

7.4   Assuming the fill in Problem 7.2 is dumped very rapidly, what would be the value of pore water pressure at the centre of the clay layer after a period of 3 years? The layer is open and the value of c_v is 7·5 x 10^{-8} m^2/s.

7.5   An open clay layer is 6 m thick, the value of c_v being 3·2 x 10^{-8} m^2/s. The initial distribution of excess pore water pressure varies linearly from 60 kN/m^2 at the top of the layer to zero at the bottom. Using the finite difference approximation of the one-dimensional consolidation equation, plot the isochrone after consolidation has been in progress for a period of 3 years and from the isochrone determine the average degree of consolidation in the layer.

7.6   A 10 m depth of sand overlies an 8 m layer of clay, below which is a further depth of sand. For the clay m_v = 8·3 x 10^{-4} m^2/kN and c_v = 1·4 x 10^{-7} m^2/s. The water table is at surface level but is to be lowered permanently by 4 m, the initial lowering taking place over a period of 40 weeks. Calculate the final settlement due to consolidation of the clay, assuming no change in the weight of the sand, and the settlement 2 years after the start of lowering.

7.7   A foundation 4 m by 3 m carrying a net foundation pressure of 350 kN/m^2 is situated at a depth of 1 m in a layer of sand 6 m thick; the water table is 4 m below the surface. Below the sand is a 6 m layer of clay resting on an impermeable stratum. Determine the final settlement of the centre of the foundation due to consolidation of the clay, using the one-dimensional method and the time for 90% of this settlement to take place. The saturated unit weight for both the sand and the clay is 19 kN/m^3: above the water table the unit weight of the sand is 17 kN/m^3.

The relationship between void ratio and effective stress (kN/m^2) for the clay is given by:

$$e = 0.72 - 0.18 \log \frac{\sigma'}{100}$$

and the coefficient of consolidation is 3.5×10^{-8} m^2/s.

7.8   A net foundation pressure of 165 kN/m^2 is carried on a raft 20 m in diameter, 1·5 m below ground level. The soil profile is as follows:

depth	0–4·5 m	:	sand ($\gamma = 17$ kN/m^3)
	4·5 m	:	water table
	4·5–6·0 m	:	sand ($\gamma_{sat} = 19$ kN/m^3)
	6·0–15·0 m	:	clay ($\gamma_{sat} = 20$ kN/m^3)
	below 15·0 m	:	sand.

The results from an oedometer test on a specimen of the clay are as follows:

Pressure (kN/m^2)	54	107	214	429
Void ratio	0·905	0·862	0·794	0·690

The coefficient of consolidation for the clay is 8.0×10^{-8} m^2/s and the value of the pore pressure coefficient A is 0·75. Calculate the final settlement of the centre of the foundation due to consolidation of the clay using the Skempton–Bjerrum method.

7.9   A half-closed clay layer is 8 m thick and it can be assumed that $c_v = c_h$. Vertical sand drains 300 mm in diameter, spaced at 3 m centres in a square pattern, are to be used to increase the rate of consolidation of the clay under the increased vertical stress due to the construction of an embankment. Without sand drains the degree of consolidation at the time the embankment is due to come into use has been calculated as 25%. What degree of consolidation would be reached with the sand drains at the same time?

7.10   A layer of saturated clay is 10 m thick, the lower boundary being impermeable; an embankment is to be constructed above the clay. Determine the time required for 90% consolidation of the clay layer. If 300 mm diameter sand drains at 4 m centres in a square pattern were installed in the clay, in what time would the same overall degree of consolidation be reached? The coefficients of consolidation in the vertical and horizontal directions respectively are 3.0×10^{-7} m^2/s and 4.4×10^{-7} m^2/s.

References

7.1   Barron, R. A. (1948): 'Consolidation of Fine Grained Soils by Drain Wells', *Transactions ASCE*, Vol. 113.

7.2   British Standard 1377 (1967): *Methods of Testing Soils for Civil Engineering Purposes*, British Standards Institution, London.

7.3   Christie, I. F. (1959): 'Design and Construction of Vertical Drains to Accelerate the Consolidation of Soils', *Civil Engineering and Public Works Review*, Nos. 2, 3, 4.

7.4   Cour, F. R. (1971): 'Inflection Point Method for Computing c_v', Technical Note, *Journal ASCE*, Vol. 97, No. SM5.

7.5   Gibson, R. E. (1963): 'An Analysis of System Flexibility and its Effects on Time Lag in Pore Water Pressure Measurements', *Geotechnique*, Vol. 13, No. 1.

7.6   Gibson, R. E. and Lumb, P. (1953): 'Numerical Solution of Some Problems in the Consolidation of Clay, *Proceedings ICE*, Part I.

7.7   Lambe, T. W. (1964): 'Methods of Estimating Settlement', *Journal ASCE*, Vol. 90, No. SM5.

7.8   Lambe, T. W. (1967): 'Stress Path Method', *Journal ASCE*, Vol. 93, No. SM6.

7.9   Muir Wood, A. M. (1959): Correspondence, *Geotechnique*, Vol. 9, p. 29.

7.10   Naylor, A. H. and Doran, I. G. (1948): 'Precise Determination of Primary Consolidation', *Proceedings 2nd International Conference SMFE, Rotterdam*, Vol. 1.

7.11   Schmertmann, J. H. (1953): 'Estimating the True Consolidation Behaviour of Clay from Laboratory Test Results', *Proceedings ASCE*, Vol. 79.

7.12   Scott, R. F. (1961): 'New Method of Consolidation Coefficient Evaluation', *Journal ASCE*, Vol. 87, No. SM1.

7.13   Skempton, A. W. and Bjerrum, L. (1957): 'A Contribution to the Settlement Analysis of Foundations on Clay', *Geotechnique*, Vol. 7, No. 4.

7.14   Taylor, D. W. (1948): *Fundamentals of Soil Mechanics*, John Wiley and Sons, New York.

7.15   Terzaghi, K. (1943): *Theoretical Soil Mechanics*, John Wiley and Sons, New York.

CHAPTER 8

Bearing Capacity

8.1 Introduction

This chapter is concerned with the bearing capacity of soils on which foundations are supported. A foundation is that part of a structure which transmits loads directly to the underlying soil. If the soil near the surface is capable of adequately supporting the structural loads it is possible to use either *footings* or a *raft*, these being referred to as spread foundations. A footing is a relatively small slab giving separate support to part of the structure. A footing supporting a single column is referred to as an individual footing, one supporting a group of columns as a combined footing and one supporting a load-bearing wall as a strip footing. A raft is a large single slab supporting the structure as a whole. If the soil near the surface is incapable of adequately supporting the structural loads, *piers* or *piles* are used to transmit the loads to suitable soil (or rock) at greater depth, piers being much shorter and having a greater cross-sectional area than piles. Spread foundations should be constructed below the depth which is subject to frost action (around 0·5 m in Great Britain) and the depth to which seasonal swelling and shrinkage of the soil takes place.

A foundation must satisfy two fundamental requirements, (1) the factor of safety with respect to shear failure of the supporting soil must be adequate, a value of three being a common specification, (2) the settlement of the foundation should be tolerable and, in particular, differential settlement should not cause any unacceptable damage. The *allowable* bearing capacity (q_a) is defined as the maximum pressure that may be applied to the soil such that the two fundamental requirements are satisfied. An indirect requirement is that the foundation, and the operations involved in its construction, should have no adverse effect on adjacent structures and services.

For preliminary design purposes CP 2004 [8.5] gives *presumed bearing values* (Table 8.1), being the allowable bearing capacities normally considered appropriate for particular types of soil under vertical static load. The shortcomings of such a table lie in the fact that the classification of the soil types is based on properties that are not the most important from the point of view of bearing capacity.

If the settlement of a structure is uniform, no structural damage should be caused although the result may be inconvenient and services may be damaged. If differential settlement occurs, however, there is a danger of structural damage. The angular distortion between two points under a structure is equal to the differential settlement

Table 8.1   Presumed bearing values (CP 2004: 1972)

Soil type	Bearing value (kN/m^2)	Remarks
Compact gravel or compact sand and gravel	> 600	Width of foundation (B) not less than 1 m. Water table at least B below base of foundation
Medium dense gravel or medium dense sand and gravel	200–600	
Loose gravel or loose sand and gravel	< 200	
Compact sand	> 300	
Medium dense sand	100–300	
Loose sand	< 100	
Very stiff boulder clays and hard clays	300–600	Susceptible to long-term consolidation settlement
Stiff clays	150–300	
Firm clays	75–150	
Soft clays and silts	< 75	
Very soft clays and silts	—	

between the points divided by the distance between them. Angular distortion limits proposed by Bjerrum as a general guide for a number of conditions are given in Table 8.2. For the usual type of framed building with panel walls and for load-bearing walls, a limit of 1/300 is suggested.

Table 8.2   Angular distortion limits

1/150	Structural damage of general buildings expected
1/300	Cracking in panel walls expected.
	Difficulties with overhead cranes
1/500	Limit for buildings in which cracking is not permissible
1/600	Overstressing of structural frames with diagonals
1/750	Difficulties with machinery sensitive to settlement

Results from elastic theory (Fig. 6.6) indicate that the increase in vertical stress in the soil below the centre of a strip footing of width B is approximately 20% of the foundation pressure at a depth of $3B$. In the case of a square foundation the corresponding depth is $1·5B$. For practical purposes these depths can normally be accepted as the limits of the zones of influence of the respective foundations and are called the *significant depths*. It is essential that the soil conditions are known within the significant depth of any foundation.

8.2   Ultimate Bearing Capacity

The least pressure that will cause complete shear failure of the soil in the vicinity of the foundation is defined as the ultimate bearing capacity (q_f). If the pressure on a foundation is steadily increased to the value q_f the soil in the vicinity of the foundation changes from the state of elastic equilibrium to the state of plastic equilibrium. The change starts at the edges of the foundation, gradually spreading downwards then outwards on each side of the foundation. Eventually all the soil between the failure surfaces and ground level reaches the state of plastic equilibrium and complete shear failure takes place with the foundation breaking into the soil.

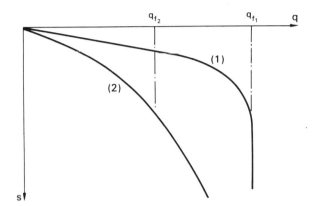

Figure 8.1   General and local shear failure.

If the soil is dense or stiff the strains prior to failure will be relatively small and the pressure–settlement relationship will be of the form of curve (1) in Fig. 8.1. The ultimate bearing capacity is well-defined and failure of this type is referred to as *general* shear failure. If, on the other hand, the soil is loose or soft the strains prior to failure will be relatively large and the pressure–settlement relationship will be of the form of curve (2) in Fig. 8.1. In this case, large settlements, which would be unacceptable in practice, occur before plastic equilibrium is fully developed and failure is taken arbitrarily at a point where the curve becomes relatively steep and straight. Failure of this type is referred to as *local* shear failure.

No rigorous solution for ultimate bearing capacity has been obtained and in practice approximate solutions are used. Initially, the mechanism of failure under a strip footing with a *smooth* base will be considered.

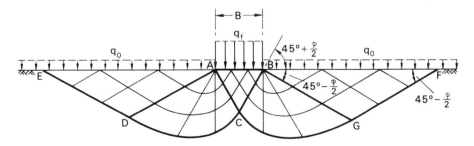

Figure 8.2   Failure under a shallow strip footing with a smooth base.

A strip footing of width B and semi-infinite length carrying a uniform pressure q on the surface of a semi-infinite, homogeneous and isotropic soil is shown in Fig. 8.2. The shear strength parameters for the soil are c and ϕ but the unit weight is assumed to be zero. When the pressure becomes equal to the ultimate bearing capacity q_f the footing is pushed downwards into the soil mass producing a state of plastic equilibrium below the footing. Since the surface AB is smooth the active Rankine state is developed within the wedge ABC, the angles ABC and BAC being $(45° + \phi/2)$. The downward movement of the wedge ABC forces the adjoining soil sideways, producing outward lateral forces on both sides of the wedge. Passive Rankine zones ADE and BGF therefore develop on both sides of the active wedge, the angles DEA and GFB being $(45° - \phi/2)$. The transition between the downward movement of the active wedge and the lateral movement of the passive wedge takes place through zones of radial shear ACD and BCG, the surfaces CD and CG being logarithmic spirals to which the failure planes of the active and passive wedges are tangential. A state of plastic equilibrium thus exists above the surface EDCGF, the remainder of the soil being in a state of elastic equilibrium. For this case the following solution was obtained by Prandtl:

$$q_{fc} = c \cot \phi\{\exp(\pi \tan \phi) \tan^2(45° + \phi/2) - 1\} \tag{8.1}$$

If the shear strength parameter c is zero, the bearing capacity of a weightless soil is zero. A pressure on the strip footing can then be supported only if a surcharge pressure (q_0) exists on the soil surface. The solution in this case is:

$$q_{fq} = q_0\{\exp(\pi \tan \phi) \tan^2(45° + \phi/2)\} \tag{8.2}$$

8.3 Terzaghi's Theory of Bearing Capacity

Terzaghi's theory, although not rigorous, enables the ultimate bearing capacity of a *shallow* strip footing of width B to be determined with sufficient accuracy for use in practice. A shallow footing is defined as one whose depth D below the surface is not greater than the width B. The shear strength of the soil between the surface and depth D is neglected, this soil being considered only as a surcharge imposing a uniform pressure $q_0 = \gamma D$ on the horizontal plane at foundation level. The theory assumes that general shear failure takes place and that the volume of the soil remains unchanged prior to failure.

It is assumed that the base of the footing is *rough* and that friction (and, if appropriate, adhesion) prevents shear displacement of the soil adjoining the base. The active Rankine state, therefore, cannot be developed under the footing. A wedge of soil, ABC in Fig. 8.3, adjoining the base remains in a state of elastic equilibrium and is effectively part of the footing. At failure the soil on either side of the elastic

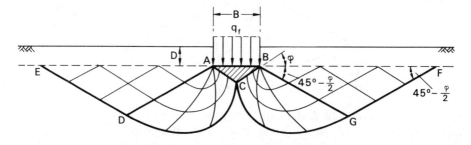

Figure 8.3   Failure under a shallow strip footing with a rough base.

wedge ABC is in a state of plastic equilibrium within a zone of radial shear and a passive Rankine zone.

The lower boundaries AC and BC of the elastic wedge are failure planes. The failure surfaces CDE and CGF are taken to be vertical at C and since the angle of intersection between two sets of failure planes is $(90° + \phi)$, as was shown in Chapter 5, the planes AC and BC are then inclined at angle ϕ to the horizontal.

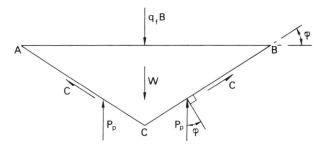

Figure 8.4   Forces on wedge ABC.

The footing cannot break into the soil until the total passive resistance of the soil masses ACDE and BCGF has been overcome. The inclined boundaries AC and BC become the equivalent of a wall surface on which the shear strength parameters c and ϕ replace the wall adhesion and the angle of wall friction, respectively.

Referring to Fig. 8.4, the forces acting on the planes AC and BC are the total passive resistance P_P, acting in the vertical direction (i.e. at angle $\delta = \phi$ to the normal), and the adhesion force C acting along the planes, where:

$$C = \frac{cB}{2 \cos \phi}$$

The weight of the wedge ABC is given by:

$$W = \gamma \frac{B^2}{4} \tan \phi$$

Considering the equilibrium of the wedge ABC:

$$q_f B = 2P_P + 2C \sin \phi - W \tag{8.3}$$

In general the normal component of passive pressure can be expressed by an equation of the form:

$$p_{Pn} = K_{P\gamma} \gamma z + c K_{Pc} + q_0 K_{Pq}$$

The total passive resistance, acting at angle δ to the normal, on a surface of vertical height H inclined at angle α to the horizontal is given by:

$$P_P = \frac{1}{\sin \alpha \cos \delta} \int_0^H p_{Pn} \, dz$$

$$= \frac{1}{\sin \alpha \cos \delta} (\tfrac{1}{2} K_{P\gamma} \gamma H^2 + c K_{Pc} H + q_0 K_{Pq} H)$$

For the surfaces AC and BC, $H = (B/2) \tan \phi$, $\alpha = (180° - \phi)$ and $\delta = \phi$, therefore:

$$P_P = \frac{1}{2 \cos^2 \phi} (\tfrac{1}{4} K_{P\gamma} \gamma B^2 \tan \phi + c K_{Pc} B + q_0 K_{Pq} B)$$

Hence from equation 8.3:

$$q_f = \tfrac{1}{2} \gamma B \left\{ \tfrac{1}{2} \tan \phi \left(\frac{K_{P\gamma}}{\cos^2 \phi} - 1 \right) \right\} + c \left(\frac{K_{Pc}}{\cos^2 \phi} + \tan \phi \right) + q_0 \left(\frac{K_{Pq}}{\cos^2 \phi} \right) \qquad (8.4)$$

Equation 8.4 shows that the ultimate bearing capacity is influenced by the width of the footing, the unit weight of the soil, the shear strength of the soil, represented by parameters c and ϕ, and the surcharge pressure $q_0 = \gamma D$. Since the terms in brackets are functions of ϕ only, the ultimate bearing capacity can be written in the form:

$$q_f = \tfrac{1}{2} \gamma B N_\gamma + c N_c + \gamma D N_q \qquad (8.5)$$

where N_γ, N_c and N_q are dimensionless bearing capacity factors depending only on the value of ϕ. The ultimate bearing capacity can be evaluated in terms of either total stress or effective stress.

Terzaghi considered that the bearing capacity was due to contributions from the following sources:

(1) the weight of the soil, with zero surcharge pressure;

(2) the constant component of shear strength (represented by the parameter c), assuming the soil has zero unit weight and zero surcharge pressure;

(3) the surcharge pressure acting on the surface of the soil, assuming the soil has zero unit weight.

It should be realised that different failure surfaces are involved in the determination of the contribution from source (1) and those from sources (2) and (3). Superposition of the contributions from the above sources gives a conservative approximation to the bearing capacity in a form which is very convenient for use in practice.

For any value of ϕ the passive pressure coefficient $K_{P\gamma}$ can be determined by means of the ϕ-circle or logarithmic spiral methods referred to in Chapter 5: the corresponding bearing capacity factor N_γ can then be evaluated. Terzaghi derived the following expressions for the factors N_q and N_c by extending the simplified solution due to Prandtl:

$$N_q = \frac{\exp\{(3\pi/2 - \phi) \tan \phi\}}{2 \cos^2 (45° + \phi/2)} \qquad (8.6)$$

$$N_c = \cot \phi \, (N_q - 1) \qquad (8.7)$$

Values of Terzaghi's bearing capacity factors are given in terms of ϕ in Fig. 8.5. When $\phi = 0$ the values are $N_\gamma = 0$, $N_c = 5 \cdot 7$ and $N_q = 1$. It should be noted that the plane strain value of ϕ is appropriate in the case of a strip footing.

Alternative values of the bearing capacity factors have been given by Meyerhof [8.10] and are represented by the dotted lines in Fig. 8.6. Meyerhof varied the value of the angles ABC and BAC (Fig. 8.3) between ϕ and $(45° + \phi/2)$ in order to obtain a minimum value of N_γ. The values of N_c and N_q are determined from equations 8.1 and 8.2, respectively.

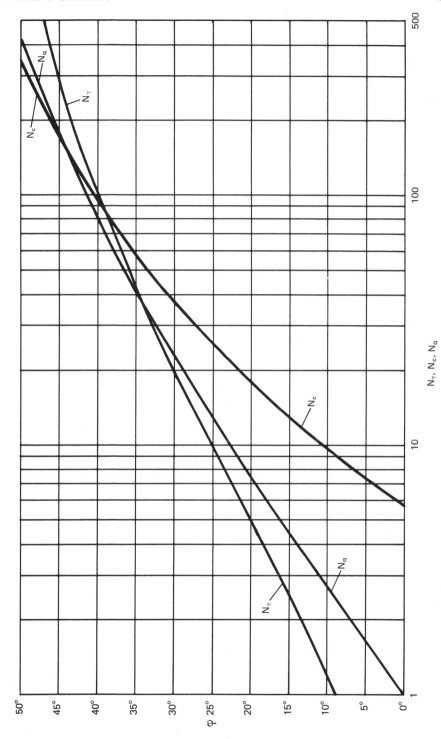

Figure 8.5   Bearing capacity factors for shallow footings.

Terzaghi proposed empirical adjustments to the shear strength parameters to cover the case of local shear failure. The parameters c_l and ϕ_l should be used for local shear, the bearing capacity factors being those corresponding to ϕ_l, where

$$c_l = \tfrac{2}{3}c \tag{8.8}$$

and

$$\phi_l = \tan^{-1}(\tfrac{2}{3}\tan\phi) \tag{8.9}$$

Terzaghi also proposed shape factors for the extension of the two-dimensional theory for strip footings to the three-dimensional cases of square and circular footings. For a square footing of dimension B, the ultimate bearing capacity is given by:

$$q_f = 0\cdot4\gamma B N_\gamma + 1\cdot3cN_c + \gamma D N_q \tag{8.10}$$

and for a circular footing of diameter B:

$$q_f = 0\cdot3\gamma B N_\gamma + 1\cdot3cN_c + \gamma D N_q \tag{8.11}$$

For rectangular footings (dimensions $B \times L$) linear interpolation between the values for strip footings ($B/L = 0$) and square footings ($B/L = 1$) may be used.

The actual pressure on the soil due to the weight of the structure is called the *total* foundation pressure (q). The *net* foundation pressure (q_n) is the increase in pressure at foundation level, being the total foundation pressure less the weight of soil per unit area permanently removed, i.e.;

$$q_n = q - \gamma D \tag{8.12}$$

The factor of safety (F) with respect to shear failure is defined in terms of the net ultimate bearing capacity (q_{nf}), i.e.:

$$F = \frac{q_{nf}}{q_n} = \frac{q_f - \gamma D}{q - \gamma D} \tag{8.13}$$

Eccentric and Inclined Loading

Footings may be subjected to eccentric and inclined loading and such conditions lead to a reduction in bearing capacity. If e is the eccentricity of the resultant load on the base of a footing of width B, it was suggested by Meyerhof that an effective foundation width B' be used in equation 8.5, where:

$$B' = B - 2e \tag{8.14}$$

The resultant load is assumed to be uniformly distributed over the effective width B'.

The effect of inclined loading on bearing capacity can be taken into account by means of inclination factors proposed by Meyerhof. If the angle of inclination of the resultant load is α to the vertical then the bearing capacity factors N_γ, N_c and N_q should be multiplied respectively by the following factors:

$$i_\gamma = (1 - \alpha/\phi)^2 \tag{8.15a}$$

$$i_c = i_q = (1 - \alpha/90°)^2 \tag{8.15b}$$

8.4 Meyerhof's Theory

Meyerhof [8.9] developed a general theory of bearing capacity for a strip footing at any depth. The assumed failure mechanism is similar to that in Terzaghi's theory but the failure surfaces are extended above foundation level so that the shear strength of the soil above this level is taken into account. The assumed failure surfaces for shallow and deep footings are shown in Fig. 8.6, the curves CD and CG being logarithmic spirals in each case. The central zone ABC again acts as part of the footing if the base is assumed to be rough. Adjoining zone ABC are zones of radial shear ACD and BCG extending above foundation level. In zones ADEH and BGFJ the soil varies between the states of radial and plane shear.

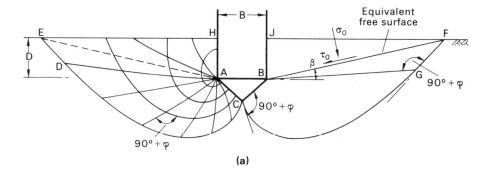

(a)

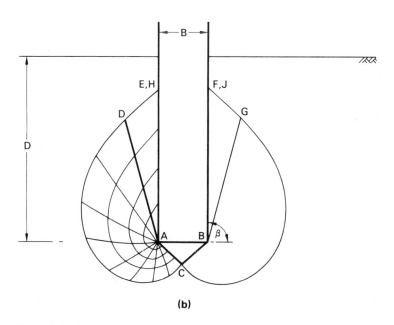

(b)

Figure 8.6   Failure mechanisms in Meyerhof's general theory.

The planes AE and BF are referred to as the 'equivalent free surfaces', inclined at angle β to the horizontal. The angle β is related to the depth/breadth ratio of the footing. The ultimate bearing capacity is given by the equation:

$$q_f = \tfrac{1}{2}\gamma BN_\gamma + cN_c + \sigma_0 N_q \tag{8.16}$$

where σ_0 is the average normal stress on the equivalent free surface. Shape factors can be applied in the cases of square and circular footings. The bearing capacity factors depend principally on the shear strength parameter ϕ and the angle β. Due to the dependence on β and the necessity of determining the stress σ_0, the theory is inconvenient for use in practice.

Meyerhof presented the following simplified solutions for the ultimate bearing capacity of a strip footing.

When the shear strength parameter ϕ is zero:

$$q_f = cN_{cq} + \gamma D \tag{8.17}$$

where N_{cq} is a resultant bearing capacity factor depending on the depth/breadth ratio of the footing and on the adhesion on the sides of the footing. For a depth/breadth ratio of 2, N_{cq} reaches a maximum value of 8·3 when the adhesion is zero and a maximum value of 8·8 when the adhesion is equal to the shear strength parameter c.

When the shear strength parameter c is zero:

$$q_f = \tfrac{1}{2}\gamma BN_{\gamma q} \tag{8.18}$$

where $N_{\gamma q}$ is a resultant bearing capacity factor depending on the shear strength parameter ϕ, the lateral pressure coefficient on the sides of the footing and the angle of friction between the soil and the sides of the footing.

Skempton's Values of N_c

In a review of bearing capacity theory, Skempton [8.13] concluded that in the case of saturated clays under undrained conditions ($\phi_u = 0$) the ultimate bearing capacity of a footing could be expressed by the equation:

$$q_f = c_u N_c + \gamma D \tag{8.19}$$

the factor N_c being a function of the shape of the footing and the depth/breadth ratio. Skempton's values of N_c are given in Fig. 8.7. The factor for a rectangular footing of dimensions $B \times L$ (where $B < L$) is the value for a square footing multiplied by:

$$(0·84 + 0·16\, B/L)$$

Example 8.1

A footing 2·25 m square is located at a depth of 1·5 m in a sand, the shear strength parameters being $c' = 0$ and $\phi' = 38°$. Determine the ultimate bearing capacity (a) if the water table is well below foundation level, (b) if the water table is at the surface. The unit weight of the sand above the water table is 18 kN/m^3: the saturated unit weight is 20 kN/m^3.

For a square footing the ultimate bearing capacity (with $c = 0$) is given by:

$$q_f = 0·4\gamma BN_\gamma + \gamma DN_q$$

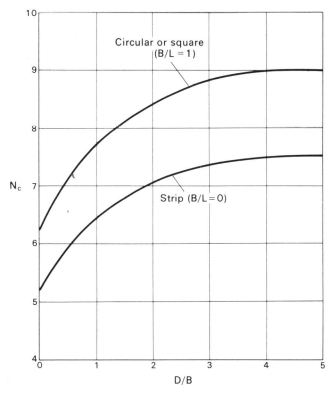

Figure 8.7 Skempton's values of N_c for $\phi_u = 0$.

For $\phi = 38°$ the bearing capacity factors are $N_\gamma = 75$ and $N_q = 60$.

$$\therefore \qquad q_f = (0\cdot4 \times 18 \times 2\cdot25 \times 75) + (18 \times 1\cdot5 \times 60)$$
$$= 1215 + 1620$$
$$= 2835 \text{ kN/m}^2$$

When the water table is at the surface, the ultimate bearing capacity is given by:

$$q_f = 0\cdot4\gamma'BN_\gamma + \gamma'DN_q$$
$$= (0\cdot4 \times 10\cdot2 \times 2\cdot25 \times 75) + (10\cdot2 \times 1\cdot5 \times 60)$$
$$= 688 + 918$$
$$= 1606 \text{ kN/m}^2$$

Example 8.2

A strip footing is to be designed to carry a load of 800 kN/m at a depth of 1 m in a firm soil of unit weight 18 kN/m³. The appropriate shear strength parameters are $c_u = 15$ kN/m² and $\phi_u = 30°$. Determine the width of the footing if a factor of safety against shear failure of 3 is specified.

The values of Terzaghi's bearing capacity factors are obtained from Fig. 8.5. For $\phi = 30°$:

$$N_\gamma = 20; \quad N_c = 37; \quad N_q = 22$$

The ultimate bearing capacity (units kN/m^2) is given by:

$$\begin{aligned} q_f &= 0 \cdot 5\gamma B N_\gamma + cN_c + \gamma D N_q \\ &= (0 \cdot 5 \times 18 \times B \times 20) + (15 \times 37) + (18 \times 1 \times 22) \\ &= 180B + 951 \end{aligned}$$

$\therefore \qquad q_{nf} = q_f - \gamma D = 180B + 933$

The net foundation pressure is:

$$q_n = \frac{800}{B} - 18$$

Then for a factor of safety of 3:

$$\tfrac{1}{3}(180B + 933) = \frac{800}{B} - 18$$

Hence,

$$B = 1 \cdot 83 \text{ m}$$

Example 8.3

A footing 2 m square is located at a depth of 4 m in a stiff clay of saturated unit weight 21 kN/m^3. The undrained strength of the clay at a depth of 4 m is given by the parameters $c_u = 120$ kN/m^2 and $\phi_u = 0$. For a factor of safety of 3 with respect to shear failure, what load could be carried by the footing?

In this case $D/B = 2$ and from Fig. 8.7 the value of N_c for a square footing is 8·4. The ultimate bearing capacity is given by:

$$q_f = c_u N_c + \gamma D$$

$\therefore \qquad q_{nf} = c_u N_c = 120 \times 8 \cdot 4 = 1008 \text{ } kN/m^2$

For $F = 3$, $q_n = 1008/3 = 336$ kN/m^2

$\therefore \qquad \begin{aligned} q &= q_n + \gamma D \\ &= 336 + (21 \times 4) \\ &= 420 \text{ } kN/m^2 \end{aligned}$

Allowable load = $420 \times 2^2 = 1680$ kN

8.5 Allowable Bearing Capacity of Sands

The allowable bearing capacity of a sand depends mainly on the relative density, the position of the water table relative to foundation level, the lateral confining pressure and the size of the foundation. Of secondary importance are particle shape and size distribution. Most sands are non-homogeneous and the allowable bearing capacity is usually limited by settlement considerations except in the case of very narrow foundations. Settlement in a sand is rapid and occurs almost entirely during construction.

The relative density has a dominating influence on the value of the shear strength parameter ϕ' and on the form of the pressure–settlement curve. Disturbance of the natural condition of the sand during construction may result in a change in relative density. The water table position affects both the ultimate bearing capacity and the settlement. If the sand within the significant depth is fully saturated the effective unit weight is roughly halved, resulting in a lower bearing capacity, and a reduction in lateral confining pressure with a corresponding increase in settlement. Loss of lateral confining pressure due to any other cause, for example adjacent excavation, will also result in increased settlement. The size of the foundation governs the significant depth. If the sand is very loose, vibration or shock may result in volume decrease, causing appreciable settlement. Very loose sand should be compacted or piles should be used.

Differential settlement between a number of footings is governed mainly by the variations in homogeneity of the sand within the significant depth and to a lesser extent by variations in foundation pressure. According to Terzaghi and Peck [8.17], settlement records indicate that the differential settlement of footings of approximately equal size carrying the same pressure is unlikely to exceed 50% of the maximum settlement. If the footings are of different sizes the differential settlement will be greater. The maximum settlement of footings carrying the same pressure increases with increasing footing size. There is no appreciable difference between the settlement of square and strip footings of the same width. For a given footing size and pressure the settlement decreases slightly with increasing footing depth because of the higher lateral confining pressure. Even under extreme variations of footing size and depth it is unlikely that differential settlement will be greater than 75% of the maximum settlement.

A reasonable design criterion for footings is an allowable maximum settlement of 25 mm, i.e. the largest footing should not settle by more than 25 mm even if it were situated on the most compressible pocket of sand. The differential settlement between any two footings is then unlikely to exceed 18 mm. Differential settlement may be decreased by reducing the size of the smallest footings as long as the factor of safety with respect to shear strength remains at least 3.

The settlement distribution of a raft is different from that for a series of footings. The settlement of footings is governed by the soil characteristics relatively near the surface and any one footing may be influenced by a weak pocket of soil. The settlement of a raft, on the other hand, is governed by the properties of the soil over a much greater depth. Weak pockets of soil may occur at random within this depth and their influence tends to be compensating or they are bridged over. A raft carrying a uniform pressure on sand will settle fairly uniformly if situated at a depth of at least 2·5 m below ground level, this depth usually being sufficient to prevent significant lateral yield in the sand. The differential settlement of a raft as a percentage of the maximum settlement is roughly half the corresponding percentage for a footing. Thus for a differential settlement of 18 mm, the same as for a number of footings, the criterion for the maximum settlement of a raft is 50 mm.

In practice the relative density of a sand is normally estimated indirectly by means of empirical correlations based on the results of in-situ bearing tests or penetration tests. This approach is considered more reliable than the use of presumed bearing values. The approach has also been applied liberally to medium or dense non-plastic silts.

The Plate Bearing Test

The sand is loaded through a steel plate at least 300 mm square. Readings of load and settlement are observed up to failure or to at least 1·5 times the estimated allowable bearing capacity. The load increments should be approximately one-tenth of the estimated allowable bearing capacity. The test plate should be located at foundation level in a pit at least 1·5 m square. The test is reliable only if the sand is reasonably uniform over the significant depth of the full-scale footing. Minor local weaknesses near the surface may influence the results of the test while having an insignificant effect on the full-scale foundation. On the other hand, a weak stratum below the significant depth of the test plate but within the significant depth of the foundation, as shown in Fig. 8.8, would have no influence on the test results: the weak stratum, however, would have a significant effect on the performance of the foundation.

Settlement increases as the size of the foundation increases and Terzaghi and Peck proposed the following empirical relationship for settlement within the linear part of the pressure–settlement curve:

$$s_B = s_b \left(\frac{2B}{B + b} \right)^2 \tag{8.20}$$

where

s_b = settlement of test plate of dimension b,

s_B = settlement of footing of width B.

Bjerrum and Eggestad [8.3], however, in a review of published settlement measurements, presented a plot of settlement ratio s_B/s_b against width ratio B/b which showed that there can be a considerable scatter of points about the curve representing equation 8.20.

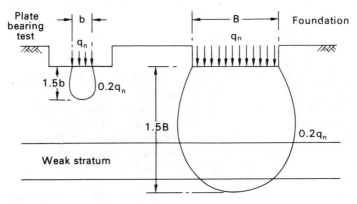

Figure 8.8   Influence of weak stratum.

The Standard Penetration Test

A split barrel sampler (Fig. 8.9a), 50·8 mm in diameter, is driven into the sand at the bottom of a borehole by means of a 63·5 kg mass falling freely through a distance of 760 mm. After an initial drive of 150 mm, the number of blows required to drive the sampler through a depth of 305 mm is determined. This number is called the *standard penetration resistance* (*N*) and has been correlated empirically with the relative density of the sand. Tests should be carried out at intervals of 760 mm within the significant depth. Full details of the test are given in BS 1377 [8.2]. The average *N* value for each borehole is determined and the lowest average should be used

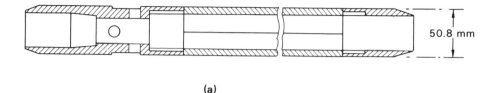

(a)

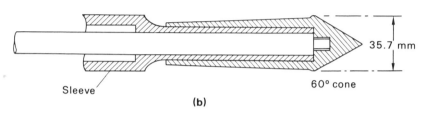

(b)

Figure 8.9   (a) Split-barrel sampler, (b) Dutch cone.

in design. For fine sands and non-plastic silts below the water table the measured *N* value, if greater than 15, is reduced to N', where:

$$N' = 15 + \tfrac{1}{2}(N - 15) \tag{8.21}$$

Terzaghi and Peck presented curves showing the relationship between standard penetration resistance and the bearing pressure limiting maximum settlement to 25 mm and differential settlement to 18 mm. The curves, shown in Fig. 8.10, are based on the assumption that the position of the water table is not less than 2*B* below the footing, where *B* is the least footing dimension. If the sand at foundation level is saturated the pressures obtained from Fig. 8.10 should be halved in the case of shallow footings and reduced by one-third if the depth/breadth ratio is greater than unity. For intermediate positions of the water table the appropriate pressure may be obtained by interpolation.

An approximate correlation between standard penetration resistance and the shear strength parameter ϕ', proposed by Peck, Hanson and Thornburn [8.12] is given in Fig. 8.11.

An important factor ignored by Terzaghi and Peck is the influence of lateral confining pressure on the standard penetration resistance. At constant relative density the standard penetration resistance increases with increasing confining pressure. Confining pressure is a function of the effective overburden pressure. Gibbs and Holtz [8.7] showed how standard penetration resistance is related to relative density and effective overburden pressure and their results are shown in Fig. 8.12. The Terzaghi and Peck relationship between standard penetration resistance and relative density is also represented in Fig. 8.12. Relative density is also influenced to a limited extent by particle shape and size distribution but these factors are not taken into account in the above relationships.

Measured values of standard penetration resistance near the surface result in very conservative values of allowable bearing capacity. If the standard penetration resistance is adjusted in terms of effective overburden pressure, more realistic values of bearing capacity are obtained. If, for example, the measured N value is 10 at a

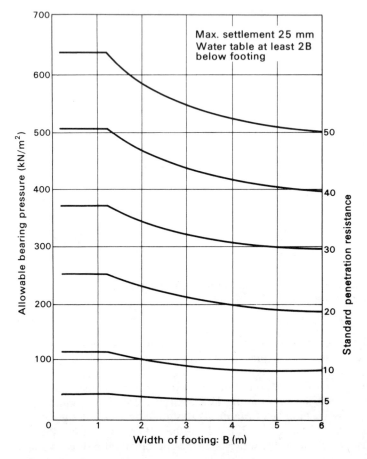

Figure 8.10   Relationship between standard penetration resistance and allowable bearing pressure (Terzaghi and Peck [8.17]).

depth at which the effective overburden pressure is 50 kN/m², the method of obtaining the corrected N value from Fig. 8.12 is shown by the dotted line. From the value $N = 10$ on the vertical axis a horizontal line is drawn to intersect the curve for an effective overburden pressure of 50 kN/m². From this point of intersection a vertical line is drawn to intersect the Terzaghi and Peck curve and from this point a second horizontal line is drawn to meet the vertical axis at a corrected N value of 30.

The Dutch Cone Test

The Dutch cone (Fig. 8.10b) is a penetrometer having an apex angle of 60° and an end area of 1000 mm² (35·7 mm diameter). The cone is attached to rods running

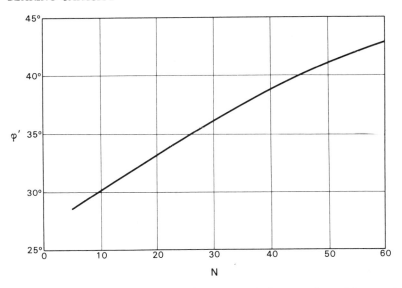

Figure 8.11   Approximate correlation between standard penetration resistance and shear strength parameter ϕ' (Peck, Hanson and Thornburn [8.12]).

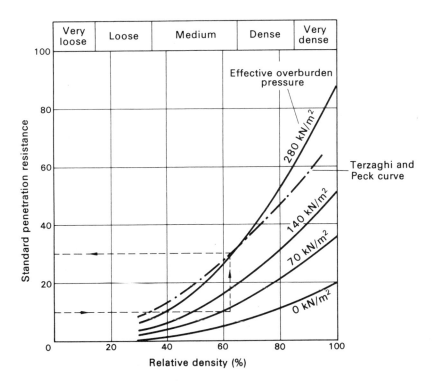

Figure 8.12   Relationship between standard penetration resistance and effective overburden pressure (Gibbs and Holtz [8.7]).

inside a sleeve. The cone and sleeve can be pushed independently into the sand by means of a hydraulic jack, no boring being required. The cone is pushed a distance of 500 mm into the sand at a rate of 10 mm/s and the load measured by use of a pressure gauge. The load divided by the end area is termed the *cone penetration resistance* (C_r).

A compressibility constant C can be obtained by means of an empirical relationship proposed by Buisman:

$$C = 1 \cdot 5 \frac{C_r}{\sigma_0'}$$

(8.22)

where σ_0' is the effective overburden pressure at the point of measurement. Settlement can then be estimated from the equation:

$$s = \frac{H}{C} \ln \frac{\sigma_0' + \Delta\sigma}{\sigma_0'}$$

(8.23)

where s is the settlement of a layer of thickness H and $\Delta\sigma$ is the increment of vertical stress at the centre of the layer.

8.6   Allowable Bearing Capacity of Clays

The allowable bearing capacity of a clay may be limited either by the requirement of an adequate factor of safety with respect to shear strength or by settlement considerations. Shear strength, and hence the factor of safety, will increase whenever consolidation takes place. The factor of safety should therefore be checked for the condition immediately after construction, using the undrained shear strength parameters. The methods of estimating the immediate settlement under undrained conditions and the long-term consolidation settlement are detailed in Chapters 6 and 7 respectively.

The settlement of foundations on overconsolidated clays depends on the overconsolidation ratio, the higher the ratio the lower the settlement for a given foundation. If possible the bearing capacity should be limited so that the preconsolidation pressure is not exceeded. In the case of footings, differential settlement may be reduced by increasing the size of the largest footings above that required by the allowable bearing capacity. Foundations are not usually constructed on normally-consolidated clays because the resulting consolidation settlement would almost certainly be excessive.

Medium and dense plastic silts can be dealt with in roughly the same way as clays. Loose silts should not be used to support foundations.

If a stratum of soft clay lies below a firm stratum in which footings are located, there is a possibility that the footings may break through into the soft stratum. Such a possibility can be avoided if the vertical stresses at the top level of the clay are less than the allowable bearing capacity of the clay by an adequate factor.

8.7   Bearing Capacity of Piles

Piles may be divided into two main categories according to their method of installation. The first category consists of driven piles of steel or precast concrete and piles formed by driving tubes or shells (fitted with a driving shoe) which are filled with concrete after driving. Also included in this category are piles formed by placing concrete as the driven tube is withdrawn. The installation of any type of driven pile causes displacement and disturbance of the soil around the pile. The second category consists of piles which are installed without soil displacement. Soil is removed by boring or drilling to form a shaft, concrete then being cast in the shaft to form the pile. The shaft may be lined or unlined, depending on the type of soil. In clays the shaft may be enlarged at its base by a process known as under-reaming: the resultant pile consequently has a larger base area in contact with the soil.

Pile Driving Formulae

A number of formulae have been proposed in which the dynamics of the pile driving operation is considered in a very idealistic way and the dynamic resistance to driving is assumed to be equal to the static bearing capacity of the pile, an assumption for which there is no theoretical justification.

Upon striking the pile, the kinetic energy of the driving hammer is assumed to be:

$$Wh - \text{(energy losses)}$$

where W is the weight of the hammer and h is the equivalent free fall. The energy losses may be due to friction, heat, hammer rebound, vibration and elastic compression of the pile, the packing assembly and the soil. The net kinetic energy is equated to the work done by the pile in penetrating the soil. The work done is Rs where R is the average resistance of the soil to penetration and s is the set or penetration of the pile per blow. The smaller the set the greater the resistance to penetration.

The *Engineering News* formula takes into account the energy loss due to temporary compression (c_p) resulting from elastic compression of the pile. Thus:

$$R(s + c_p/2) = Wh \tag{8.24}$$

from which R can be determined. In practice, empirical values are given to the term $c_p/2$ (e.g. for drop hammers $c_p/2 = 25$ mm).

The Hiley formula takes into account the energy losses due to elastic compression of the pile, the soil and the packing assembly on top of the pile, all represented by a term c, and the energy losses due to impact, represented by an efficiency factor η. Thus:

$$R(s + c/2) = \eta Wh \tag{8.25}$$

The elastic compression of the pile and the soil can be obtained from the driving trace of the pile (Fig. 8.13). The compression of the packing assembly must be estimated separately by assuming a value of the stress in the assembly during driving.

Driving formulae should be used only for piles in sands and gravels and if possible should be calibrated against the results of load tests.

Bearing Capacity from Soil Properties

The bearing capacity of a pile (or a pier) is equal to the sum of the base or end resistance and the shaft resistance. The base resistance is the product of the cross-sectional area (A) and the ultimate bearing capacity (q_f) at base level: the value of q_f is estimated from bearing capacity theory. The shaft resistance is the product of the perimeter area of the shaft (A_s) and the ultimate shearing resistance (f_s), referred to as the 'skin friction', between the pile and the soil. The weight of soil removed or displaced is assumed to be equal to the weight of the pile. Thus the ultimate load (Q_f) that can be applied to the pile is given by the equation:

$$Q_f = A q_f + A_s f_s \tag{8.26}$$

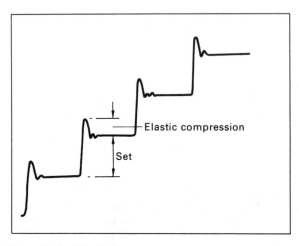

Figure 8.13   Pile driving trace.

The bearing capacity of piles driven in *sands* depends mainly on the relative density of the sand. During driving the relative density adjoining the pile is increased (unless in the case of dense sands) as the result of compaction due to soil displacement and vibration. The bearing capacity is thus higher than that corresponding to the relative density of the undisturbed soil.

Current test data has shown that Meyerhof's theory overestimates the bearing capacity of deep foundations but that a theory developed by Berezantzev, Khristoforov and Golubkov [8.1] gives reasonable results. In this theory, failure is assumed to have taken place when the failure surfaces reach the level of the base as shown in Fig. 8.14. The surcharge pressure at base level consists of the pressure due to the weight of an annulus of soil surrounding the pile, reduced by the frictional force on the outer surface of the annulus. The ultimate bearing capacity can be expressed in the form:

$$q_f = \gamma' B N_\gamma + \gamma' L N_q \tag{8.27}$$

where B is the lateral dimension of the pile and L is the length. The factors N_γ and N_q are of the same order of magnitude and since B is small compared to L the first term in equation 8.27 can be neglected. Then:

$$q_f = \gamma' L N_q \tag{8.28}$$

The factor N_q depends on the shear strength parameter ϕ' and the ratio L/B. For a given value of ϕ' the value of N_q decreases with increasing L/B ratio. Values of N_q for an L/B ratio of 25 are given in Table 8.3. Extrapolated values for an L/B ratio of 50 are shown in brackets.

The lateral effective stress at any depth z can be written as:

$$\sigma'_x = K \gamma' z$$

where K is the appropriate lateral pressure coefficient, depending on the lateral dimension of the pile and the relative density of the sand. Therefore the average skin friction on a pile of length L can be expressed theoretically as:

$$f_s = \tfrac{1}{2} K \gamma' L \tan \delta \qquad\qquad (8.29)$$

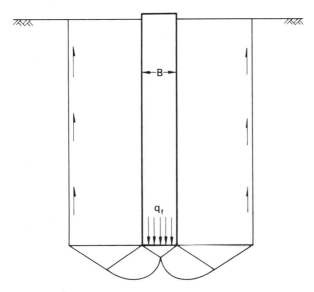

Figure 8.14   Failure mechanism in theory of Berezantzev, Khristoforov, and Golubkov.

where δ is the angle of friction between the pile and the soil. For concrete piles driven in sand, suggested values of K are 1·0 and 2·0 for loose and dense sands respectively. These values should be halved for steel H piles. Suggested values of δ are $0·75\phi'$ for concrete piles and $20°$ for steel piles.

The relevant shear strength for the determination of the base resistance of a pile in *clay* is the undrained strength at base level. The ultimate bearing capacity is expressed as:

$$q_f = c_u N_c \qquad\qquad (8.30)$$

Table 8.3   Berezantzev, Khristoforov and Golubkov theory.
Relationship between ϕ' and N_q

ϕ'	28°	30°	32°	34°	36°	38°	40°
N_q	12	17	25	40	58	89	137
	(9)	(14)	(22)	(37)	(56)	(88)	(136)

Based on theoretical and experimental studies, the value of N_c can be taken as 9 (Skempton's value) for design purposes.

The skin friction can be related empirically to the average undrained strength $(\bar{c}_u)$ of the undisturbed clay between the top and bottom of the pile, i.e.:

$$f_s = \alpha \bar{c}_u \qquad\qquad (8.31)$$

where α is a coefficient depending on the type of clay, the method of installation and the pile material.

In the case of piles driven entirely in the clay the shear strength adjoining the pile, and hence the skin friction, is reduced to the remoulded value. If the clay is non-fissured there is also a significant increase in pore water pressure in the vicinity of the pile. As drainage takes place the shear strength gradually increases from the remoulded value, with a corresponding increase in skin friction, a phenomenon known as 'take up'. Most of this increase takes place within a few months, therefore the value of skin friction after 'take up' is normally used in design. The appropriate value of the coefficient α is estimated from the results of load tests. Driving a pile in clay also results in heave around the pile, the clay being displaced upwards as well as laterally, and this can cause a reduction in the bearing capacity of adjacent piles.

In the case of bored piles there is an increase in the water content of the clay adjoining the shaft, mainly due to stress release and as a result of the clay being in contact with the wet concrete. This softening of the clay causes a reduction in shear strength and in the value of skin friction when the pile has been installed. If the clay is fissured the strength of a small laboratory specimen will be greater than the in-situ strength because it will be relatively less fissured than the mass of soil in the vicinity of the pile base and a reduction factor should be applied to the laboratory strength.

Negative skin friction can occur on the perimeter of a pile driven through a layer of clay undergoing consolidation (for example, due to a fill recently placed on top of the clay) into a firm stratum (Fig. 8.15). The consolidating clay exerts a downward drag on the pile and the direction of skin friction in this layer is reversed. The force due to this downward or negative skin friction is thus carried by the pile instead of helping to support the pile load.

Penetration Tests

In the case of piles in sands an approximate value of the shear strength parameter ϕ' (necessary for use with equations 8.28 and 8.29) can be obtained from the results of standard penetration tests, using the correlation given in Fig. 8.11. Another approach is to use correlations, published by Meyerhof [8.11], between the results of load tests on piles and standard penetration tests. These correlations show that the end bearing capacity of a pile in sand should not be less than:

$$q_f = 250N \text{ (kN/m}^2) \tag{8.32}$$

where N is the lowest value of standard penetration resistance at or just below base level. Meyerhof also suggested that the average value of skin friction can be estimated from the relationship:

$$f_s = 2\overline{N} \text{(kN/m}^2) \tag{8.33}$$

where $\overline{N}$ is the average value of standard penetration resistance between the top and bottom of the pile.

The Dutch cone test can also be used, the cone and tube resistances being determined separately. The end bearing capacity of a pile in sand is given approximately by the product of the cross-sectional area of the pile and the cone penetration resistance at base level. The direct application of cone penetration resistance ignores

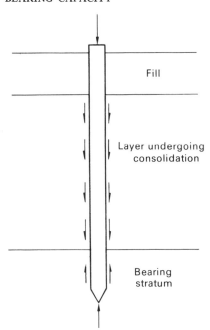

Figure 8.15   Negative skin friction.

the scale effect between the penetrometer and the pile but De Beer [8.6] proposed a design method which allows for the scale effect. The skin friction on the penetrometer tube will be lower than that on the pile because different volumes of soil will be displaced in the two cases. The penetrometer skin friction should be scaled up by the ratio of the pile to the tube circumferences.

Load Tests

The loading of a test pile enables the ultimate bearing capacity to be determined directly and provides a means of assessing the accuracy of calculated values of bearing capacity. Tests may also be carried out in which loading is stopped when the proposed working load has been exceeded by an adequate amount. The results from a test on a particular pile will not necessarily reflect the performance of other piles on the same site and an adequate number of tests are required, depending on the extent of the site investigation.

Two test procedures are detailed in CP 2004 [8.5]. In the *maintained load test* the load/settlement relationship for the test pile is obtained by loading in suitable increments, allowing sufficient time between increments for settlement to be substantially complete. The ultimate bearing capacity is normally taken as the load corresponding to a specified settlement (e.g. 10% of the pile diameter). In the *constant rate of penetration* (*CRP*) test the pile is made to penetrate the soil at a constant rate, the load applied in order to maintain this rate being continuously measured. The test is continued until shear failure of the soil takes place, at which stage the ultimate bearing capacity of the pile has been reached. The settlement under a maintained load cannot be estimated from the results of a CRP test.

Pile Groups

Piled foundations usually consist of a group of piles fairly close together and in general the bearing capacity of the group is not equal to the sum of the bearing capacities of the individual piles designed singly. For piles in clay the group bearing capacity is less than the sum of the single pile bearing capacities because the clay adjoining any particular pile is further disturbed by the installation of adjacent piles, to an extent

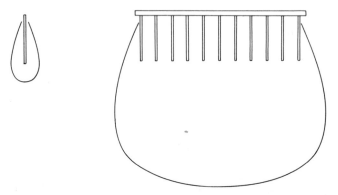

Figure 8.16   Bulbs of pressure for a single pile and a pile group.

depending on the pile spacing. A closely-spaced group of piles in clay may fail as a unit on the perimeter of the group. Tests by Whitaker [8.18] on model piles showed that for groups comprising a given number of piles of a given length there was a critical spacing at which the method of failure changed. For spacings above the critical value, failure occurred below individual piles; for spacings below the critical value the group failed as a unit. The bearing capacity of a pile group which fails as a unit is given by equation 8.26 with A equal to the base area of the group and A_s equal to the perimeter area of the group.

In the case of loose to medium sands the driving of a group of piles causes compaction of the sand between the piles, with an increase in the value of ϕ'. As a result the group bearing capacity is greater than the sum of the single pile capacities. Pile driving in dense sands, on the other hand, results in a loosening of the sand with a reduction in the value of ϕ'.

The bulbs of pressure of a single pile and a closely-spaced group of piles of the same length are of the form illustrated in Fig. 8.16. The settlement of a pile group is thus influenced by the soil to an appreciable depth below the base level of the piles and is always greater than the corresponding settlement of a single pile.

Whitaker [8.19] suggests that a rough estimate of the consolidation settlement of a pile group in clay can be obtained by assuming that the total load is carried by an 'equivalent raft', of the same area as the group, located at a level $L/3$ above the pile bases (where L is the length of the piles), the load spreading outwards from the edges of the raft at an angle of 30° to the vertical.

The settlement of a pile group in sand can be estimated from the standard penetration resistance or the cone penetration resistance of the sand below base level. The total load is assumed to be carried on an equivalent raft, of the same area as the group, at base level. If the sand overlies clay, the settlement due to consolidation of the clay can be estimated by assuming a 30° load spread from the edges of the equivalent raft at base level of the piles.

Example 8.4

A 750 mm diameter bored pile is to extend from a depth of 2 m to a depth of 22 m in a stiff clay. The undrained strength of the clay varies with depth as follows:

Depth (m)	4	8	12	16	20	24
c_u (kN/m²)	78	102	130	151	174	200

Determine the maximum load that may be applied to the pile if a load factor of 2 is specified and if $\alpha = 0.45$.

> At a depth of 22 m the value of c_u is 187 kN/m².
>
> The average undrained strength ($\bar{c}_u$) between 2 and 22 m is 127 kN/m².
>
> The ultimate load is given by:
>
> $$Q_f = A c_u N_c + A_s \alpha \bar{c}_u$$
>
> $$= \left(\frac{\pi}{4} \times 0.75^2 \times 187 \times 9\right) + (\pi \times 0.75 \times 20 \times 0.45 \times 127)$$
>
> $$= 740 + 2690$$
>
> $$= 3430 \text{ kN}$$
>
> With a load factor of 2, a load of 1715 kN may be applied to the pile.

Problems

8.1 A load of 425 kN/m is carried on a strip footing 2 m wide at a depth of 1 m in a stiff clay of saturated unit weight 21 kN/m³, the water table being at the surface. Calculate the factor of safety with respect to shear failure (a) when $c_u = 105$ kN/m² and $\phi_u = 0$, (b) when $c' = 10$ kN/m² and $\phi' = 28°$.

8.2 A strip footing 1·5 m wide is located at a depth of 0·75 m in a sand of unit weight 18 kN/m³, the water table being well below foundation level. The shear strength parameters are $c' = 0$ and $\phi' = 38°$. The footing carries a load of 500 kN/m. Determine the factor of safety with respect to shear failure (a) if the load is vertical, (b) if the load is inclined at 10° to the vertical.

8.3 Determine the load which could be carried on a foundation 4·50 m x 2·25 m at a depth of 3·50 m in a stiff clay if a factor of safety of 3 with respect to shear failure is specified. The saturated unit weight of the clay is 20 kN/m³ and the relevant shear strength parameters are $c_u = 135$ kN/m² and $\phi_u = 0$.

8.4 A square footing is required to carry a load of 1000 kN at a depth of 1 m in a loose, dry sand of unit weight 16 kN/m³. The shear strength parameters are $c' = 0$ and $\phi' = 34°$. The design is to be based on the criterion of local shear failure. Determine the size of the footing for a factor of safety of 3·5 with respect to shear failure.

8.5 A footing 2·5 m square carries a uniform pressure of 400 kN/m² at a depth of 1 m in a sand. The saturated unit weight of the sand is 20 kN/m³ and the unit weight above the water table is 17 kN/m³. The shear strength parameters are $c' = 0$

and $\phi' = 40°$. Determine the factor of safety with respect to shear failure for the following cases:

(a) the water table is 5 m below the surface;
(b) the water table is 1 m below the surface;
(c) the water table is at the surface and there is seepage vertically upwards under a hydraulic gradient of 0·2.

8.6   A footing 4 m square is located at a depth of 1 m in a layer of saturated clay 13 m thick, the water table being at the surface. The following parameters are known for the clay: $c_u = 100$ kN/m^2, $\phi_u = 0$, $c' = 15$ kN/m^2, $\phi' = 27°$, $m_v = 6·5 \times 10^{-5}$ m^2/kN, $\gamma_{sat} = 21$ kN/m^3. Determine the allowable bearing capacity if the factor of safety with respect to shear failure is not to be less than 3 and if the maximum consolidation settlement is to be limited to 30 mm.

8.7   A load of 1000 kN is to be carried on a square footing in a sand. A plate bearing test carried out on a 300 mm square plate at foundation level yielded the following results:

Load (kN)	5	10	15	20	30	40	50
Settlement (mm)	1·78	3·81	5·55	7·87	19·05	52·50	152·00

On the basis of equation 8.20, what should be the size of the footing if the settlement is not to exceed 25 mm?

8.8   The following column loads are to be carried on individual footings at a depth of 1 m in a sand of unit weight 18 kN/m^3:

500, 550, 850, 900, 1075, 1200, 880, 700 kN.

Standard penetration tests were carried out in four boreholes on the site, the recorded N values being as follows:

Depth (m)	BH 1	BH 2	BH 3	BH 4
0·75	5	8	6	4
1·50	7	11	5	8
2·25	11	9	8	10
3·00	12	12	10	11
3·75	15	14	12	16
4·50	19	17	11	16

The water table is at a depth of 5 m. Determine the allowable bearing capacity for the design of the footings.

8.9   A concrete pile 250 mm square is driven to a depth of 12 m in a sand of saturated unit weight 20 kN/m^3, the water table being at the surface of the sand. For the sand $\phi' = 36°$, $\delta = 27°$ and the earth pressure coefficient K is taken to be 1·5. Determine the ultimate load that may be applied to the pile.

References

8.1   Berezantzev, V.G., Khristoforov, V.S. and Golubkov, V.N. (1961): 'Load Bearing Capacity and Deformation of Piled Foundations', *Proceedings 5th International Conference SMFE, Paris*, Vol. 2.

8.2   British Standard 1377 (1967): *Methods of Testing Soils for Civil Engineering Purposes*, British Standards Institution, London.

8.3   Bjerrum, L. and Eggestad, A. (1963): 'Interpretation of Loading Tests on Sand', *Proceedings European Conference SMFE, Wiesbaden*, Vol. 1.

8.4   British Standard Code of Practice, CP 101 (1972): *Foundations and Substructures for Non-industrial Buildings of not more than Four Storeys*, British Standards Institution, London.

8.5   British Standard Code of Practice, CP 2004 (1972): *Foundations*, British Standards Institution, London.

8.6   DeBeer, E. E. (1963): 'The Scale Effect in the Transposition of the Results of Deep Sounding Tests on the Ultimate Bearing Capacity of Piles and Caisson Foundations', *Geotechnique*, Vol. 13, No. 1.

8.7   Gibbs, H. J. and Holtz, W. G. (1957): 'Research on Determining the Density of Sands by Spoon Penetration Testing', *Proceedings 4th International Conference SMFE, London*, Vol. 1, Butterworths.

8.8   Leonards, G. A. (1962): *Foundation Engineering*, McGraw-Hill, New York.

8.9   Meyerhof, G. G. (1951): 'The Ultimate Bearing Capacity of Foundations', *Geotechnique*, Vol. 2, No. 4.

8.10   Meyerhof, G. G. (1955): 'Influence of Roughness of Base and Groundwater Conditions on the Ultimate Bearing Capacity of Foundations', *Geotechnique*, Vol. 5, No. 3.

8.11   Meyerhof, G. G. (1956): 'Penetration Tests and Bearing Capacity of Cohesionless Soils', *Proceedings ASCE*, Vol. 82, No. SM1.

8.12   Peck, R. B., Hanson, W. E. and Thornburn, T. H. (1953): *Foundation Engineering*, John Wiley and Sons, New York.

8.13   Skempton, A. W. (1951): 'The Bearing Capacity of Clays', *Proceedings Building Research Congress*, Vol. 1.

8.14   Skempton, A. W. (1959): 'Cast-in-situ Bored Piles in London Clay', *Geotechnique*, Vol. 9, No. 4.

8.15   Sutherland, H. B. (1963): 'The Use of In-situ Tests to Estimate the Allowable Bearing Pressure of Cohesionless Soils', *The Structural Engineer*, Vol. 41, No. 3.

8.16   Terzaghi, K. (1943): *Theoretical Soil Mechanics*, John Wiley and Sons, New York.

8.17   Terzaghi, K. and Peck, R. B. (1967): *Soil Mechanics in Engineering Practice*, John Wiley and Sons, New York.

8.18   Whitaker, T. (1957): 'Experiments with Model Piles in Groups', *Geotechnique*, Vol. 7, No. 4.

8.19   Whitaker, T. (1970): *The Design of Piled Foundations*, Pergamon Press, Oxford.

CHAPTER 9

Stability of Slopes

9.1 Introduction

Gravitational and seepage forces tend to cause instability in natural slopes, in slopes formed by excavation and in the slopes of embankments and earth dams. The most important types of slope failure are illustrated in Fig. 9.1. In *rotational* slips the shape of the failure surface in section may be a circular arc or a non-circular curve. In general, circular slips are associated with homogeneous soil conditions and non-circular slips with non-homogeneous conditions. *Translational* and *compound* slips occur where the form of the failure surface is influenced by the presence of an adjacent stratum of significantly different strength. Translational slips tend to occur where the adjacent stratum is at a relatively shallow depth below the surface of the slope: the failure surface tends to be plane and roughly parallel to the slope. Compound slips usually occur where the adjacent stratum is at greater depth, the failure surface consisting of curved and plane sections.

In practice, limiting equilibrium methods are used in the analysis of slope stability. It is considered that failure is on the point of occurring along an assumed or a known

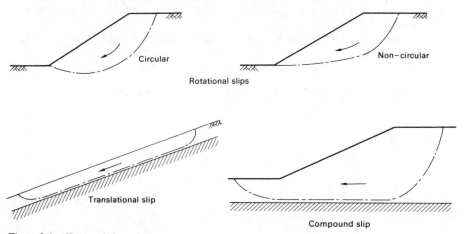

Figure 9.1   Types of slope failure.

failure surface. The shear strength required to maintain a condition of limiting equilibrium is compared with the available shear strength of the soil, giving the average factor of safety along the failure surface. The problem is considered in two dimensions, conditions of plane strain being assumed. It has been shown that a two-dimensional analysis gives a conservative result for a failure on a three-dimensional (dish-shaped) surface.

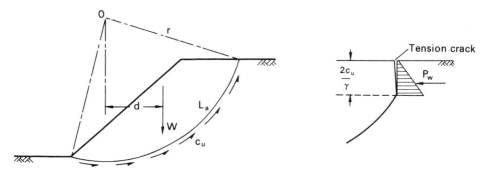

Figure 9.2   The $\phi_u = 0$ analysis.

9.2   Analysis for the Case of $\phi_u = 0$

This analysis, in terms of total stress, covers the case of a fully-saturated clay under undrained conditions, i.e. for the condition immediately after construction. Only moment equilibrium is considered in the analysis. In section, the potential failure surface is assumed to be a circular arc. A trial failure surface (centre O, radius r and length L_a) is shown in Fig. 9.2. Potential instability is due to the total weight of the soil mass (W per unit length) above the failure surface. For equilibrium the shear strength which must be mobilised along the failure surface is expressed as:

$$\tau_m = \frac{\tau_f}{F} = \frac{c_u}{F}$$

where F is the factor of safety with respect to shear strength. Equating moments about O:

$$Wd = \frac{c_u}{F} L_a r$$

$$\therefore \qquad F = \frac{c_u L_a r}{Wd} \qquad\qquad (9.1)$$

The moments of any additional forces must be taken into account. In the event of a tension crack developing, as shown in Fig. 9.2, the arc length L_a is shortened and a hydrostatic force will act normal to the crack if the crack fills with water. It is necessary to analyse the slope for a number of trial failure surfaces in order that the minimum factor of safety can be determined.

Example 9.1

A 45° slope is excavated to a depth of 8 m in a deep layer of saturated clay of unit weight 19 kN/m^3: the relevant shear strength parameters are c_u = 65 kN/m^2 and ϕ_u = 0. Determine the factor of safety for the trial failure surface specified in Fig. 9.3.

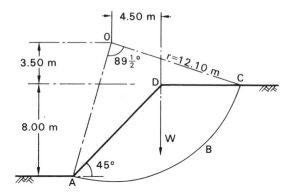

Figure 9.3   Example 9.1.

In Fig. 9.3, the cross-sectional area ABCD is 70 m^2.

The weight of the soil mass = 70 x 19 = 1330 kN/m.

The centroid of ABCD is 4·5 m from O.

The angle AOC is $89\frac{1}{2}°$ and radius OC is 12·1 m.

The arc length ABC is calculated as 18·9 m.

The factor of safety is given by:

$$F = \frac{c_u L_a r}{W d}$$

$$= \frac{65 \times 18·9 \times 12·1}{1330 \times 4·5}$$

$$= 2·48$$

This is the factor of safety for the trial failure surface selected and is not necessarily the minimum factor of safety.

9.3   The ϕ-Circle Method

The analysis is in terms of total stress. A trial failure surface, a circular arc (centre O, radius r) is selected as shown in Fig. 9.4. If the shear strength parameters are c_u and ϕ_u, the shear strength which must be mobilised for equilibrium is:

$$\tau_m = \frac{\tau_f}{F} = \frac{1}{F} (c_u + \sigma \tan \phi_u)$$

$$= c_m + \sigma \tan \phi_m$$

where F is the factor of safety with respect to shear strength. For convenience the following notation is introduced:

$$c_m = \frac{c_u}{F_c} \qquad (9.2)$$

$$\tan \phi_m = \frac{\tan \phi_u}{F_\phi} \qquad (9.3)$$

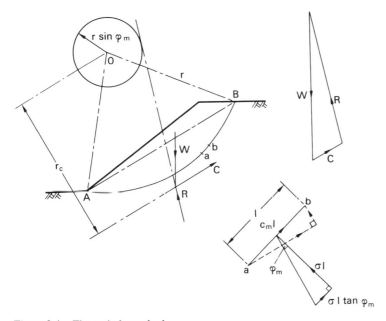

Figure 9.4   The ϕ-circle method.

it being a requirement that:

$$F_c = F_\phi = F$$

An element ab, of length l, of the failure surface is considered, the element being short enough to be approximated to a straight line. The forces acting on ab (per unit dimension normal to the section) are as follows:

(1) the total normal force σl;
(2) the component of shearing resistance $c_m l$;
(3) the component of shearing resistance $\sigma l \tan \phi_m$.

If each force $c_m l$ along the failure surface is split into components perpendicular and parallel to the chord AB, the perpendicular components sum to zero and the sum of the parallel components is given by:

$$C = c_m L_c \qquad (9.4)$$

where L_c is the *chord* length AB. The force C is thus the resultant, acting parallel to the chord AB, of the forces $c_m l$. The line of application of the resultant force C can be determined by taking moments about the centre O. If the force C acts at distance r_c from O, then:

$$Cr_c = r \Sigma c_m l$$

i.e.,

$$c_m L_c r_c = r c_m L_a$$

where $L_a = \Sigma l$ is the *arc* length AB.
Thus,

$$r_c = \frac{L_a}{L_c} r \tag{9.5}$$

The resultant of the forces σl and $\sigma l \tan \phi_m$ on the element ab acts at angle ϕ_m to the normal and is therefore tangential to a circle, centre O, of radius $r \sin \phi_m$: this circle is referred to as the ϕ-circle. The same technique was used in Chapter 5. The overall resultant (R) for the arc AB is *assumed* to be tangential to the ϕ-circle. Strictly, the resultant R is tangential to a circle of radius slightly greater than $r \sin \phi_m$ but the error involved in the above assumption is generally insignificant.

The soil mass above the trial failure surface is in equilibrium under its total weight (W) and the shear resultants C and R. The force W is known in magnitude and direction; the direction only of the resultant C is known. Initially a trial value of F_ϕ is selected and the corresponding value of ϕ_m is calculated from equation 9.3. For equilibrium the line of application of the resultant R must be tangential to the ϕ-circle and pass through the point of intersection of the forces W and C. The force diagram can then be drawn, from which the value of C can be obtained. Then:

$$c_m = \frac{C}{L_c}$$

and

$$F_c = \frac{c_u}{c_m}$$

It is necessary to repeat the analysis at least three times, starting with different values of F_ϕ. If the calculated values of F_c are plotted against the corresponding values of F_ϕ, the factor of safety corresponding to the requirement $F_c = F_\phi$ can be determined. The whole procedure must be repeated for a series of trial failure surfaces in order that the minimum factor of safety is obtained.

For an effective stress analysis the total weight W is combined with the resultant boundary water force on the failure mass and the effective stress parameters c' and ϕ' are used.

Based on the principle of geometric similarity, Taylor [9.13] published *stability coefficients* for the analysis of homogeneous slopes in terms of total stress. For a slope of height H the stability coefficient (N_s) for the failure surface along which the factor of safety is a minimum is:

$$N_s = \frac{c_u}{F \gamma H} \tag{9.6}$$

Values of N_s, which is a function of the slope angle β and the shear strength parameter ϕ_u, can be obtained from Fig. 9.5. For $\phi_u = 0$, the value of N_s also depends on the depth factor D, where DH is the depth to a firm stratum.

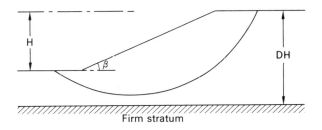

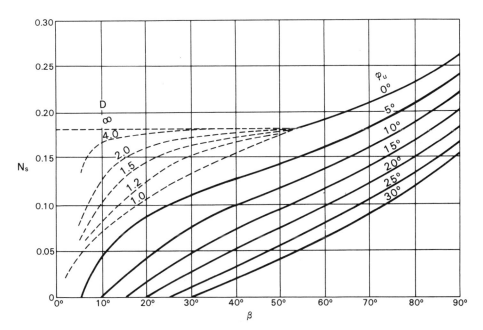

Figure 9.5 Taylor's stability coefficients.

In example 9.1, $\beta = 45°$, $\phi_u = 0$, and assuming D is large, the value of N_s is 0·18. Then from equation 9.6:

$$F = \frac{c_u}{N_s \gamma H}$$

$$= \frac{65}{0·18 \times 19 \times 8}$$

$$= 2·37$$

Gibson and Morgenstern [9.4] published stability coefficients for slopes in normally-consolidated clays in which the undrained strength c_u ($\phi_u = 0$) varies linearly with depth.

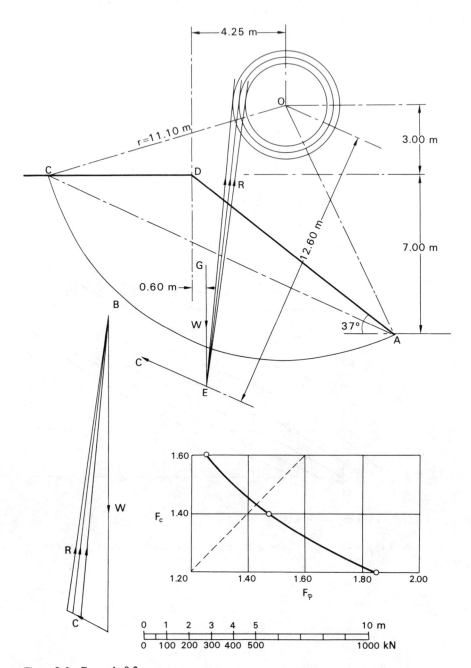

Figure 9.6   Example 9.2.

Example 9.2

An embankment slope is detailed in Fig. 9.6. For the given failure surface, determine the factor of safety in terms of total stress using the ϕ-circle method. The appropriate shear strength parameters are $c_u = 15$ kN/m^2 and $\phi_u = 15°$: the unit weight of the soil is 20 kN/m^3.

The area ABCD is 68 m^2 and the centroid (G) is 0·60 m from the vertical through D. The radius of the failure arc is 11·10 m. The arc length AC is 19·15 m and the chord length AC is 16·85 m.

The weight of the soil mass is:

$$W = 68 \times 20 = 1360 \text{ kN/m}$$

The position of the resultant C is given by:

$$r_c = \frac{L_a}{L_c} r$$

$$= \frac{19·15}{16·85} \times 11·10 = 12·60 \text{ m}$$

Now:

$$\phi_m = \tan^{-1}\left(\frac{\tan 15°}{F_\phi}\right)$$

Trial values of F_ϕ are chosen, the corresponding values of $r \sin \phi_m$ are calculated and the ϕ-circles drawn as shown in Fig. 9.6. The resultant C (for any value of F_ϕ) acts in a direction parallel to the chord AC and at distance r_c from O. The forces C and W intersect at point E. The resultant R, corresponding to each value of F_ϕ, passes through E and is tangential to the appropriate ϕ-circle. The force diagrams are drawn and the values of C determined.

The results are tabulated below.

F_ϕ	ϕ_m	$r \sin \phi_m$ (m)	C (kN/m)	$c_m = C/L_c$ (kN/m^2)	$F_c = \dfrac{c_u}{c_m}$
1·20	12°35′	2·42	137	8·1	1·85
1·40	10°50′	2·08	172	10·2	1·47
1·60	9°30′	1·83	203	12·1	1·24

If F_c is plotted against F_ϕ (Fig. 9.6) it is apparent that:

$$F = F_c = F_\phi = 1·43$$

9.4 The Method of Slices

In this method the potential failure surface, in section, is again assumed to be a circular arc with centre O and radius r. The soil mass (ABCD) above a trial failure surface (AC) is divided by vertical planes into a series of slices of width b, as shown in Fig. 9.7. The base of each slice is assumed to be a straight line. For any slice the inclination of the base to the horizontal is α and the height, measured on the centre-line, is h. The factor of safety is defined as the ratio of the available shear strength (τ_f) to the shear strength (τ_m) which must be mobilised to maintain a condition of limiting equilibrium, i.e.:

$$F = \frac{\tau_f}{\tau_m}$$

The factor of safety is taken to be the same for each slice, implying that there must be mutual support between slices, i.e. forces must act between the slices.

The forces (per unit dimension normal to the section) acting on a slice are listed below.

(1) The total weight of the slice, $W = \gamma bh$ (γ_{sat} where appropriate).
(2) The total normal force on the base, N. In general this force has two components, the effective normal force N' (equal to $\sigma' l$) and the boundary water force ul, where u is the pore water pressure at the centre of the base and l is the length of the base.
(3) The shear force on the base, $T = \tau_m l$.
(4) The total normal forces on the sides, E_1 and E_2.
(5) The shear forces on the sides, X_1 and X_2.

Any external forces must also be included in the analysis.

The problem is statically indeterminate and in order to obtain a solution assumptions must be made regarding the inter-slice forces E and X: the resulting solution for factor of safety is not exact.

Considering moments about O, the sum of the moments of the shear forces T on the failure arc AC must equal the moment of the weight of the soil mass ABCD. For any slice the lever arm of W is $r \sin \alpha$, therefore:

$$\Sigma Tr = \Sigma Wr \sin \alpha$$

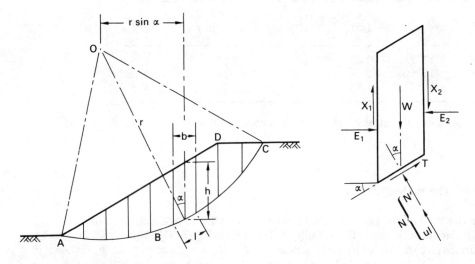

Figure 9.7   The method of slices.

Now,

$$T = \tau_m l = \frac{\tau_f}{F} l$$

$$\therefore \qquad \sum \frac{\tau_f}{F} l = \Sigma W \sin \alpha$$

$$\therefore \qquad F = \frac{\Sigma \tau_f l}{\Sigma W \sin \alpha}$$

For an analysis in terms of effective stress:

$$F = \frac{\Sigma (c' + \sigma' \tan \phi')l}{\Sigma W \sin \alpha}$$

or,

$$F = \frac{c' L_a + \tan \phi' \Sigma N'}{\Sigma W \sin \alpha} \qquad (9.7)$$

where L_a is the arc length AC. Equation 9.7 is exact but approximations are introduced in determining the forces N'. For a given failure arc the value of F will depend on the way in which the forces N' are estimated.

The Fellenius Solution

In this solution it is assumed that for each slice the resultant of the inter-slice forces is zero. The solution involves resolving the forces on each slice normal to the base, i.e.:

$$N' = W \cos \alpha - ul$$

Hence the factor of safety in terms of effective stress (equation 9.7) is given by:

$$F = \frac{c' L_a + \tan \phi' \Sigma (W \cos \alpha - ul)}{\Sigma W \sin \alpha} \qquad (9.8)$$

The components $W \cos \alpha$ and $W \sin \alpha$ can be determined graphically for each slice. Alternatively, the value of α can be measured or calculated. Again, a series of trial failure surfaces must be chosen in order to obtain the minimum factor of safety. This solution underestimates the factor of safety: the error, compared with more accurate methods of analysis, is usually within the range 5–20%.

For an analysis in terms of total stress the parameters c_u and ϕ_u are used and the value of u in equation 9.8 is zero. If $\phi_u = 0$ the factor of safety is given by:

$$F = \frac{c_u L_a}{\Sigma W \sin \alpha} \qquad (9.9)$$

As N' does not appear in equation 9.9 an exact value of F is obtained.

The Bishop Simplified Solution

In this solution it is assumed that the resultant forces on the sides of the slices are horizontal, i.e.

$$X_1 - X_2 = 0$$

For equilibrium the shear force on the base of any slice is:

$$T = \frac{1}{F}(c'l + N' \tan \phi')$$

Resolving forces in the vertical direction:

$$W = N' \cos \alpha + ul \cos \alpha + \frac{c'l}{F} \sin \alpha + \frac{N'}{F} \tan \phi' \sin \alpha$$

$$\therefore \qquad N' = \left(W - \frac{c'l}{F} \sin \alpha - ul \cos \alpha\right) \Bigg/ \left(\cos \alpha + \frac{\tan \phi' \sin \alpha}{F}\right) \qquad (9.10)$$

It is convenient to substitute:

$$l = b \sec \alpha$$

From equation 9.7, after some rearrangement:

$$F = \frac{1}{\Sigma W \sin \alpha} \sum \{c'b + (W - ub) \tan \phi'\} \left[\frac{\sec \alpha}{1 + \dfrac{\tan \alpha \tan \phi'}{F}}\right] \qquad (9.11)$$

The pore water pressure can be related to the total 'fill pressure' at any point by means of the dimensionless *pore pressure ratio*, defined as:

$$r_u = \frac{u}{\gamma h} \qquad (9.12)$$

(γ_{sat} where appropriate).
For any slice,

$$r_u = \frac{u}{W/b}$$

Hence equation 9.11 can be written:

$$F = \frac{1}{\Sigma W \sin \alpha} \sum \left[\{c'b + W(1 - r_u) \tan \phi'\} \frac{\sec \alpha}{1 + \dfrac{\tan \alpha \tan \phi'}{F}}\right] \qquad (9.13)$$

As the factor of safety occurs on both sides of equation 9.13 a process of successive approximation must be used to obtain a solution but convergence is rapid. The method is very suitable for solution on the computer. In the computer program the slope geometry can be made more complex, with soil strata having different properties and pore pressure conditions being introduced.

In most problems the value of the pore pressure ratio r_u is not constant over the whole failure surface but, unless there are isolated regions of high pore pressure, an average value (weighted on an area basis) is normally used in design. Again, the factor of safety determined by this method is an underestimate but the error is unlikely to exceed 7% and in most cases is less than 2%.

Spencer [9.12] proposed a method of analysis in which the resultant inter-slice forces are parallel and in which both force and moment equilibrium are satisfied.

Spencer showed that the accuracy of the Bishop simplified method, in which only moment equilibrium is satisfied, is due to the insensitivity of the moment equation to the slope of the inter-slice forces.

Dimensionless stability coefficients for homogeneous slopes, based on equation 9.13, have been published by Bishop and Morgenstern [9.3]. It can be shown that for a given slope angle and given soil properties the factor of safety varies linearly with r_u and can thus be expressed as:

$$F = m - nr_u \tag{9.14}$$

where m and n are the stability coefficients. The coefficients m and n are functions of β, ϕ', the dimensionless number $c'/\gamma H$ and the depth factor D.

Example 9.3

Using the Fellenius method of slices, determine the factor of safety in terms of effective stress of the slope shown in Fig. 9.8 for the given failure surface. The distribution of pore water pressure along the failure surface is given in the figure. The unit weight of the soil is 20 kN/m^3 and the relevant shear strength parameters are $c' = 10$ kN/m^2 and $\phi' = 29°$.

The factor of safety is given by equation 9.8. The soil mass is divided into slices 1·5 m wide. The weight (W) of each slice is given by:

$$W = \gamma bh = 20 \times 1·5 \times h = 30h \text{ kN/m}$$

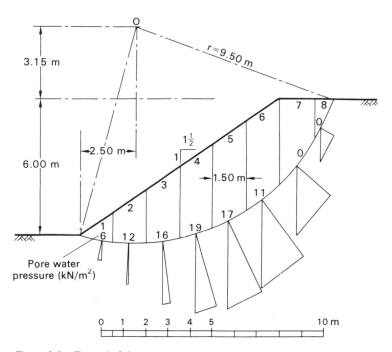

Figure 9.8   Example 9.3.

The height h for each slice is set off below the centre of the base and the normal and tangential components $h \cos \alpha$ and $h \sin \alpha$ respectively are determined graphically, as shown in Fig. 9.8. Then:

$$W \cos \alpha = 30h \cos \alpha$$

and

$$W \sin \alpha = 30h \sin \alpha$$

The arc length (L_a) is calculated as 14·35 m. The results are tabulated below:

Slice No.	$h \cos \alpha$ (m)	$h \sin \alpha$ (m)	u (kN/m^2)	l (m)	ul (kN/m)
1	0·75	−0·15	6	1·55	9·3
2	1·80	−0·10	12	1·50	18·0
3	2·70	0·40	16	1·55	24·8
4	3·25	1·00	19	1·60	30·4
5	3·45	1·75	17	1·70	28·9
6	3·10	2·35	11	1·95	21·4
7	1·90	2·25	0	2·35	0
8	0·55	0·95	0	2·15	0
	17·50	8·45		14·35	132·8

$$\Sigma W \cos \alpha = 30 \times 17\cdot50 = 525 \text{ kN/m}$$
$$\Sigma W \sin \alpha = 30 \times 8\cdot45 = 254 \text{ kN/m}$$
$$\Sigma(W \cos \alpha - ul) = 525 - 132\cdot8 = 392\cdot2 \text{ kN/m}$$

$$F = \frac{c'L_a + \tan \phi' \ \Sigma(W \cos \alpha - ul)}{\Sigma W \sin \alpha}$$

$$= \frac{(10 \times 14\cdot35) + (0\cdot554 \times 392\cdot2)}{254}$$

$$= \frac{143\cdot5 + 217}{254}$$

$$= 1\cdot42$$

9.5   Analysis of a Plane Translational Slip

It is assumed that the potential failure surface is parallel to the surface of the slope and is at a depth that is small compared with the length of the slope. The slope can then be considered as being of infinite length, with end effects being ignored. The slope is inclined at angle β to the horizontal and the depth of the failure plane is z, as shown in section in Fig. 9.9. The water table is taken to be parallel to the slope at a height of mz $(0 < m < 1)$ above the failure plane. Steady seepage is assumed to be taking place in a direction parallel to the slope. The forces on the sides of any vertical slice are equal and opposite and the stress conditions are the same at every point on the failure plane.

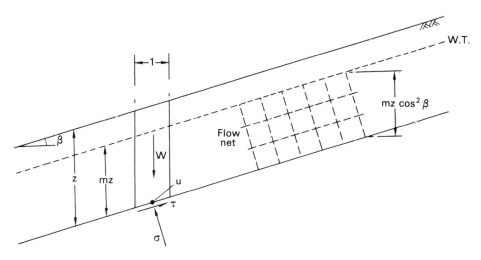

Figure 9.9   Plane translational slip.

In terms of effective stress, the shear strength of the soil along the failure plane is:

$$\tau_f = c' + (\sigma - u) \tan \phi'$$

and the factor of safety is:

$$F = \frac{\tau_f}{\tau}$$

The expressions for σ, τ and u are as follows:

$$\sigma = \{(1 - m)\gamma + m\gamma_{sat}\} z \cos^2 \beta$$
$$\tau = \{(1 - m)\gamma + m\gamma_{sat}\} z \sin \beta \cos \beta$$
$$u = mz\gamma_w \cos^2 \beta$$

The following special cases are of interest, If $c' = 0$ and $m = 0$ (i.e. the soil between the surface and the failure plane is not fully saturated), then:

$$F = \frac{\tan \phi'}{\tan \beta} \tag{9.15}$$

If $c' = 0$ and $m = 1$ (i.e. the water table coincides with the surface of the slope), then:

$$F = \frac{\gamma' \tan \phi'}{\gamma_{sat} \tan \beta} \tag{9.16}$$

It should be noted that when $c' = 0$ the factor of safety is independent of the depth z. If c' is greater than zero, the factor of safety is a function of z, and β may exceed ϕ' provided z is less than a critical value.

For a total stress analysis the shear strength parameters c_u and ϕ_u are used and the value of u is zero.

Example 9.4

A long natural slope in a fissured overconsolidated clay is inclined at $12°$ to the horizontal. The water table is at the surface and seepage is roughly parallel to the slope. A slip has developed on a plane parallel to the surface at a depth of 5 m. The saturated unit weight of the clay is 20 kN/m³. The peak strength parameters are $c' = 10$ kN/m³ and $\phi' = 26°$; the residual strength parameters are $c'_r = 0$ and $\phi'_r = 18°$. Determine the factor of safety along the slip plane (a) in terms of the peak strength parameters, (b) in terms of the residual strength parameters.

With the water table at the surface ($m = 1$), at any point on the slip plane:

$$\sigma = \gamma_{sat} z \cos^2 \beta$$
$$= 20 \times 5 \times \cos^2 12° = 95 \cdot 5 \text{ kN/m}^2$$
$$\tau = \gamma_{sat} z \sin \beta \cos \beta$$
$$= 20 \times 5 \times \sin 12° \times \cos 12° = 20 \cdot 3 \text{ kN/m}^2$$
$$u = \gamma_w z \cos^2 \beta$$
$$= 9 \cdot 8 \times 5 \times \cos^2 12° = 46 \cdot 8 \text{ kN/m}^2$$

Using the peak strength parameters:

$$\tau_f = c' + (\sigma - u) \tan \phi'$$
$$= 10 + (48 \cdot 7 \times \tan 26°) = 33 \cdot 8 \text{ kN/m}^2$$

Then the factor of safety is given by:

$$F = \frac{\tau_f}{\tau} = \frac{33 \cdot 8}{20 \cdot 3} = 1 \cdot 66$$

Using the residual strength parameters, the factor of safety can be obtained from equation 9.16:

$$F = \frac{\gamma' \; \tan \phi'_r}{\gamma_{sat} \; \tan \beta}$$

$$= \frac{10 \cdot 2}{20} \times \frac{\tan 18°}{\tan 12°} = 0 \cdot 78$$

9.6   The Morgenstern–Price Analysis

Morgenstern and Price [9.8] developed a general analysis in which all boundary and equilibrium conditions are satisfied and in which the failure surface may be any shape, circular, non-circular or compound. The soil mass above the failure plane is divided into sections by a number of vertical planes and the problem is rendered statically determinate by assuming a relationship between the forces E and X on the vertical boundaries between each section. This assumption is of the form:

$$X = \lambda f(x) E \tag{9.17}$$

where $f(x)$ is an arbitrary function describing the pattern in which the ratio X/E varies across the soil mass and λ is a scale factor. The value of λ is obtained as part of the solution along with the factor of safety F. The values of the forces E and X and the point of application of E can be determined at each vertical boundary. For any assumed function $f(x)$ it is necessary to examine the solution in detail to ensure that it is physically reasonable. The choice of the function $f(x)$ does not appear to influence the computed value of F by more than about 5% and $f(x) = 1$ is a common assumption.

The analysis involves a complex process of iteration for the values of λ and F, described by Morgenstern and Price [9.9], and the use of a computer is essential.

9.7   End-of-Construction and Long-Term Stability

When a slope is formed either by excavation or by the construction of an embankment the changes in total stress result in changes in pore water pressure in the vicinity of the slope and, in particular, along a potential failure surface. Prior to construction the initial pore water pressure (u_0) at any point is governed either by a static water table level or by a flow net for conditions of steady seepage. The change in pore water pressure at any point is given theoretically by equation 4.17 or 4.18. The final pore water pressure, after dissipation of the excess pore water pressure is complete, is governed by the static water table level or the steady seepage flow net for the final conditions after construction.

If the permeability of the soil is low, a considerable time will elapse before any significant dissipation of excess pore water pressure will have taken place. At the end of construction the soil will be virtually in the undrained condition and a total stress analysis will be relevant. In principle an effective stress analysis is also possible for the end of construction condition using the pore water pressure (u) for this condition, where:

$$u = u_0 + \Delta u$$

However, because of its greater simplicity, a total stress analysis is generally used. It should be realised that the same factor of safety will not generally be obtained from a total stress and an effective stress analysis of the end-of-construction condition. In a total stress analysis it is implied that the pore water pressures are those for a failure condition: in an effective stress analysis the pore water pressures used are those predicted for a non-failure condition. In the long-term, the fully-drained condition will be reached and only an effective stress analysis will be appropriate.

If, on the other hand, the permeability of the soil is high, dissipation of excess pore water pressure will be largely complete by the end of construction. An effective stress analysis is relevant for all conditions with values of pore water pressure being obtained from the static water table level or the appropriate flow net.

Pore water pressure may thus be an independent variable, determined from the static water table level or from the flow net for conditions of steady seepage, or may be dependent on the total stress changes tending to cause failure.

It is important to identify the most dangerous condition in any practical problem in order that the appropriate shear strength parameters are used in design.

Excavated and Natural Slopes in Saturated Clays

Equation 4.17, with $B = 1$ for a fully-saturated clay, can be rearranged as follows:

$$\Delta u = \tfrac{1}{2}(\Delta \sigma_1 + \Delta \sigma_3) + (A - \tfrac{1}{2})(\Delta \sigma_1 - \Delta \sigma_3) \qquad (9.18)$$

For a typical point P on a potential failure surface (Fig. 9.10) the first term in equation 9.18 is negative and the second term will also be negative if the value of A is

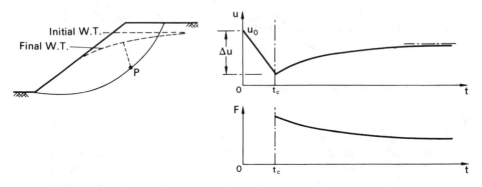

Figure 9.10   Pore pressure dissipation and factor of safety (After Bishop and Bjerrum [9.2]).

less than 0·5. Overall, the pore water pressure change Δu is negative. The effect of the rotation of the principal stress directions is neglected. As dissipation proceeds the pore water pressure increases to the final value as shown in Fig. 9.10. The factor of safety will therefore have a lower value in the long-term, when dissipation is complete, than at the end of construction.

Residual shear strength is relevant to the long-term stability of slopes in *over-consolidated fissured clays.* A number of cases are on record in which failures in this type of clay have occurred long after dissipation of excess pore water pressure had been completed. Analysis of these failures showed that the average shear strength at failure was well below the peak value. In clays of this type it is suspected that large strains can occur locally due to the presence of fissures, resulting in the peak strength being reached, followed by a gradual decrease towards the residual value. The development of large local strains can lead eventually to a progressive slope failure. Fissures may not be the only cause of progressive failure: there is considerable non-uniformity of shear stress along a potential failure surface and local overstressing may initiate progressive failure. It should be realised, however, that the residual strength is reached only after a considerable slip movement has taken place and the strength relevant to 'first-time' slips lies between the peak and residual values. Analysis of failures in natural slopes in overconsolidated fissured clays has indicated that the residual shear strength is ultimately attained, probably as a result of successive slipping.

9.8   Stability of Earth Dams

In the design of earth dams the factor of safety of both slopes must be determined as accurately as possible for the most critical conditions. For economic reasons an unduly conservative design must be avoided. In the case of the upstream slope the most critical stages are at the end of construction and during rapid drawdown of the reservoir level. The critical stages for the downstream slope are at the end of construction and during steady seepage when the reservoir is full. The pore water pressure distribution at any stage has a dominant influence on the factor of safety and in large earth dams it is common practice to install a piezometer system so that the actual pore water pressures can be measured at any stage and compared with the predicted values used in design (provided an effective stress analysis has been used). Remedial action can then be taken if the factor of safety, based on the measured values, is considered too low.

(a) *End of Construction*

The construction period of an earth dam is likely to be long enough to allow partial dissipation of excess pore water pressure before the end of construction, especially in a dam with internal drainage. A total stress analysis, therefore, would result in too conservative a design. An effective stress analysis is preferable, using predicted values of r_u.

The pore pressure (u) at any point can be written as:

$$u = u_0 + \Delta u$$

where u_0 is the initial value and Δu is the change in pore water pressure under undrained conditions. In terms of the change in total major principal stress:

$$u = u_0 + \overline{B}\Delta\sigma_1$$

Then:

$$r_u = \frac{u_0}{\gamma h} + \overline{B}\frac{\Delta\sigma_1}{\gamma h}$$

If it is assumed that the increase in total major principal stress is approximately equal to the fill pressure along a potential failure surface, then:

$$r_u = \frac{u_0}{\gamma h} + \overline{B} \tag{9.19}$$

The soil is partially saturated when compacted, therefore the initial pore water pressure (u_0) is negative. The actual value of u_0 depends on the placement water content, the higher the water content the closer the value of u_0 to zero. The value of $\overline{B}$ also depends on the placement water content, the higher the water content the higher the value of $\overline{B}$. Thus for an upper bound:

$$r_u = \overline{B} \tag{9.20}$$

The value of $\overline{B}$ must correspond to the stress conditions in the dam. Equations 9.19 and 9.20 assume no dissipation during construction. A factor of safety as low as 1·3 may be acceptable at the end of construction provided there is reasonable confidence in the design data.

If high values of r_u are anticipated, dissipation of excess pore water pressure can be accelerated by means of horizontal drainage layers incorporated in the dam, drainage taking place vertically towards the layers: a typical dam section is shown in Fig. 9.11. The efficiency of drainage layers has been examined theoretically by Gibson and Shefford [9.5] and it was shown that in a typical case the layers, in order to be fully effective, should have a permeability at least 10^6 times that of the embankment soil: an acceptable efficiency would be obtained with a permeability ratio of about 10^5.

Equations 9.19 and 9.20 can be applied in the case of any embankment (other than an earth dam). The construction period for a typical embankment is short and

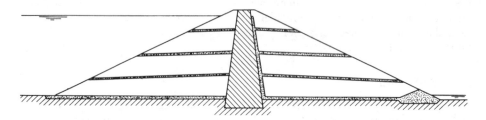

Figure 9.11   Horizontal drainage layers.

no significant dissipation is likely during construction: accordingly, a total stress analysis is normal for the end of construction condition. Dissipation proceeds after the end of construction with the pore water pressure decreasing to the final value in the long-term. The factor of safety of the embankment at the end of construction is therefore lower than that in the long-term.

(b) Steady Seepage

After the reservoir has been full for some time, conditions of steady seepage become established through the dam with the soil below the top flow line in the fully-saturated state. This condition must be analysed in terms of effective stress with values of pore pressure being determined from the flow net. Values of r_u up to 0·45 are possible in homogeneous dams but much lower values can be achieved in dams having internal drainage. The factor of safety for this condition should be at least 1·5.

(c) Rapid Drawdown

After a condition of steady seepage has become established, a drawdown of the reservoir level will result in a change in the pore water pressure distribution. If the permeability of the soil is low, a drawdown period measured in weeks may be 'rapid' in relation to the dissipation time and the change in pore water pressure can be assumed to take place under undrained conditions. Referring to Fig. 9.12, the pore

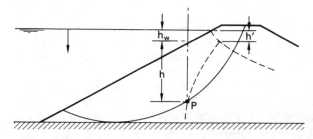

Figure 9.12   Rapid drawdown conditions (After Bishop and Bjerrum [9.2]).

water pressure before drawdown at a typical point P on a potential failure surface
is given by:

$$u_0 = \gamma_w(h + h_w - h')$$

where h' is the loss in total head due to seepage between the upstream slope surface
and the point P. It is again assumed that the total major principal stress at P is equal
to the fill pressure. The change in total major principal stress is due to the total or
partial removal of water above the slope on the vertical through P. For a drawdown
depth exceeding h_w:

$$\Delta\sigma_1 = -\gamma_w h_w$$

and the change in pore water pressure is then given by:

$$\Delta u = \bar{B}\Delta\sigma_1$$
$$= -\bar{B}\gamma_w h_w$$

Therefore the pore water pressure at P immediately after drawdown is:

$$u = u_0 + \Delta u$$
$$= \gamma_w\{h + h_w(1 - \bar{B}) - h'\}$$

Hence:

$$r_u = \frac{u}{\gamma_{sat} h}$$

$$= \frac{\gamma_w}{\gamma_{sat}}\left\{1 + \frac{h_w}{h}(1 - \bar{B}) - \frac{h'}{h}\right\} \tag{9.21}$$

For total stress decreases the value of $\bar{B}$ is slightly greater than 1. A conservative value
of r_u could be obtained by assuming $\bar{B} = 1$ and neglecting h'. Typical values of r_u
immediately after drawdown are within the range 0·3 to 0·4. A minimum factor of
safety of 1·2 may be acceptable after rapid drawdown.

Morgenstern [9.7] published stability coefficients for the approximate analysis
of homogeneous slopes after rapid drawdown.

The pore water pressure distribution after drawdown in soils of high permeability
varies as pore water drains out of the soil above the drawdown level. The saturation
line moves downwards at a rate depending on the permeability of the soil. A series
of flow nets can be drawn for different positions of the saturation line and values of
pore water pressure obtained. The factor of safety can thus be determined, using an
effective stress analysis, for any position of the saturation line.

Problems

9.1   For the given failure surface, determine the factor of safety in terms of total
stress for the slope detailed in Fig. 9.13. The unit weight for both soils is 19 kN/m³.
For soil (1) the relevant shear strength parameters are $c_u = 20$ kN/m² and $\phi_u = 0$:

for soil (2) $c_u = 35$ kN/m² and $\phi_u = 0$. What is the factor of safety if allowance is made for the development of a tension crack which fills with water?

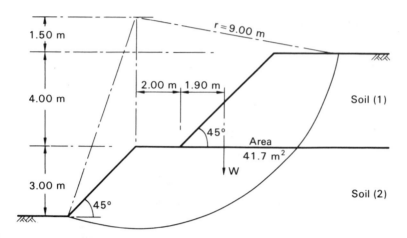

Figure 9.13   Problem 9.1.

9.2   A cutting 9 m deep is to be excavated in a saturated clay of unit weight 19 kN/m³. The relevant shear strength parameters are $c_u = 30$ kN/m² and $\phi_u = 0$. A hard stratum underlies the clay at a depth of 11 m below ground level. Using Taylor's stability coefficients, determine the slope angle at which failure would occur. What is the allowable slope angle if a factor of safety of 1·2 is specified?

9.3   A slope inclined at 34° to the horizontal is excavated to a depth of 8 m in a soil of unit weight 20 kN/m³. A trial failure surface is selected, a circular arc of radius 13·6 m, passing through the toe of the slope and intersecting the ground surface 7·5 m behind the top of the slope. Using the Fellenius method of slices, determine the factor of safety in terms of total stress for the specified failure surface. The appropriate shear strength parameters are $c_u = 20$ kN/m² and $\phi_u = 14°$.

9.4   For the given failure surface, determine the factor of safety in terms of effective stress for the slope detailed in Fig. 9.14, using the Fellenius method of slices. The unit weight of the soil is 21 kN/m³ and the relevant shear strength parameters are $c' = 8$ kN/m² and $\phi' = 32°$.

9.5   Repeat the analysis of the slope detailed in Problem 9.4 using the Bishop simplified method of slices.

9.6   A slope is to be constructed in a soil for which $c' = 0$ and $\phi' = 36°$. It is to be assumed that the water table may occasionally reach the surface of the slope, with seepage taking place parallel to the slope. Determine the maximum slope angle for a factor of safety of 1·5, assuming a potential failure surface parallel to the slope. What would be the factor of safety of the slope, constructed at this angle, if the water table should be well below the surface? The saturated unit weight of the soil is 19 kN/m³.

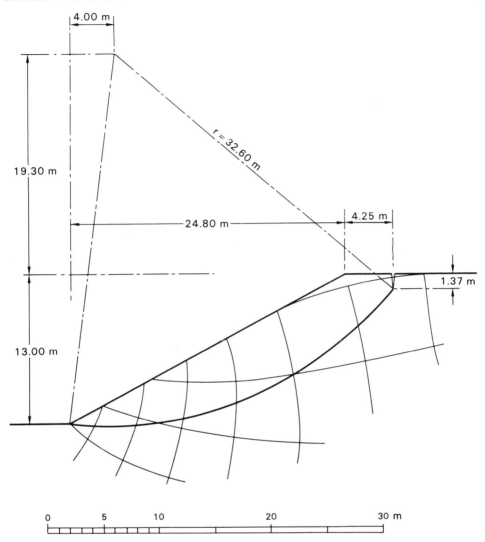

Figure 9.14   Problem 9.4.

References

9.1   Bishop, A. W. (1955): 'The Use of the Slip Circle in the Stability Analysis of Slopes', *Geotechnique*, Vol. 5, No. 1.

9.2   Bishop, A. W. and Bjerrum, L. (1960): 'The Relevance of the Triaxial Test to the Solution of Stability Problems', *Proceedings ASCE Research Conference on Shear Strength of Cohesive Soils, Boulder, Colorado*, p. 437.

9.3   Bishop, A. W. and Morgenstern, N. R. (1960): 'Stability Coefficients for Earth Slopes', *Geotechnique*, Vol. 10, No. 4.

9.4   Gibson, R. E. and Morgenstern, N. R. (1962): 'A Note on the Stability of Cuttings in Normally Consolidated Clays', *Geotechnique*, Vol. 12, No. 3.

9.5   Gibson, R. E. and Shefford, G. C. (1968): 'The Efficiency of Horizontal
       Drainage Layers for Accelerating Consolidation of Clay Embankments',
       Geotechnique, Vol. 18, No. 3.

9.6   Lo, K. Y. (1965): 'Stability of Slopes in Anisotropic Soils', *Journal ASCE*,
       Vol. 91, No. SM4.

9.7   Morgenstern, N. R. (1963): 'Stability Charts for Earth Slopes During Rapid
       Drawdown', *Geotechnique*, Vol. 13, No. 2.

9.8   Morgenstern, N. R. and Price, V. E. (1965): 'The Analysis of the Stability of
       General Slip Surfaces', *Geotechnique*, Vol. 15, No. 1.

9.9   Morgenstern, N. R. and Price, V. E. (1967): 'A Numerical Method for
       Solving the Equations of Stability of General Slip Surfaces', *Computer
       Journal*, Vol. 9, p. 388.

9.10   Skempton, A. W. (1964): 'Long-Term Stability of Clay Slopes', *Geotechnique*,
       Vol. 14, No. 2.

9.11   Skempton, A. W. (1970): 'First-Time Slides in Overconsolidated Clays'
       (Technical Note), *Geotechnique*, Vol. 20, No. 3.

9.12   Spencer, E. (1967): 'A Method of Analysis of the Stability of Embankments
       Assuming Parallel Inter-Slice Forces, *Geotechnique*, Vol. 17, No. 1.

9.13   Taylor, D. W. (1937): 'Stability of Earth Slopes', *Journal of the Boston
       Society of Civil Engineers*, Vol. 24, No. 3.

9.14   Whitman, R. V. and Bailey, W. A. (1967): 'Use of Computers for Slope
       Stability Analysis', *Journal ASCE*, Vol. 93, No. SM4.

Principal Symbols

A, a	Area
A	Air content
$A, \bar{A}$	Pore pressure coefficients
a'	Modified shear strength parameter (effective stress)
a	Dial gauge reading in oedometer test
B	Width of footing
$B, \bar{B}$	Pore pressure coefficients
C_U	Coefficient of uniformity
C_C	Coefficient of curvature
C_s	Isotropic compressibility of soil skeleton
C_{s0}	Uni-axial compressibility of soil skeleton
C_v	Compressibility of pore fluid
C_c	Compression index
C_α	Rate of secondary compression
C_r	Cone penetration resistance
c	Shear strength parameter
c_u	Undrained (total stress) shear strength parameter
c'	Drained (effective stress) shear strength parameter
c_r'	Drained residual shear strength parameter
c_w	Wall adhesion
c_v	Coefficient of consolidation (vertical drainage)
c_h	Coefficient of consolidation (horizontal drainage)
D	Depth of footing
D	Depth factor
D	Particle size
d	Length of drainage path
d	Depth of penetration
d	Diameter
E	Young's modulus
e	Void ratio
e	Eccentricity
F	Factor of safety
f_s	Skin friction

G_s	Specific gravity of solid particles
g	$9 \cdot 8 \text{ m/s}^2$
H, h	Height
H	Layer or specimen thickness
h	Total head
I	Influence factor
I_P	Plasticity index (or PI)
I_L	Liquidity index (or LI)
I_D	Relative density (or RD)
I_B	Brittleness index
i	Hydraulic gradient
i	Inclination factor
J	Seepage force
j	Seepage pressure
K	Lateral pressure coefficient
K_A	Active pressure coefficient
K_P	Passive pressure coefficient
K_0	Coefficient of earth pressure at-rest
K	Absolute permeability
k	Coefficient of permeability
L, l	Length
LL	Liquid limit (or w_L)
LI	Liquidity index (or I_L)
LS	Linear shrinkage
M	Mass
m_v	Coefficient of volume change
N	Standard penetration resistance
N_d	Number of equipotential drops
N_f	Number of flow channels
N_γ	Bearing capacity factor
N_c	Bearing capacity factor
N_q	Bearing capacity factor
N_s	Stability coefficient
n	Porosity
n_d	Equipotential number
P_A	Total active thrust
P_P	Total passive resistance
PL	Plastic limit (or w_P)
PI	Plasticity index (or I_P)
p	Pressure
p_A	Active pressure
p_P	Passive pressure
p_0	At-rest pressure
Q	Surface load
Q_f	Ultimate load
q	Flow per unit time
q	Surface pressure; total foundation pressure
q_n	Net foundation pressure
q_a	Allowable bearing capacity
q_f	Ultimate bearing capacity

q_{nf}	Net ultimate bearing capacity
R, r	Radius
RD	Relative density (or I_D)
r	Compression ratio
r_u	Pore pressure ratio
S_r	Degree of saturation
s	Settlement
s_c	Consolidation settlement
s_i	Immediate settlement
T_v	Time factor (vertical drainage)
T_r	Time factor (radial drainage)
t	Time
U	Boundary water force
U	Degree of consolidation
u, u_w	Pore water pressure
u_a	Pore air pressure
V	Volume
v	Discharge velocity
v'	Seepage velocity
W	Weight
w	Water content
w_L	Liquid limit (or LL)
w_P	Plastic limit (or PL)
z	Depth coordinate
z	Elevation head
α'	Modified shear strength parameter (effective stress)
α	Pile adhesion coefficient
β	Slope angle
γ	Unit weight
γ_d	Dry unit weight
γ_{sat}	Saturated unit weight
γ'	Buoyant unit weight
γ_w	Unit weight of water
δ	Angle of wall friction
η	Dynamic viscosity
ν	Poisson's ratio
ρ	Bulk density
ρ_d	Dry density
ρ_{sat}	Saturated density
ρ_w	Density of water
σ	Total normal stress
σ'	Effective normal stress
$\sigma_1, \sigma_2, \sigma_3$	Total principal stresses
$\sigma_1', \sigma_2', \sigma_3'$	Effective principal stresses
τ	Shear stress
τ_f	Shear strength; peak shear strength
τ_r	Residual shear strength
ϕ	Potential function
ϕ	Shear strength parameter
ϕ_u	Undrained (total stress) shear strength parameter

ϕ' Drained (effective stress) shear strength parameter

ϕ'_r Drained residual shear strength parameter

χ Parameter in effective stress equation for partially-saturated soil

ψ Flow function

Answers to Problems

Chapter 1

1.1	SW, SM, ML, CH
1.2	0·55, 46·7%, 2100 kg/m^3, 20·3%
1.3	15·7 kN/m^3, 19·7 kN/m^3, 9·9 kN/m^3, 18·7 kN/m^3, 19·3%
1.4	97%
1.5	1920 kg/m^3, 0·38, 83·5%, 4·5%
1.6	15·2%, 1830 kg/m^3, 3·5%

Chapter 2

2.1	4·9 x 10^{-8} m/s
2.2	1·3 x 10^{-6} m^3/s (per m)
2.3	5·9 x 10^{-5} m^3/s (per m), 316 kN
2.4	2·0 x 10^{-6} m^3/s (per m)
2.5	4·1 x 10^{-6} m^3/s (per m)
2.6	1·0 x 10^{-6} m^3/s (per m)
2.7	1·8 x 10^{-5} m^3/s (per m)
2.8	0·9 x 10^{-5} m^3/s (per m)

Chapter 3

3.1	48·5 kN/m^2
3.2	51·4 kN/m^2, 33·4 kN/m^2
3.3	105·9 kN/m^2
3.4	(a) 94·0 kN/m^2, 154·2 kN/m^2, (b) 94·0 kN/m^2, 133·8 kN/m^2
3.5	10·0 kN, 73° below horizontal
3.6	30·2 kN/m^2, 10·6 kN/m^2
3.7	1·5, 15 kN/m^2, 90 kN/m^2
3.8	2·0, 0·67 m.

Chapter 4

4.1	113 kN/m^2
4.2	44°
4.3	110 kN/m^2, 0°

4.4   205 kN/m^2
4.5   55 kN/m^2, 17°
4.6   0, 25$\frac{1}{2}$°, 170 kN/m^2
4.7   15 kN/m^2, 28°
4.8   76 kN/m^2
4.9   0·76
4.10   0·96, 0·23

Chapter 5

5.1   76·5 kN/m, 122 kN/m
5.2   222 kN/m, 267 kN/m
5.3   306 kN/m, 50°, 65°, 7$\frac{1}{2}$°, 82$\frac{1}{2}$°
5.4   390 kN/m
5.5   300 kN/m
5.6   174 kN/m^2, 69 kN/m^2, 1·9
5.7   3·95 m
5.8   5·60 m, 235 kN
5.9   7·80 m, 172 kN
5.10   110 kN

Chapter 6

6.1   96 kN/m^2
6.2   277 kN/m^2
6.3   45 kN/m^2
6.4   66 kN/m^2
6.5   76 kN
6.6   6 mm

Chapter 7

7.1 $c_v = 8·4 \times 10^{-8}$ m^2/s, $m_v = 9·7 \times 10^{-4}$ m^2/kN, $k = 8·0 \times 10^{-10}$ m/s
7.2   318 mm, 37 mm (four sub-layers)
7.3   2·63 years, 0·95 years
7.4   65·5 kN/m^2
7.5   0·65
7.6   130 mm, 85 mm
7.7   70 mm (three sub-layers), 27·7 years
7.8   310 mm (three sub-layers)
7.9   0·80
7.10   8·95 years, 0·72 years

Chapter 8

8.1   3·1, 3·5
8.2   5·6, 3·7
8.3   4100 kN
8.4   2·95 m
8.5   8·4, 6·4, 4·0
8.6   120 kN/m^2

8.7 220 kN/m^2
8.8 300 kN/m^2
8.9 1000 kN

Chapter 9

9.1 $1\cdot43, 1\cdot27$
9.2 $50°, 27°$
9.3 $1\cdot53$
9.4 $0\cdot92$
9.5 $1\cdot02$
9.6 $13°, 3\cdot1$

Index